CARING ACROSS GENERATIONS

Caring across Generations

The Linked Lives of Korean American Families

Grace J. Yoo and Barbara W. Kim

NEW YORK UNIVERSITY PRESS
New York and London

NEW YORK UNIVERSITY PRESS
New York and London
www.nyupress.org

References to Internet websites (URLs) were accurate at the time of writing.
Neither the author nor New York University Press is responsible for URLs that
may have expired or changed since the manuscript was prepared.

LIBRARY OF CONGRESS CATALOGING-IN-PUBLICATION DATA

Yoo, Grace J.
  Caring across generations : the linked lives of Korean American families / Grace J. Yoo and
Barbara W. Kim.
     pages cm
  Includes bibliographical references and index.
  ISBN 978-0-8147-6897-6 (hardback) — ISBN 978-0-8147-6999-7 (paper)
  1. Korean Americans—Social conditions. 2. Korean Americans—Family relationships.
3. Older immigrants—United States—Social conditions. 4. Adult children of immigrants—
United States. 5. Adult children of aging parents—United States. 6. Immigrant families—
United States—Social conditions. I. Kim, Barbara W. II. Title.
  E184.K6Y756 2014
  973'.04957—dc23
                                  2014002558

New York University Press books are printed on acid-free paper,
and their binding materials are chosen for strength and durability.
We strive to use environmentally responsible suppliers and materials
to the greatest extent possible in publishing our books.

Manufactured in the United States of America
10 9 8 7 6 5 4 3 2 1

Also available as an ebook

To my parents, Frank and Wendy Yoo
And my sisters, Joyce and Alice
GJY

To my parents, Susie and Yong Chae Kim
And my brothers, Richard and Edward
BWK

CONTENTS

ACKNOWLEDGMENTS

Our friendship spans over twenty years of working in various capacities towards the development of Asian American studies on college campuses, as well as writing grants and researching health and social issues impacting the Korean immigrant community. Through a 2005 Community Grant Award from the Korean American Economic Development Center, we surveyed more than 268 Korean immigrant small-business owners in the state of California on their health insurance and retirement savings needs. Somewhere in the midst of this research collaboration and family updates, we realized that the complex issues facing Korean immigrants also impacted their adult children. As children of Korean immigrants, we joked that we were our parents' retirement plans, although we had no clear idea of how others in similar predicaments actually cared for and supported parents in retirement.

The desire to understand these experiences was rooted in the journeys of supporting our own aging parents. At various moments in our research collaboration, we also experienced numerous changes in our parents' health and losses in our extended families, and we wondered how other adult children with competing demands could be there for their immigrant parents. We knew that demographically, we were not alone in grappling with this question. As the first cohort of the largely post-1965 Korean immigrants (of the larger baby boomer generation) entered older adulthood, we wanted to understand how adult children of Korean immigrants were preparing to care or currently caring for their aging parents and how family histories and past relations affected care-giving attitudes, expectations, and practices. The California State University's Office of Community Service Learning awarded us a Collaboration Minigrant through its Multi-Campus Engaged Scholarship Initiatives Program and got us started in 2006. Research, Scholarly, and

Creative Activities (RSCA) awards from California State University, Long Beach provided time to work on the book project while awards from San Francisco State University helped fund a research assistant and participant incentives.

Our book would not have been possible without the support of a large community of people. First, we would like to thank our research assistants: Kathie Ahn, Steve Chae, Jeanelle Chang, Jason Chung, Veronica Gomez, Ellie Hong, Charles Kim, Enoch Kim, Amy Lee, Jonathan Lee, Man Ng, Gabriel Oh, Eunjung Park, and Jenny Suh. We would like to thank students from the Fall 2006 and Spring 2007 AAS 380 Koreans in America course at San Francisco State who assisted with data collection. Students in the Fall 2011 ASAM 495/595 Seminar in Asian American Studies at CSULB read transcripts and manuscript drafts and provided feedback. Margaret Rhee became involved in this project as a graduate research assistant and eventually co-authored an article on adult children, love, and marriage; we are so thankful for her invaluable assistance with data collection and analysis during the early stages of the project. We are also thankful to our students, many of whom are children of immigrants and/or the first generation in their families to go to college, for their enthusiasm and support for this project.

Our colleagues generously listened, read, and offered advice at different stages and helped us develop a conceptual framework over the years. Michael Omi provided guidance and feedback at its initial stages. We are grateful to those who commented on earlier drafts, shared theory with us and/or provided encouragement throughout this process including Caryn Aviv, Karra Bikson, Edith Chen, Ellen G. Levine, Judy Goldstein, Linda Juang, Mai Nhung Le, Allen LeBlanc, Alan Oda, Gabriela Segovia-McGahan, Amy Sueyoshi, Barbara Ustanko and Emily Han Zimmerman. Russell Jeung provided constructive criticism at all stages and read the final chapters. We are especially indebted to Wei Ming Dariotis, who read and edited the manuscript while caring for her ailing father

We want to thank our colleagues at SFSU and CSULB who have provided congenial and supportive academic homes. Special acknowledgements in the College of Ethnic Studies and the Asian American Studies Department at SFSU go to Laureen Chew, Wei Ming Dariotis, Lorraine Dong, Robert Fung, Daniel Phil Gonzales, Marlon Hom, Russell Jeung,

Betty Kano, Ben Kobashigawa, Mai Nhung Le, Jonathan Lee, Kenneth Monteiro, Becky Mou, Isabelle Pelaud, Eric Pido, Valerie Soe, Anantha Sudhakar, Allyson Tintiangco-Cubales, Wesley Ueunten, and Jeannie Woo. Barbara Kim would like to thank Chi-Ah Chun, Linda España-Maram, Henry Fung, Lawrence Hashima, Simon Kim, Karen Nakai, Alan Nishio, Karen Quintiliani, Mary Ann Takemoto, Dean Toji, John Tsuchida, Kris Zentgraf, and colleagues in the Department of Asian and Asian American Studies at CSULB. John M. Liu and Gail M. Nomura provided exuberant and unflagging mentorship, professional and personal, over the years; we thank you.

It takes a village to complete a book. Grace Yoo thanks sister Alice, nieces Michelle and Jeanelle, babysitters Erin McCoy and Silvia Garcia, and the wonderful community of parents in the city of Pacifica who organized a carpool and provided a playdate for Albert and Jeremy so another paragraph could be written. Barbara Kim thanks Elizabeth Berger, Deana Chuang, Nancy Yum Gil, Patricia-Anne Johnson, Joanne Kim, Young Kwak, Anne Manalili, Linda Maram, Karen Moon, Allyson Nakamoto, Hyun Joo Oh, Eve Oishi, Rowena Robles, Maythee Rojas, Anna Sandoval, Julie Wong, Alice Yoo, Anne Yu, and Sunny Yun, who enriched this project and her life with their friendships, wisdom, laughter, and good food in more ways than they can know.

A credit card left behind by mistake at the New York University Press table at a conference led to a follow-up conversation with Executive Editor Ilene Kalish, who remembered the project and requested a proposal. We thank Ilene for believing in this book. We also appreciate the encouragement and constructive comments of our anonymous reviewers and the editorial expertise of Caelyn Cobb and Alexia Traganas.

We thank our families for their love and support. Jason, Jeremy, and Albert provide the best reasons to find balance between work and family. Derek offered the most unexpected and welcome distraction and unwavering support over the life of this project. We thank our siblings Alice, Joyce, Mike, Richard, Riae, Edward, and Amy and look forward to growing old together. The Chang family—including older siblings, nieces and nephews—showed not only love and care, but strength and compassion for parents, Hui Son and Ok Kim Chang, until their passing. The Li sisters have welcomed its newest member with open arms, and their joint care-giving of their mother and my mother-in-law, Wai

Tong Li, embody the spirit of this book; thank you for your example. Our paternal grandfather, Yong Chang Park and our maternal grandmothers, Bong Dan Park and Jung Eui Kim, immigrated as older adults and raised their grandchildren when their children were busy at work; we thank them for their hard work, love, and prayers. The growing number of nephews and nieces through birth and marriage brings us great joy as they pass through various milestones, and we hope this book illuminates the linked generations and lives among us. To our parents—Frank Sungkun Yoo, Wendy Wangsook Yoo, Yong Chae Kim and Susie Kim—we offer our deepest gratitude and love.

Finally, we owe a great debt to all the participants, identified by pseudonyms in the study, who graciously took time from their demanding schedules to share their lives with honesty, humor, and patience. Passionate about their families, work, neighbors, faith, community, and various social and political issues, they inspired us with their generosity and thoughtful reflections and insights about growing up and aging as children of immigrants. The interviews often ended with the participant glad to know they were not the only ones going through a particular issue with their parent and curious about what other adult children were doing about it. We are most grateful to our respondents for allowing us to tell their stories.

Introduction

Caring across a Lifetime

When we immigrated to the United States, the relationship was more of a 180-degree type of thing. I became pretty much the parent to my parents and my younger brother. It meant that when we had documents to review and take care of [it was my responsibility]. My parents were not able to do that because their English was non-existent. I had to explain what it was that they were signing, whether it be school documents, documents from work, things like that. So the relationship was more business-like, more parenting the parent than the child that I was.
—Joel

In 1979, Joel's parents decided to emigrate from South Korea to the United States. They were seeking better opportunities for their sons, Joel, thirteen at the time, and his younger brother, who was eleven, and they settled in Los Angeles near other Korean immigrants. Both parents were college-educated. Joel's father had worked in Korea as a mid-level manager, and his mother had been a homemaker. After immigration, however, the family's life changed dramatically. His father faced downward mobility and his mother needed to find work to help support the family. While she found a job as a seamstress at a local Korean immigrant-owned garment factory, he worked as a laborer at a manufacturing plant. Reproducing a pattern common for immigrants, Joel's parents began to rely on their older son, the most fluent English speaker in the household, to interact with the dominant English-speaking American society. Now in his forties, Joel reflects on how migration brought on major changes in the family, in particular the role reversals between his parents and himself. Although Joel's story is that of a child of Korean immigrants, his narrative resonates with those of others who, like Joel, play a unique role that is intimately linked to their parents' lives as immigrants.

Throughout childhood and into middle age, while negotiating various life transitions including careers, marriage, and parenthood, the children of immigrants serve their parents as brokers of culture and language. Their life paths are often impacted by their parents' pre-immigration lives, which can include war or other forms of political and economic turmoil. Daily struggles with the realities of being immigrants—including racism and discrimination—affect not only the immigrant parents but also the children who act as their intercessors in the English-speaking world and especially in governmental, legal, educational, and medical institutions. Because their parents may have immigrated specifically to give the next generation a better life, the children of these immigrants also deeply consider their parents' hopes and dreams as they make major life decisions of their own. Their successes are often seen within the family as the fulfillment of their parents' sacrifices.

As they explore the meaning of their parents' culture in the context of passing on certain aspects to their own children, the adult children of immigrants may also be entering another phase of their relationship with their now increasingly elderly parents, care-giver by providing financial assistance and health aid, and emotional care work. While children of non-immigrants may also see caring for their parents as recompense for the way their parents cared for them during childhood, children of immigrants have already played pseudo-parental roles in their families as they negotiated the English-speaking world on their parents' behalf. And while children of non-immigrants may also have taken on parental responsibilities at a young age, their reasons for doing so differ from those of immigrant children, whose family histories have a distinct dynamic. When immigrant parents face declining health, their adult children become advocates, translators, educators, and care-givers. These roles take on a deeper meaning when an immigrant parent's health starts to decline. Mee Jin, the youngest of three American-born sisters, had graduated from college and had recently been promoted at work when her father was diagnosed with cancer. Mee Jin tried to juggle her new job and care-giving, driving about one hundred and twenty miles each day, but finally she quit her job and moved in with her parents in order to take care of her father full-time. She provided support to her dying father on many different levels, such as taking him to chemotherapy, interacting with doctors, and being present when her father passed on. She remembers:

> You don't ever think you're ever going to have to go through that—to think about seeing your parents die in front of you. . . . You just think that everybody is going to be okay and then he's going to die in [his] sleep or whatever. It's a life changing event, that role reversal and having to help [your parents] go to the bathroom. . . . Seeing your parents take their last breath, it's hard.

Mee Jin's father's illness and passing dramatically shifted the family dynamics from one in which independent parents and their grown children lived separate lives to one in which children advocated for an ill father and then cared for a grieving mother. Although one of her sisters moved in with their mother, Mee Jin notes, "My mom felt like I was the stronger one of the three daughters so she turns to me if she has a problem or doesn't know how to do something. . . . Whatever it is, she'll call me first." Even though her father's passing was emotionally devastating for her as well, Mee Jin had to be strong for her mother who relied on her more than ever. The care work Joel and Mee Jin provide has been deeply informed by their parents' lives as immigrants. Unlike their peers in non-immigrant households, the children of Korean immigrants play a major supportive role in their parents' lives from childhood to adulthood by bridging communication gaps and negotiating the structural and institutional disparities that immigrants typically encounter. This book chronicles the reflections of adult children of Korean immigrants who, as children, have supported immigrant parents working long hours, struggling with language issues, racism and discrimination, and who, as adults, not only provide their aging parents tangible and emotional support but also work to ensure that cultural traditions are not forgotten and are revisited and passed on to the next generation.

Linked Lives: Care and Emotion Work
of Children of Immigrants

This study is rooted in the theoretical concept of linked lives in which "lives are lived interdependently and socio-historical influences are expressed through this network of shared relationships."[1] As this theory suggests, the challenges and successes faced by each generation are influenced by the preceding generation and impact the next generation. Each generation's trajectory is interdependent and life-long.[2] At the same time, individuals also construct their own human agency within the opportunities and constraints provided by history and social structures.[3] Proposed by sociologist Glen H. Elder, Jr., the concept of linked lives derives from a focus on socio-historical factors and their impact on families in the context of the Great Depression. While it has not yet been applied to the issue of human agency on the part of immigrants and to the subsequent socialization of American-born generations in terms of a wide range of historical, cultural, and economic constraints, this theoretical construct does provide a basis for understanding how immigrant family members adapt, relate to, and care for each other. The concept of linked lives suggests that the hardships of immigrant parents in one generation, experienced through social inequities and cultural and language barriers, are interdependently linked with the struggles and successes of the next generation.[4]

Inasmuch as the theory of linked lives provides a structural lens to examine families across generations, the various processes that link generations for immigrants and their children have not been fully studied. We suggest that the process of linking lives for immigrant parents and their children involves care work that comes not only in the form of tangible support but also through emotion work.[5] In particular, we examine how this dynamic operates as parents enter old age. The literature of care work has traditionally focused on the role of women in looking after ill and older family members. Elaine Brody, in *Women in the Middle: Their Parent-Care Years*, documents how daughters have been the main caregivers to aging parents and how this role is fraught with juggling competing demands (spouses, children, and work) and causes exhaustion for the women in the middle.[6] In *The Managed Heart: Commercializing of Human Feeling* and in other works, sociologist Arlie Russell Hochschild argues that women do emotion work in their lives to elicit feelings in others and also to adhere to gendered "feeling" norms and expectations. Research has shown that mothers and daughters do this work, thus serving as the glue that holds families together over a lifetime.[7] In immigrant families, emotional labor performed by children can take on forms similar to that performed by mothers in non-immigrant families. Both male and female children of immigrants serve as bridges for their parents in ways that not only entail cultural and language brokering but also involve emotional labor ranging from doing well in school in childhood to being present for aging immigrant parents in later life. We suggest that the children of Korean immigrants observe and recognize personal sacrifices and institutional disadvantages that their parents experience in American society and that trying to do well in school, attend top-notch colleges, pursue professional careers, marry a co-ethnic, have children, and observe and reinvent cultural traditions are all forms of emotional labor that they perform for their families over a lifetime.

Several insightful studies discuss intergenerational relations within the broad context of non-white immigrant populations who have arrived since the 1960s, and in particular the need felt by many children of immigrants to "give back" to their parents in old age. But since the majority of these studies focus on young adulthood, they do not consider how these feelings may develop over the life course, and how these intentions are fulfilled or challenged in middle adulthood.[8] Meanwhile, studies that examine immigrant older adults and care-giving in the United States tend to focus on the population who are the *grandparents* of the children of immigrants.[9] These studies leave unanswered questions and demonstrate a need for future research on the unique experiences of children of post-1960s immigrants who are entering middle age in the United States.

Immigrant Children and Their Parents

Children with at least one foreign-born parent now comprise almost one-fourth of U.S. children under age eighteen.[10] Recent studies illustrate that in addition to financial hardships and limitations in English language proficiency, immigrant parents experience significantly higher levels of parental aggravation than non-immigrant parents and that they have less knowledge about supportive resources on parenting as well.[11] In the United States, immigrants continually struggle with belonging, psychological distress, and discrimination.[12] Asian Americans, immigrant and non-immigrant, face racial micro-aggressions related to being perceived as "perpetual foreigners," which can result in psychological distress.[13] The children of immigrants, whether born in the United States or having arrived as young children, look at the world through such a lens. They are observers of and witnesses to the difficulties encountered by immigrant parents who must navigate a new language, new culture, new social networks, and new institutional structures. In a sense, as witnesses and observers, these children are linked to the hardships experienced by the immigrant generation.

In the context of studying how the intersections of culture, migration, class, language, and racism impact children of immigrants, one understudied area concerns how they navigate the concerns and needs of their families over the course of their lives. We do know that children, throughout their lives, serve as links to their immigrant parents' past and present and that they support their parents' well-being. We also know that those children of immigrants who become familiar with the English language and American culture faster than their parents and other family members provide significant work as language and cultural brokers, helping their parents and families adapt to and navigate life in the United States.[14] From a young age, they contribute to their families by translating, interpreting, and writing legal letters and contracts; filling out business forms; accompanying their parents to doctors' offices to interpret medical information; and interacting with various officials (e.g., lawyers, doctors) of authority and power.[15] Children of immigrants, as language and cultural brokers, bridge and mediate gaps of communication and meaning between their non-fluent parents and mainstream social institutions and practices.[16] Children may view these responsibilities as burdensome or stressful if they feel inadequate about their ability to accurately translate or interpret concepts and meanings. Conversely, brokering can build their self-confidence, interpersonal skills, and language abilities as they actively contribute to their families' survival and well-being.[17]

The narratives in this study provide a unique lens for examining intergenerational relations and cultural contexts in Korean American families as immigrant parents and children age. The notion of filial piety plays a significant role in Korean and Korean American families. Although practices of filial piety are being redefined in South Korea in response to social and economic changes, children in Korea are still typically expected to care for parents in their old age.[18] In the context of Korean and many Asian immigrant families in the United States, we argue that ideas of filial piety are not just cultural, but also structurally rooted in the documented everyday experiences of racialized immigrants—experiences that include prejudice, racism, and institutional barriers.[19]

Understanding how older immigrants and their adult children navigate old age is important. From 1990 to 2010, the population of those aged sixty-five and older has increased from 29.6 million to 38.6 million, and is now the fastest growing segment of the population by age in the United States.[20] Within this segment, foreign-born elderly persons make up an increasing portion of the population. Due to the language and cultural barriers that immigrants face, as well as the disparities they experience over their lifetime, their children's care work may begin earlier and may involve more and qualitatively different tasks than that for non-immigrant aging parents. This may be due to multiple factors, including a lack of extended family members in the immediate area as migration often results in geographic separation from kin. While cultural and linguistic brokering may start during childhood as they negotiate for their working immigrant parents, such brokering continues as a lifelong process as parents age and face health issues.

Core Questions

Framing the study of Korean American families in a life-course perspective, this book examines how adult children of immigrants view and make meaning of their experiences growing up in Korean immigrant households, as well as how they interpret the past and current concerns and cultural values of their parents as they make their own life choices. Specifically, the book answers the following questions:

1. How, and to what extent, does being a child of an immigrant shape life-course experiences from childhood to young and middle adulthood? What types of work do children of immigrants do for immigrant parents over their lifetimes? How does this work, especially cultural brokering

and care work, shift and change during different life stages, including childhood, college, marriage, and child-rearing?

2. How do children of immigrants interpret their childhoods in relation to the life experiences of their immigrant parents?

3. As children of immigrants enter middle adulthood and make major life decisions, in what ways do these adult children recognize their parents' histories and sacrifices, while also recognizing their own need for self-care?

4. How have adult children of immigrants experienced and viewed their affinity, attachment, and identity in relation to culture, and how have they been perceived by co-ethnics in these terms? How do children of Korean immigrants as adults carry forward and reinterpret Korean cultural traditions? In this process, how do they negotiate concepts of authenticity?

5. How and when do adult children of Korean immigrants step in to support relatively healthy immigrant parents dealing with aging and the various changes and losses it brings? Who among the siblings in a family do so?

6. How do adult children of aging immigrants adjust to their parents' declining health? How do they navigate structural and economic barriers (e.g., racism, language, health insurance) for access to quality health care when aging immigrant parents are faced with chronic or debilitating health conditions and the prospects of dying?

Methods

This study draws from in-depth interviews with 137 Korean American adult children of immigrants in order to explore the questions outlined above. Our participants were recruited and interviewed between the years 2006 and 2012, and resided in the greater Los Angeles or San Francisco Bay metropolitan areas. At the time of the interviews, respondents had at least one parent aged fifty-five or older, were themselves age eighteen or older, and were either 1.5 generation or second-generation. Social scientists define members of the 1.5 generation as foreign-born persons who came to the United States before the age of thirteen (the term is similar to that of the "knee-high" generation used in the Japanese American communities in Hawaii), while members of the second generation are those born in the United States to foreign-born parents.[21] We chose age fifty-five of one or more parent as an eligibility criteria because parents were close to thinking about retirement and approaching the age of sixty, or *hwangap*, which in traditional Korean society signifies both completion of a significant life cycle and longevity, and thus is a milestone celebrated by family and friends.[22] While we conducted many interviews and all follow-up interviews, trained undergraduate and graduate student interviewers also assisted under our supervision.

There has been an ongoing debate among social scientists about how a researcher's positionality, including his or her race, class, gender, sexuality, age, and experiences, can pose unique "insider" and "outsider" challenges and possibilities in social science research.[23] For more than a decade, we have researched disparities impacting the Korean American community, in particular the high rates of uninsured persons among Korean American immigrants. We also fit into the study parameters in being 1.5- and second-generation Korean Americans with aging immigrant parents who have retired after decades of living and working in the United States. And thus we posit that our "insider" identities helped us recruit participants and gain entry into the lives of adult 1.5- and second-generation Korean Americans who also juggle work, marriage, children, community engagement/activism, and/or aging parents.[24] While we recognize that our insider status, ethnic and generational, may have helped us connect with our respondents in some ways, we also recognize that being as close to the subject as we are can present its own challenges, including enticing us to focus on those issues that are salient to our own situations. For example, as we examine the lack of retirement planning and low rates of health care access for Korean immigrants, we wonder how they and their adult children deal with their impending old age and with accompanying questions such as financial costs of care and living arrangements and acknowledge that as children of aging immigrant parents, we ourselves ask these questions, too. Our life decisions and celebrations, crises, additions, and losses in relationship to our own immigrant parents inevitably informed and shaped the questions we asked our respondents. Perhaps other researchers would have asked different questions and made different interpretations.

Most participants were more than willing to share their reflections and struggles; in fact, many agreed to participate because they wanted to affirm that they were not the only ones experiencing issues with care-giving for their parents. As co-researchers, we brought different parental dispositions and immigration and health histories, as well as our own personal biographies into the project. Despite—or perhaps because of—these differences, our shared position as daughters of Korean immigrants provides a unique lens for understanding the lives of adult children of immigrants, who, like us, arrived as young children or were born in the United States and who navigate and care for their parents over a lifetime.

Outline of the Book

Chapter 1, "Brokering Dreams," explores the respondents' childhoods in Korean immigrant households. Respondents discuss the pressures and challenges of growing up as children of parents pursuing the "Korean American dream" of financial and social stability, with much of their dreams pinned on and invested in their children's educational achievements.[25] This chapter sheds light on different types of care work that the respondents provided in childhood. Whether they immigrated as children or were born in the United States, these respondents often found themselves brokering their parents' interactions with official worlds during their childhoods. This labor, visible (physical) and invisible (emotional), was sometimes not asked for explicitly, but was understood and observed by the children as being essential to the survival of their families and the well-being of their immigrant parents.

In chapter 2, "Giving Back," adult children of Korean immigrants in their twenties, thirties, and forties share how they are navigating and remembering their parents' traumatic, war-inflected pre-migration histories; giving back for their parents' challenges and sacrifices as immigrants; and pursuing their dreams for themselves and their children. Significantly, this chapter illustrates how the immigration experience intricately links American born and/or raised adult children to the traumatic war histories of their immigrant parents. Finally, this chapter discusses how adult children recognize their own feelings around obligations and duty to their parents as they reflect on their own dreams, passions, and needs for self-care.

Chapter 3, "Caring about Culture," delves into how respondents practice cultural traditions while also reclaiming and re-making their culture and interpreting it in new ways that provide meaning in their Korean

American contexts. Although the cultural experiences of reclaiming and remaking what is Korean vary, a unifying theme related by respondents is their deep desire to retain the value of respect towards elders and to care for their parents in old age. This chapter further explores how respondents re-make culture for their own children—the third generation—especially in relation to respecting and caring for older adults.

In chapter 4, "Gender at Work," the focus turns to how adult children become more aware of changes and losses happening in their parents' lives, including retirement from work, selling businesses, marital difficulties, and death of close friends and family members. In our study, adult daughters, both near and far, are more acutely aware of and responsive to changes happening in their parents' lives. Adult daughters do emotion work by maintaining close ties with their parents, but are also more aware of and empathetic to changes their parents experience as they age. This chapter also explores the negotiations that take place between spouses and among siblings in providing financial and other types of support to aging parents.

Chapter 5, "In the Midst of Caring for Ill Parents," explores how respondents navigate health care options for their parents, many of whom have lived in the United States for decades but still face language barriers. In considering the personal limitations and challenges that individuals face in caring for their parents, this chapter also examines how the respondents fulfill the roles of advocate and intermediary in order to secure health care and wellness for their parents.

Finally, "Linked Lives: Where Do We Go from Here?" looks at intergenerational costs and benefits of linked lives, and examines how adult children of aging immigrants find meaning through caring across lifetimes, while functioning at maximum capacity. Given that the older adult population is increasing in racial, ethnic, and generational diversity, the impact this is having on families, communities, and local, state, and national budgets and policies is a complex issue that requires dialogue within and beyond the family.[26] Hence, this chapter explores policy implications and the importance of community and support in the face of the cultural, political, and structural challenges facing older immigrants and their adult children.

* * *

This book chronicles experiences of Korean American families from the perspective of the 1.5 and second generations and analyzes the often invisible work children of immigrants provide from childhood into middle adulthood. The goal of this book is that it will reveal the work that children do in immigrant families. Immigrants experience disruptions in culture, language, status, friendships, and family relationships; they also encounter racism and prejudice. Witnessing and responding to these difficulties, children of immigrants also give back in recognition of these hardships.

For Korean American adult children, experiences caring for immigrant parents in their childhoods lay the groundwork for the types of care that they continue to do into middle adulthood. Emotion work and other forms of care work learned early on, such as language and cultural brokering, continue throughout lifetimes to preserve and pass on culture, understand parents' past, and support them as they face retirement and losses in their lives. The journey of children's care and concern for immigrant parents starts at migration and is not without its ongoing frustrations, conflicts, and ambivalence. Nonetheless, intergenerational relations do change as immigrant parents and children age, even as they remain linked. As the narratives of respondents illuminate, children of immigrants in their middle adulthood continue to serve as brokers for their parents' dreams and their futures, and in the process, help redefine social, cultural, and political life in the contemporary United States.

1

Brokering Dreams

When we were growing up, we went to art classes on Satur-
days. That was because of my mom, she wanted us to make
art. And we played the violin because she wanted me to play
the violin. And, of course, you're supposed to have good
grades, and you're supposed to help them out in their business. . . . So while my parents worked long hours we would
come home and take care of ourselves and eat, whatever. And
all weekend, we would have to work, whatever it was. And
of course, they would pay you by giving you food. . . . You
know, you never get any kind of praise, any compliments, no
hugs. It was just—ah, criticism.
—Lauren

Lauren emigrated with her family from Korea when she was five years
old. Her parents ran a number of small businesses until they retired in
the early 2000s. Today, Lauren remembers the pressure to "do it all" in
her childhood. In addition to taking art and music lessons, studying for
good grades, and helping out in her parents' business, Lauren assumed
the role of the primary translator/interpreter in the family as a child. As
a teenager, she took a part-time job to earn personal spending money,
but her parents needed her paychecks to cover household bills. She
filled out college financial aid forms for her older sibling and tended
to her parents' business, legal, and medical matters. Now in their thirties, Lauren and her sibling pay the mortgage and all the bills for their
retired parents. Lauren has filled out applications for Medicare and
senior housing and goes grocery shopping and translates mail for them.

Lauren jokes that much to her surprise, her parents have become more open and affectionate as they aged: "Now that I'm older and they want to give me hugs. It's like, ugh, what are you doing?" Her parents relied on their children's help when they were young because, as Lauren says, "We [as a family] had to survive." Lauren and her sister will continue to support their parents "because we've been doing it for a while." For Lauren, caring for her parents throughout her life is not simply a cultural mandate or value, but a practical and necessary result of how immigration made the children's labor vital to the family's overall establishment in the United States.

* * *

By 2008, almost 30 percent of young adults aged eighteen to thirty-four in the United States were either foreign-born or had at least one foreign-born parent. Scholars predict that "as this generation reaches adulthood in large numbers within the next decade or two, its impact will be increasingly and widely felt throughout the society."[1] The transition to adulthood differs widely by generation, ethnicity, national origin, and nativity/citizenship status and with respect to education, work, marriage, and birth rate. Studying the processes by which new Americans acculturate in relation to their families helps make sense of the collective immigrant experience, and suggests broader implications for American politics, economy, and culture against the backdrop of global economic restructuring.

The children of immigrants are coming of age at a critical time in American society, as it experiences dramatic demographic shifts through immigration and aging. In recent decades, ethnic, racial, and socioeconomic diversity has been fueled by international migration resulting from the liberalization of U.S. civil rights and immigration laws in the latter half of the twentieth century.[2] Like many other immigrants, those from Korea have faced multiple issues including language and cultural barriers, underemployment, and downward mobility.[3] At the same time, Korean immigrants have played a unique role in small business entrepreneurship.[4] Compared to other racial/ethnic and immigrant groups in the United States, Korean immigrants have the highest self-employment rate.[5]

In the larger context of contemporary U.S. immigration, studies of Korean immigrant families have focused on the experiences of the first generation and their economic and social adaptation to the United States. These studies have highlighted changing post-migration family dynamics, focusing on issues such as the impact of ethnic entrepreneurship and labor participation on spousal relations and gender roles.[6] Meanwhile, studies from the perspective of children of Korean immigrants, or the second generation, have thoughtfully explored educational goals/expectations, intergenerational conflicts, and racial, ethnic, class, political, and religious identities in relation to the broader American society.[7] Further studies have explored how children of Korean and other Asian immigrants contribute critically to the collective survival and well-being of the family as laborers in family businesses and as primary translators and interpreters for their households.[8] In one of the first studies to focus on the practices and perspectives of children in labor-intensive ethnic/family/immigrant entrepreneurship, Miri Song compared the labor of Chinese children in their immigrant parents' take-away restaurants in England to the caring labor that adult children, usually daughters, provide for elderly parents.[9] Song writes:

> Described as a labor of love, looking after elderly parents is based upon intense feelings of obligation and guilt, as well as love and concern. Such caring work for elderly parents is said to be difficult, in part, because it seems to reverse the traditional parent-child relationship—rather than parents caring for their children, adult children, in turn, look after their parents in infirmity and illness. . . . While this kind of work seems almost universal for adult daughters, the performance of caring work by children or adolescents, rather than adults, is relatively unusual in most contemporary Western societies.[10]

Korean immigrants experience a similar dynamic: children help with their family's economic survival, and roles reverse as these children—at young ages—navigate culture, language, and racism for their immigrant parents and care for their economic survival. As introduced by Lauren's story above, this chapter explores the pressures and challenges of growing up with parents who invested in their children's educational and other opportunities while also relying on their children as mediators, translators, and workers for survival and stability. By getting good grades, cultural and language brokering, working in family businesses, and managing family relations, young children and teenagers have provided care and solace to their immigrant parents in ways this chapter illustrates in detail. While the kind of labor that children of immigrants provide is a labor of love, as Miri Song notes, it is not without pressures, conflicts, and negotiations; nor are feelings about such childhoods free from ambivalence.

Caring Starts Early: Emotion Work in Childhood

Studies of immigrant families illustrate that the parents face many more hardships, including financial challenges and English proficiency, than native U.S.-born parents. Indeed, a recent study indicates that immigrant parents face significantly elevated levels of parental aggravation and have significantly fewer resources compared to American-born parents.[11] In keeping with these findings, most respondents remembered high stress levels in their households as parents struggled to find and maintain work or start up small businesses. They recalled the additional difficulties their parents faced due to limited English reading and speaking abilities, cultural unfamiliarity, and encounters with racism and discrimination at work and in public spaces.

Children of immigrants in our study not only empathized with their immigrant parents' plights but often actively sought to make things better for their parents. That is, they performed "emotion work," which sociologist Arlie Hochschild defines as "the act of trying to change in degree or quality an emotion or feeling."[12] Hochschild argues that one who engages in emotion work tries to evoke, shape, or suppress one's (or another's) inner feelings for the purpose of caring for family and loved ones. A growing body of literature describes how women engage in the bulk of emotion work within their intimate relationships and families as they assume responsibility for maintaining familial ties and the emotional care-taking of others.[13] Like others who have engaged in emotion work, the respondents in our study were involved in varying levels of care for their immigrant parents.[14]

Although respondents of all genders discussed emotion work that they provided to their parents over a lifetime, daughters most often talked about this type of work as care and of their necessary role in soothing parents. Trying to ease their parents' stresses over and worries about immigrant survival, female respondents sought to shield their parents from the external society through brokering language and culture, doing well in school, or otherwise acting on behalf of their parents. While the work that daughters more often mentioned entailed emotion work, sons discussed physical work such as chores at home or at the family business which they provided as a form of care giving. In both cases, the facets of emotional and physical work in childhood were intended to help parents survive and feel better in the present and hopeful about the future.

Scholars have found that children are aware of the difficulties and challenges their parents face in migrating to the United States, and feel pressure and responsibility to make up for these through academic, professional, and financial achievements in the future.[15] Many respondents in our study experienced similar pressure to varying degrees as they observed how their parents' education and work experiences in Korea often did not translate to equivalent work in America. What many remembered from their childhoods was the toll that that this rupture between pre-immigration education and work experience and post-immigration opportunities took on their parents and family relations. As children, many respondents tried to manage the negative emotions that resulted. Many recalled how their parents fought with each other over language difficulties, financial uncertainties, and downward social mobility.

Nancy, for one, witnessed many fights between her parents, especially when they left a comfortable, more "privileged life" in Korea to struggle financially in the United States:

> There were lots and lots of fights. I think they were like, on the brink of divorce so often I can't even count them. You know they're both hot-tempered. They're typical Koreans, and they'd throw things and yell. My brothers and sister and I would tell them "Stop fighting! It's too loud!" You know, I was never scared that they were going to hurt each other, or that we were going to get hurt. It was never like that, but more like "stop, stop, stop"—it's just too much. It's too loud, too often. So just memories of just lots of yelling, about money, about the pressures of being an immigrant

and finding housing for all of us. Where are we going to live? How are we going to get money for the next car payment? How are we going to pay for food, for the next month? You know, just the ongoing struggle not being able to speak that much English. They left a pretty, middle-class to upper-middle-class lifestyle to being lower-middle class or just sometimes, just being straight impoverished in the States. So I think that was hard for them. Like, oh, they roll the dice and they came out against them.

Like Nancy, many respondents shared memories of watching struggling parents trying to make it in America. These difficulties often served as catalysts for children of immigrants to attempt to make things better for their families. These efforts included getting good grades; helping at home and at work; working to be their parents' voice in an English-speaking world; and running errands to get their parents' favorite food or drinks.

Getting Good Grades

As documented in previous studies, children's academic success was a source of pride for many immigrant parents (and conversely, source of great conflict for children who did not do as well in school), especially for those parents who viewed such success as a stepping stone to future opportunities for their children and the collective household.[16] Doing well in school was one way that respondents addressed their parents' difficult work and lowered social status. For those in our sample, getting good grades was also a way for respondents to manage their parents' emotions, not only by soothing them, but also providing their parents with status in the present and hope for the future. Across the board, respondents described childhoods that often focused on academic achievement that would ultimately impact parents' emotions. However, gender differences did exist in how "getting good grades" was interpreted and viewed by these children of immigrants. Daughters saw good grades as something that could make or break their parents' day, while sons were more ambivalent about the need to perform and manage their parents' emotions in this manner.

Connie, for example, describes how, by doing well in school, she could change the negative emotions her self-employed parents were experiencing. Her father, who worked as an engineer in Korea, came to the United

States to attend graduate school, but eventually dropped out of the program for financial reasons. For Connie, getting good grades not only was a form of emotion work, but also became a source of empowerment:

> When I brought home good grades, I couldn't wait to become the object of their bliss. As the child of first generation immigrants, I got used to seeing a tired, grim facial expression on my parents' faces. When I brought home straight A's, their faces would be transformed; happy, joyful, hopeful—all the things they rarely were, otherwise. To be the cause of such transformation made me feel not only happy, but also powerful.

Another respondent who did well in school observed that her parents used her good grades to show off among other Korean immigrants. Abigail, an executive in her forties, notes that

> The most notable memory around my report cards was that my mother would put the report card into her purse so that she could look at it during her workday and also show it to her friends to "brag." She told me that those reports cards are what made the immigration hardship worth it.

Although some respondents criticized this overt behavior of comparing children's academic achievements, others like Abigail highlighted how her grades brought some comfort and validation to her mother. In this way, adult daughters like Abigail indicated how they were empathetic to their immigrant parents' plight, and were aware that good grades could ease their difficult workdays and provide a hope for the future.

But the pressure to maintain top grades became challenging to meet as schoolwork increased in difficulty. As Connie grew older and bringing home good grades became more challenging, academics became a source of conflict, as she recalls:

> I mean one B+ on my report card. My parents were no longer happy with me. Whatever stress and strain they felt became multiplied as they began to weigh the future against this slight. It was awful.

Compared to the daughters, the sons were more likely to frame their stories of academic and parental pressures in an ambivalent fashion.

Although many males in the study did well in school as well, they tended to focus on the unfairness and relentlessness of these pressures. Dylan, for example, wryly observed that his parents, both of whom immigrated as international students, earned graduate degrees, and developed professional careers in the United States, had only one way to define achievement in school. It was through:

> the classic, unexplained, unbridled emphasis on education to the exclusion of all else. . . . I was senior class president. I was sophomore class president. I was editor-in-chief of the newspaper. I ran track. I was in the marching band four years. I was on the student council, and my parents considered me a total failure because I didn't get straight A's. You know, they told me that much, "Until you get straight A's, everything else you do is meaningless."

Dylan, now in his forties, describes how his parents did not accept his various extra-curricular activities as forms of achievement that would help him in the future, in such areas as college admissions and career opportunities. More explicitly, other male respondents observed how their childhoods were limited because their parents' worldviews were solely fixated on education. As Jeremy, who is in his thirties, recalls:

> My parents, all they did was survive. I think my parents were very stubborn. They would just see a lot of things their way —but not knowing and understanding that there is more to life than just making money, more to life than just studying and getting good grades.

Although sons did not necessarily do better or worse academically, they differed from daughters in their reactions to parental pressures. Daughters empathized with their parents' emotions, while sons were more likely to feel ambivalent about their parents and academics. Several male respondents, for example, discussed how they were so frustrated with their parents and their narrow definition of academic success that they sometimes purposely did poorly in school. Bart describes how, out of frustration with his parents who narrowly defined academic success as getting into an Ivy League university, he deliberately did badly in some classes so they would stop pressuring him to get into these schools.

Peter also experienced intense pressure to do well in school, especially from his father, who tried to motivate his son by showing his own report cards from Korea, pointing out how financially difficult it was to emigrate to the United States, and once, delivering severe corporal punishment. Like Bart, Peter reacted. He describes how the academic pressure created such a conflict between him and his parents that he purposefully did not do well in school.

> My parents are intense people; it took me a long time to realize that. We have a wonderful relationship now, but when I was growing up, it was just awful. Really awful, day after day there wasn't a day without conflicts. It was a pretty unpleasant time. You are living with your parents, they support you, but you don't want to live with them. As a result I passive aggressively got back at them, I didn't do well in school, I didn't care about that stuff. Of course, my dad wanted me to do well in school so I didn't. It was a pretty unhappy childhood.

It was not until Peter left home for college, which gave both him and his parents space and distance from each other, that his relationship with them improved. More likely than female respondents to describe how parental pressures they faced as children caused difficulty, stress, and grief, male respondents also often cited how they "acted out" because of these pressures. Another such son, Richard, discusses how he wished he'd known growing up that other children in Korean immigrants' households also experienced them. It would have helped to know he was not the only one:

> There's the rebellious stage in the young adult years. Koreans tend to be more conservative than other parents. I had thoughts like "Why can't I do this?" or "they will never understand." There were probably billions of kids like me, but I didn't know that. I didn't know I was supposed to get help so I just dealt with it.

Although some children, including daughters, criticized their parents' fixation on grades and academic success, others allowed their parents to use their academic success as a vicarious source of pride and accomplishment; this was a form of emotion work for these children.

But other children, especially sons, focused on the intensity of conflict that the pressure to perform successfully in school created in their relationship with their parents, and were more likely to discuss how they actively or "passive-aggressively" responded to the pressure.

In the long run, many respondents went on to fulfill their parents' definition of academic success—earning straight A's on report cards, receiving academic awards, and completing undergraduate and graduate degrees at prestigious colleges and universities. But many also did not fulfill this narrow definition of success: they did not earn top grades or attend elite colleges and universities; a few in the sample did not attend a four-year college. Still, regardless of the educational paths they followed, respondents indicated that their relationships with their parents improved after high school and college as grades were no longer the focus.

Picking up the Pieces for Immigrant Parents at Home and at Work

Despite the emphasis on schoolwork, many respondents had other responsibilities. They described how their parents' long work hours often meant taking on household chores such as caring for a younger sibling, doing laundry, cleaning, and preparing meals. Additionally, as about half of their parents were self-employed, many respondents helped in the family business. Other parental occupations of our sample reflect a diversity in Korean immigrant households; in addition to entrepreneurship, other occupations included assembly-line workers, garment industry workers, clerks, pastors, nurses, professors, and physicians. The emotion work that children of immigrants did, which varied depending on their parents' type of work, included adjusting to parents' absences (physical and/or emotional), coping with parents' fluctuating financial statuses, and helping out in parents' small businesses without complaining or outwardly expressing their discontent or frustration about the situations that they or their parents faced.

NON-ENTREPRENEUR PARENTS

With their non-entrepreneur parents spending most of their waking hours at work, respondents from these households recall coming home from school and passing time alone without parental supervision. For parents who were professionals and for those in the trades, work schedules were more predictable than for those who worked as entrepreneurs, but still required much time away from home. Parents in middle-class white-collar professions, employed as accountants, nurses, physicians, and so forth, afforded some material comfort for their children, relative to parents who worked blue-collar jobs or to parents who had to employ their children in their family business. Regardless of the different material resources and cultural capital that they could provide for their children in the United States, the parents expected their children to succeed. As Vivian Louie shows in her examination of class differences in Chinese immigrant families and structural access to educational opportunities, parents, based on their own experiences as racialized immigrants, pushed their children to obtain higher education and jobs in technical and licensed fields as protection in a racialized society.[17] These parents also stressed to their children the necessity of working harder than members of the dominant society as another form of protection, and took their own message to heart. They saw themselves having not only to demonstrate their competence in the mainstream labor force, but also to ensure that their households would be okay financially. The stress of economic survival and the long hours took a toll on families; respondents perceived that their parents were absent in their lives during childhood.

Ryan, whose parents worked as business professionals, understands now why his parents were so busy, but nonetheless wished his family had spent more time together.

> I've always really felt very close to my parents and I really loved them and I always sensed that they really loved me. I think, unfortunately though, they worked so much that I didn't get to see them or hang out with them as much as I think would have been nice. I think they were very focused on, you know, trying to get established and, you know, buy a house. . . . I think, to some extent, our family sort of suffered a little bit for it because we didn't get to do as many things together as a family. I don't remember seeing my dad a lot because he was working all the time. And then my mom, you know, I did see but you know, I think I felt like I wished they were home a little more.

Other respondents also remembered how their parents worked long hours, struggled with finances month to month, and juggled the care of their children without any outside help. For Chuck, who grew up with two professional parents, this meant that his father went to work during the day and took care of the children at night while his mother worked in the evenings as an artist. Lyn, whose father was employed as a technician, remembers that her mother was often "stressed" from a full week of work and juggling duties at home. Jordan grew up in a family with an engineer father and mother who worked in the public sector. Like Lyn, Jordan remembers watching her mother juggle her workload inside and outside the home. Jordan also sensed the high stress levels that often did not leave much for emotional connectivity between mother and daughter:

> I remember when my mom was working. She was very stressed out, a lot. She worked full time and she cleaned the house full time. And every Saturday, she had a certain schedule and we knew it. And every weekday, there was a certain schedule and we knew it. They were very regimented that way. Which was good, but she had to do all that work. But she didn't leave much room for the emotional aspect of it. Not that we didn't feel loved, but I knew she was always busy.

Other respondents whose parents worked in entry-level positions witnessed how their parents struggled financially. Jill's father, trained in Korea as a white collar professional, found himself unable to find comparable and consistent employment in the United States. Working as an independent consultant, Jill's father focused on trying to gain permanent residency while her mother worked under the table at a Korean-owned small business to provide for her family. While they did purchase a home—so often the symbol of achieving the "American dream"—her parents were barely able to cover their monthly mortgage and lived paycheck to paycheck. As a child, Jill carefully saved the money her relatives would give her on New Year's Day, and in high school she worked odd jobs, and then lent that money to her mother when her parents' financial situation became grave. Tearfully, Jill recalls how her father's education and training did not protect them from precarious financial situations:

> It's one of the fields where it's high skills but low pay and I think, especially if English is your second language and you're not particularly business

savvy like my dad—he's a good worker but not like a good manager and so I think he has never really figured out how to succeed in that system. . . .

I've been working since high school and I worked also in college. Then I worked for three years before going back to school. Even when I was a kid, money has always been tight. I remember when I would get money from relatives or something like that and would save it. Like there would be times I'd have to lend it to my mom. Knowing that I would never get it back. I'm sorry; this is hard to tell.

As a child, Jill was acutely aware when her immigrant parents were experiencing financial stressors, and she often prepared herself to help them. As she describes, she needed to have her childhood savings available for her parents when things were difficult. Jill worked numerous part-time jobs in college to financially support herself and did not ask for support from her parents because she knew they "always felt really bad about that, that they were not able to do more for me during that period in my life." Like other respondents, Jill tried to manage her emotions around financial stresses in order to lessen the burden on her parents and reassure them that she would be fine without their support.

ENTREPRENEUR PARENTS

Half of our respondents described growing up in a household where parents were self-employed. Children of immigrant entrepreneurs worked alongside their parents in various settings, tending cash registers, cleaning, taking orders, prepping ingredients, going to wholesale stores, and/or stocking shelves. Most respondents were not happy to work at the family business but had no choice in the matter, as their parents depended on their labor or did not have childcare alternatives. Caron remembers:

I used to go to the toy store like once a week or something. I was ten years old, working the cash register. So, I would always help. I'd go there pretty often, you know: organize the store, do cashier stuff . . .

Shelia and her sister were expected to work at their parents' store, as their parents depended on the girls' labor:

At the store my sister and I had to do minor things when we were younger, like stocking the shelves and sweeping. It progressed as we got older and we had more responsibilities. In the back, my mom had made a carryout for the food area. We would be cooking and tending the cash register, dealing with the deliveries and employees.

By the time Shelia was in high school, she worked two afternoons a week at the store. However, even as these children performed such work, they were not necessarily content about what they had to do.

Many disliked working in the family business, which included putting time in on weekends and during summers when peers were on family trips or vacation. Walter, whose parents owned a sandwich shop, recalls how he spent his summer vacations as a child:

> Working for my parents. Basically I woke up six in the morning because that was when I was still living in San Francisco. So we had to drive thirty minutes from San Francisco to South San Francisco. So, for an eleven-year-old kid to wake up six in the morning, that's pretty tough. Yeah, in summertime . . . usually it was from 6 a.m. to 6 p.m., 6 a.m. to 7 p.m., that I'll be home at night during my summer vacation and usually I'll help them cashier and bag the things that people buy and help them with the grocery shopping and things like that.

Chris describes how he would help at his family store, including stocking and translating when needed. Like Walter, he did not like working in his family's store as a child because it meant he could not play on the weekends:

> CHRIS: I did work for my dad when I was younger. I just followed him around with whatever stuff he needed me to do. And, usually, I would help him to translate stuff. Like I said he had stores, so I would, like, stock things for him. So I just helped him out wherever he needed me.
>
> INTERVIEWER: And what was that like?
>
> CHRIS: It was kind of frustrating. Because on Saturdays, I would really want to hang out with my friends. But I'm a little eleven year old or ten year old. I have to go help out my dad; do things that I really didn't want to do.

Shelia shares similar memories of her family working all the time. In particular, she remembers that her family rarely took a vacation and wonders if her experience is one that only other Korean immigrant entrepreneurial families could understand:

> They were working really hard making ends meet. I am curious what other Korean American families have gone through because of how . . . my friends that are not Korean American react when I tell them. They were surprised that my family has only gone on one vacation and that one vacation was very stressful. There were three families in one RV. It was very uncomfortable and it was stressful. I hear about going on vacation and doing this and that but not my family. I kind of envy that.

Derrick's parents worked in various blue-collar jobs until they saved up and bought a motel; all their children were required to work to help run the family business. Describing his childhood relationship with his parents as "contentious and difficult," Derrick remembered working at the motel: "It was awful. . . . Basically, I was their slave." He laughed. "It was pretty much manual labor." While he was accepted into his first-choice university, an Ivy League school, and whereas other respondents complained how their parents nagged them to be accepted at similar elite universities, Derrick's father "somehow coerced" him to attend a university closer to home instead because he needed Derrick to work at the motel on the weekends. After he graduated from college, Derrick relocated to California, away from the family business.

Timothy's parents also worked in blue-collar jobs when they first immigrated, and then eventually bought their own business; as he grew older, his hours and responsibilities increased.

> Initially, I worked in junior high on the weekends and then just Saturdays. We were closed on Sundays, so I worked pretty much the whole day, and then as I got older in high school and was able to drive, I worked there the whole day if I didn't have any other events going on. Then when I got to college, if I was on break during the summer, that enabled my parents to go on vacation, so I would be there a week or two at a time just running the place. You know, at first I didn't want to work, but I saw how difficult it was for my mother [and] that

she needed a break. That overcame—overruled— any objections that
I had.

Timothy's work contributed to his family's financial stability and
allowed his parents to take some time off; his main motivation for
working came from wanting his mother to rest. On the other hand, he
and his father fought constantly from junior high until college, when he
stayed away from his family for a couple of years. Thanks to his mother
who tried to improve the relationship between father and son, as well
as counseling that he regularly sought from the pastors and leaders at
his church, Timothy and his father eventually resolved their differences.

Over the years, Nancy and her siblings worked at her parents' many
businesses: a dry cleaner, a flea market stall, and a convenience store.
She recalls how she spent her summers working at the dry cleaners,
while her brother worked at the convenience store or picked up her
father after his shift ended at three in the morning. As Nancy noted
several times, though, she and her siblings were mindful that this work
was hardest on their parents:

> Really didn't like it, but of course, what am I going to do? I knew my dad
> needed me. You know we all had to do it. I think of how much more my
> parents went through, you know, it was heartache and just butt-kicking
> work.

Although entrepreneurship has been viewed through rose-colored
lenses as a path to social and economic mobility for immigrants, indi-
vidually and as an ethnic group, it requires intensive effort, including
reliance on unpaid and underpaid family labor, long hours with no
vacations, and fierce competition from co-ethnics.[18]

Many respondents adapted to the work lives of their parents by staying home by themselves after school and helping at the family business
after school and during weekends and vacations. Most respondents did
not enjoy working at the family business. Looking back, respondents
described feelings of envy, anger, and resentment about the work they
were forced to do that their peers did not have to do, as well as viewing their contribution as labor of love for their overworked and stressed

parents. Either way, their labor in the family business was required and integral to their collective survival.

Working to Be Their Voice: Cultural and Language Brokering

Cultural brokering is defined as "the act of bridging, linking, or mediating between groups or persons of differing cultural systems for the purpose of reducing conflict or producing change."[19] Children of immigrants, who tend to become fluent in the host society's language more quickly than their parents and use their language skills to translate, interpret, and mediate between their family and the English-speakers, are known as language brokers.[20] These youth do not just translate words; they are mediating between cultures and worldviews, often between their parents and members of the dominant groups and/or authority figures.

Much scholarship on children's contributions in immigrant families who speak a language other than English and maintain cultural practices and traditions distinct from dominant American society has focused on Spanish-speaking immigrants.[21] In *Translating Childhoods: Immigrant Youth, Language, and Culture*, Marjorie Faulstich Orellana observes, however, that language brokering is not limited to a particular group, but is a "cultural practice that is shaped by the experience of being an immigrant," because the children's "families need their skills in order to accomplish the tasks of everyday life in their new linguistic and cultural context".[22] She also argues that much of this "invisible" work contributes critically to the society and public institutions at large; teachers, sales clerks, managers, social service providers, medical professionals, and law enforcement officers also count on the ability of these child language brokers to communicate with adults whose English proficiency is limited. The respondents in our study were not exceptions. On the contrary, they recalled serving as language brokers as children and young adults, acting as their parents' compass for survival in the post-migration world.

Children of immigrants tend to report language brokering as a normal or expected task in a typical day.[23] Researchers who have studied child language brokers have found that children experience both positive and negative consequences from their work. Immigrant youth reported that in general, they liked brokering and that brokering made them more mature and independent individuals who made significant contributions to their families.[24] Language brokering also may foster both independence and interdependence in children due to years of mutual reliance between parents and children.[25] Others also found that language brokering increased cognitive and linguistic skills and academic performance in child language brokers.[26]

Unlike other studies that focus on youth and translation work, our interviews involved adults and their recollections of what they did as children. (As adults, many respondents continue to translate and interpret for their aging parents, which will be discussed in a later chapter.) In our sample, the 1.5 generation children were more likely to bring up examples of translating and interpreting for their parents than those respondents who were born in the United States. The most common examples they gave included calling utility companies and other household-related tasks, as well as performing similar functions for their parents' work or at the workplace. While both sons and daughters participated in these efforts, gender differences became manifest when it came to the meaning of such work. Sons, although willing to help their parents, were more often critical of the tasks that were imposed upon them. Daughters saw the tasks as difficult but also as a form of care they provided to parents who depended on them.

Many respondents served as translators at retail and service businesses. Sabrina, who came to the United States at the age of three, remembered the expectations and pressures that came from her father's reliance on her language brokering skills:

> I don't have a lot of fond memories of my dad. Whenever he needed something translated, I was the one who did it. And whenever he got frustrated, he always yelled at me. I always cried but I still had to get the job done. I grew up really fast because I needed to step up.

As other scholars have found, children of immigrants also negotiated important business contracts such as automobile purchases, lease agreements, and home purchases on behalf of their parents. Some of our respondents reported not only completing such transactions, but also reading over mortgage and other contracts in order to facilitate communications between parents who were professional realtors and non-Koreans in the same field.[27] Nancy, who immigrated at six years of age, is one example. Remembering how she and her siblings worked in the family businesses, and how, beginning in junior high, her father relied on Nancy as a language broker to deal with contracts and documents with "Americans," she observed:

> So, I was a translator for my dad. Whenever he would deal with real estate clients that were American, he would have me help him fill out the documents. Funny, how that I was in middle school, high school, typing these things out for him. So, he would tell me what he wanted me to write, and I would translate it and I would just write out the document what needed to be. And you know, I'm just in high school, so I don't know the right legal language. I just write what I can, and so I'm sure that they could tell it was the work of a preteen or a teenager, you know, but whatever. He would tell me how to do it, so sometimes I would just write down whatever he wanted verbatim, but other times I would do some translating on documents and also just interpreting—you know sometimes they couldn't understand his English. I remember one time he said, "Okay I see you soon at 'Mukadonalds.'" And then at the time I could hear him saying "What?" and he said, "I tell you I see you soon at 'Mukadonalds'" and it was like "McDonalds! McDonalds!" And he said, so he tried to say it again, but I had to get on the phone, "Okay he's going to meet you at McDonald's in ten minutes. . . . " And he actually had me go with him, and I did not know what I was doing, but he needed me to help him with interpreting because he tried to deal with as much as he could with Korean clients, but sometimes there's an American involved, so it was tough for him.

Many who did this brokering work as children framed it as something normal, as something that had to be done. Others remembered feeling uncomfortable translating or interpreting when it involved interactions with other adults in the context of businesses or institutions that they viewed as "adult" spaces or "adult" work. For example, Shirley, a second-generation woman in her thirties, recalled going to a vision exam as a child and having to negotiate between her mother, who had heard from her friends that hard contact lenses were better, and her optometrist, who wanted to prescribe soft contact lenses. Brokering between her mother, whom she described as losing her temper easily and often, and the professionals who belittled her non-English speaking parent, Shirley felt embarrassed:

> I'm in the middle! I don't know whom to side with, and it's embarrassing. But it's also, I feel sorry—I feel bad, you know, for my mom who doesn't understand, and then these professionals get annoyed and they start speaking slowly, clearly, you know, knowing that English is her second language, and so it's just, I remember that feeling it was just, embarrassment, shame, but it was also just kind of feeling sorry for my mom.

Some respondents noted how the immigration process created this intergenerational dependence, and how their translation work was a response to this parental sacrifice and sense of loss or displacement in their new home. Elizabeth, who immigrated at the age of nine and is the oldest child in her family, became the primary English speaker in her household, one year after arriving from Korea:

> I would have to call the gas company saying, "We moved, can you change our address?" and such. They would ask, "How old are you?" "Well, I'm ten, but my parents can't speak English," and asking me to do this, and things like that.

Elizabeth remains the main translator/interpreter for her parents, who still do not speak English fluently after living and working in the United States for over twenty years. She used to be bothered by this role as a youth, but now views it as her way of repaying her parents' "sacrifice."

> I find out how much they sacrificed to come here and how much they are still sacrificing because they're still not completely adjusted to America. I remember my mom telling me one time: "You don't know how much [it] cuts down on your pride, when you have to ask your sons and daughters for little things."

Joseph, who immigrated at the age of seven, remembers that he and his siblings were bothered when his parents asked them to call utility companies; they wanted to play like their peers, and not do tasks that in their eyes were the domain of parents and adults. Like Elizabeth, Joseph came to recognize his parents' sacrifices as an adult:

> They would ask us to call the electric company or the gas company, or ask my older brother and my sister. We were young at the time, and we were thinking, "That's your job, why can't they do that?" Looking back I realize they couldn't speak English. The perspectives as a child—we want to go play football, go play outside, but now, kids want to play PlaySta-tion. But we didn't realize that they needed us to help them because it was tough for them. . . . I truly appreciate what they did, looking back now, although, at the time, I couldn't truly understand them because I was going through my own identity crisis.

Richard, who immigrated at age nine, remembers growing up with "a lot of love" from his parents. "They were kind of hard on me in expec-tations, but they showed me so much sacrifice. They really loved us." Despite this good relationship, he observed how his parents empha-sized, as an element of "Korean culture," the importance of obeying and respecting older persons, particularly parents, without question-ing their authority; at the same time, these same parents relied on their children for performing important tasks that both affected the house-hold and in some ways subtracted from their own authority.

Richard's observations are particularly illustrative in that, while he shares Elizabeth and Joseph's recognition of the work of language brokering as necessary, he also expresses his discomfort with the con-tradiction that the brokering created between immigrant parents and their children. In other words, how can parents assume authority and demand deference when they cannot fulfill parental roles and tasks without their children's help in the United States? He states:

> When we got letters from school I had to explain to them what it meant. If we had to argue our electric bill, I would have to call the elec-tric company. It seemed odd to act as a parent when I already had par-ents. . . . Now, they trust and lean on me for a lot of things. I will always be a child in their eyes. I'm taking care of them and speaking for them, but at the same time the Korean culture is such that no matter how

old you are if they are older than you, you have to give respect. And, [you] have to say yes, even if they are wrong. There's definitely a struggle between what my role is and what their expectation of my role is and how that plays out in real life. They are thinking traditionally Korean, whereas I'm thinking we're not in Korea. This is the way I was raised. There are stressors from culture that they expect and have stressors from how life is here, which is not Korea.

Children in the Middle: Calming Stressed Parents

Our respondents detailed how their immigrant parents were "stressed out." Respondents discussed how they witnessed or heard how parents experienced incidents of racial prejudice, glass ceiling effect, and misunderstandings that stemmed from cultural and language barriers with supervisors, co-workers, and customers. Joseph states, "Even in terms of discrimination –they weren't called by their names at work. They were always called Chink this and Chink that." Shelia discussed how the sheer stress of work sometimes spilled out onto children and how it affected intergenerational relationships: "My parents were in so much stress and it carried over how it interacted with us. They were tired and quieter and more prone to be angry." In the 1970s and 1980s, when most of our respondents were children, there was a dearth of language-specific services regarding stress management available to Korean immigrants and their families. Immigrant families across all ethnicities have been known to be at increased risk to experience violence in the home.[28] Violence in immigrant families has been attributed to stressful situations within and outside the home, such as financial problems, problems at the workplace, discrimination, and language barriers.[29] When stressed, immigrants generally do not utilize mental health services and when violence erupts, they are less likely to seek help due to a combination of factors including structural barriers to accessing resources and the belief and fear that disclosure will bring negative impact and shame to the family and the ethnic community.[30]

The majority of the respondents did not mention family violence. But several respondents recalled incidents of domestic violence and abuse in their families; the abusers were fathers whose occupations in the United States included a range of professions. One person, Peter, received a beating so severe after failing a test as a young child that his school called a social worker to investigate; Peter's father never hit him again, but the effect of the corporal punishment lasted through his childhood. Derrick said, almost in passing, "They abused me, they beat me. It was very difficult, but I think it was because that's the only way they knew how to raise their kids."

Molly, a 1.5-generation respondent in her thirties, describes her current relationship with her parents as "fairly close." While she was growing up, her parents worked full-time and relied on Molly to take care of herself and her younger sibling. While the siblings grew up witnessing many fights between their parents, as children, they did not intervene or address them and often felt the only way to cope was to let it "blow over":

We didn't know and we didn't exactly care if other families were like this, but we did realize that whenever problems arose, we were, well, let's just pretend it didn't happen, and let it just blow over, and that included infidelity between my parents. That included abuse, physical and verbal, and mental abuse, and anything that was unpleasant, it was always covered up.

The survivors of the cycle of family violence described attempting to appease out-of-control fathers and care for abused family members. Sophia, a second-generation woman in her forties, recalls how she tried to calm her father down whenever he lost his temper with her mother or the children.

My siblings and I grew up in an abusive home. My father used to beat my mother. I remember as a small child, my father losing his temper suddenly and throwing dishes across the room and then going after my mother. My sister and brother would just hug each other tight and cry. The smallest thing would set him off. . . . Helping my parents' marriage is really about keeping my father happy, which is impossible. Growing up this way, I became rather enabling. I would ride my bike to KFC and get my father his favorite things: fried chicken, mashed potatoes, coleslaw even if he had just yelled at me recently for something. When he yelled at me, he would sit me down at a table and scream at me, telling me I was stupid, I was nothing like him, that I was going to be a failure for life, that I was like my mom, dumb. Stuff like that. And I remember looking at the garden clock in the kitchen. He'd start yelling at me at 1 p.m. and not finish until 3 or 4 p.m.

As the target of her father's anger and abuse along with her mother, Sophia tried her best to fulfill the impossible task of keeping her father happy. Earlier in the chapter, we discussed how children of immigrant parents tried to do well in school as a way to please their parents and live up to their expectations. Their father was extremely proud of Sophia's sister, an outstanding student who was admitted into several elite universities, but he used the overachiever sister's academic success to berate Sophia and her brother for being "losers" in comparison.

Maria also grew up in an abusive home as the favored child of her father who beat her mother and older siblings. She describes:

My dad was a very violent man. So we lived with domestic violence. And apparently, my mom says that before I was born, it was very bad—it was undiscriminating. It would just happen every day; it would happen whenever he felt like it, and destroyed the house. When I was born, she said that things changed a little bit—because I was the apple in my dad's eye. I was like the love of his life. So he only beat my mom when they fought and he only beat my brothers and [me] when he wanted to discipline us. Or if we were caught in the crossfire of his violence against my mom. Growing up, because of that, you sit between really loving your father and hating him.

Her father left her mother after Maria graduated from college and she was saving up to move away from California for work. She gave her savings to her mother and postponed the move to be with her as her mother began to rebuild her life; in the process, Maria shifted from trying to control her father's emotions and actions with what little influence she had in her family, to financially and emotionally taking care of her mother as a young adult.

The above examples illustrate the different ways in which some respondents as children and adolescents tried to shield their mothers and manage their abusive fathers. Domestic violence affects all families and cuts across race, ethnicity, and socioeconomic status, but as mentioned earlier, Korean immigrant families face cultural and structural barriers as they seek help for domestic violence or mental health issues.[31] The respondents survived and resolved their situations in different ways. Derrick moved out of state after college graduation, away from his parents. Molly and her sister are settled in their careers and are experiencing a role reversal with their parents, who will be relying on their children for financial and other forms of support in their old age. While her parents are still experiencing marital problems, Molly shared how she recently confronted her father with a resolute strength and power that she could not have had as a child.

> We recently had a situation where there was infidelity between my parents, and we dealt with it completely differently, and I chose that no more are we going to about this the same way, and let it blow over, I just confronted my dad about it, and I said I'm not going to put up with this anymore, I know this is between you and mom, but this is also a family issue. I was like, I'm not going to pretend like I didn't know what went on, and I don't want to do this anymore, in terms of, get your act together, or we have to sever ties because I can't deal with someone who's that disrespectful or hurtful to the people he supposedly loves the most.

Years later, having become a busy mother of two children juggling her family, job, and school at the time of the interview, Sophia discusses how her family has fared after the cycle of violence. Her mother eventually separated from her father, who is no longer physically and mentally abusive. While she and her siblings keep in regular contact with her father, Sophia is particularly determined to take care of her mother for the rest of her life. In adulthood, respondents like Sophia who survived family violence reclaimed parent-child relationships on their own terms with fathers who are no longer abusive. It must be reiterated that only a small minority of respondents revealed they experienced family violence as children. But their examples vividly illustrate how some respondents' work of soothing and caring for immigrant parents entailed pacifying abusive parents or bearing the brunt of the abuse themselves.

Conclusion

INTERVIEWER: If both your parents worked, who took care of you?

JOEL: Obviously, before coming to the U.S. my parents provided for me and my younger brothers. *When we immigrated, the situation changed. Although they worked, I took care of them.*

As Joel succinctly states, immigration brought changes to the Korean American family in which the first-generation parents found their roles compromised or reversed in America. Children of Korean immigrants often found themselves brokering their parents' worlds. This work, both visible (physical labor) and invisible (emotional), was often unspoken and seen as essential to the survival of many families and the well-being of immigrant parents. Not everyone did emotional or physical work in childhood because of variations in family circumstances and family dynamics; for example, respondents like Joy and Nina recalled that their parents, who earned higher degrees in the United States, spoke English fluently, and worked for mainstream companies, did not need or ask for support from their children. Moreover, there were differing degrees in how children participated in work and supporting their parents. Not all were involved in all aspects of physical work, such as cultural and language brokering or helping out at the family business, but most were involved in the emotion work of ensuring their immigrant parents were going to succeed in their new country.

The different types of work respondents did as children instilled the sense that their parents were at least partially dependent on them for their survival in the United States, and that their immigrant parents' dreams were embodied in them—the second generation. And one way that this second generation of Korean Americans, not always complicit, indeed sometimes ambivalent, tried to fulfill those dreams was through academic achievement. The respondents also worked as cultural and language brokers between the English-speaking American world and that of their Korean-speaking parents. For some, their roles also included the physical labor of caring for the family at home or at work by doing chores, creating meals, or helping at the family business. And finally, for many of our female respondents, caring for parents often took the form of soothing them by doing well in school, help-ing around the house, managing family businesses, and also sometimes calming domestic disputes between family members. Differing dispo-sitions among respondents played a part in determining which child among the siblings responded to familial emotional needs, but daugh-ters, more often than sons, performed emotional in addition to other types of labor. As we explore in other chapters, gender was and contin-ues to be a significant factor in differing sibling responses on how car-ing responsibility is divided in families.

As children, respondents also felt ambivalent about the work they did for their parents. Our findings illustrate that as immigrant youth grow older, they feel conflicted in choosing between their own respon-sibilities/interests (for example, increasing homework or wanting to spend time with friends) and helping their family. Studies have shown that there are costs involved for children, especially for Korean Ameri-can females, who translate for their parents, including higher psycho-logical symptoms of anxiety and depression.[32] Despite these difficulties, many respondents credit their "working" childhoods as making them into the persons they are today. Their memories of childhood and of immigrant parents sacrificing for their needs are what guide them today as they negotiate a new type of role reversal with parents entering older adulthood.

2

Giving Back

It's kind of a sense of debt that always haunts me. It's not
necessarily a Korean thing as much as it's like an immigrant
[thing], but more like being a child of immigrants. Like that
sense of debt that I'll never be able to repay them for everything that they did for me—to be able to go to college and go
to grad school —and I felt like I owe it to them.
—Patrick

Patrick, who is in his late twenties, sums up what many other respondents have suggested: they want to "give back" to their parents for all
their sacrifices. In many ways, Patrick's family's immigration experience sounds like a familiar narrative. His parents owned a store and
worked long hours until his mother developed serious health problems
that required around the clock care when Patrick was in college. He discussed the overwhelming sense of responsibility he felt as the eldest son
to help his father with the business and to provide care-giving for his
mother. While experiencing the pull of family pressures to do well and
to give back, Patrick has also felt the passion to follow his own dreams.

In her study of Korean immigrants in New York, Kyeyoung Park
argues that the concept of *anjong*, defined as "establishment, stability,
or security," is critical to understanding how they adapt to and make

meaning of their lives in the United States.[1] Although she focuses on the role of small business ownership as a core means to achieving *anjong*, Park distinguishes different definitions of establishment that her respondents try to obtain through different life stages. She explains:

> According to my analysis, for a single man anjong means primarily marriage and beginning a family. For a young couple, anjong means establishing their own business. For a couple operating a business successfully, anjong means having children and inviting parents in Korea to join them in America. At a later stage, anjong means buying a house in a "good" suburban neighborhood. At a more advanced stage, anjong means sending children to good universities, getting them trained as professionals, and marrying them to fellow Korean Americans.[2]

Building on Park's analysis, this chapter examines how respondents negotiate the elements that define their parents' sense of establishment and stability at this advanced stage of *anjong*.[3] As discussed in the previous chapter, many respondents recalled doing different types of work for their parents while they were children as the family adjusted financially and socially in the United States. As they grew older, they learned more about their parents' pasts, including personal and historical traumas, which may have been unspoken or unacknowledged in the family, and how these pasts related to their parents' immigrant experience. Even as they remain mindful of their parents' pasts, sacrifices, and dreams, many have learned (and are still learning) to pursue and meet their own needs in work, love, and life.

The children of immigrants in the United States grow up in a country that values individualism, self-sufficiency, autonomy, and eventual detachment from family, yet their life experiences from childhood to adulthood starkly contrast with these dominant American values.[4] The children of Korean immigrants, as mentioned in chapter 1, perform emotional labor as they broker the worlds of their parents through studying and doing well in school, helping at home and at work, and/ or by mediating culture and language for their parents. Their lives are linked to their parents' lives across generations especially because as children they could help break down real and perceived structural barriers that their parents encountered daily. Korean immigrants bring cultural orientations such as interdependency, collectivism, and respect for elders, which can be manifested in authoritarian styles of parenting; however, the structural barriers they encounter in the United States often cause them to rely on their children as they strive for stability and mobility.[5] The conflicts that arise as a result of pre-migration cultural orientations and the difficulties of life in the United States for Korean immigrants and their families can cause stress for the children.

The adolescent phase of development, in which one establishes an autonomous self while maintaining connectedness to others, is known as *individuation*.[6] What role does individuation play in the lives of the children of Korean immigrants? How do they navigate their own dreams and desires in relationship to their immigrant parents' wishes and wants? Those who have studied immigrant families have conceptualized family relationships as interdependent and involved in each other's lives.[7] Research on immigrant parents and their U.S.-born adolescent children shows that the push for autonomy happens at later ages than it does for their non-immigrant European American peers.[8] Socioeconomic status and the immigration experiences of their parents have also been thought to be factors delaying individuation in adolescents.[9] According to researchers, the positive outcome of individuation is differentiation, a balance between connectedness and separation in interfamilial relationships; once individuation and differentiation have occurred, healthy boundaries can develop between self and the family.[10]

Scholars are examining how the path to young adulthood and the conventional markers of becoming an adult have shifted dramatically in the last century in the United States, Canada, and Western Europe; these shifts can have an impact on life chances for today's young adults and the broader society.[11] Although there is significant amount of research on childhood and immigrant families in the United States, the literature is beginning to explore how relationships between immigrant parents and their American-born and raised children evolve as the latter navigate careers, dating and marriage, and other significant life choices in young adulthood.[12] As they enter middle adulthood, how do adult children of Korean immigrants interpret their parents' lives? How do they find ways to give back as a result? And how, while in this process, do they manage to care for themselves, and if applicable, their spouses/partners and children? The themes that emerge in this chapter include how children understand their parents' traumatic pasts and limitations, recognize their parents' love in the light of past and current conflicts, and give back to their parents while navigating their own major life decisions. And finally, adult children recognize their own feelings around obligations and duty to their parents as they reflect on their own dreams, passions, and need for self-care.

Understanding Intergenerational Impact of Parents' Past: The Korean War

Kyeyoung Park writes, "Korean immigration to America can be interpreted as one outcome of American political, economic, . . . missionary, and military involvement in Korea since the late nineteenth century."[13] Many respondents came to understand their parents and intergenerational relations in a new light as adults; one way to do this was by viewing their upbringing in the context of Korean history, such as the Korean War (1950–1953). Although the years during and following the Korean War were cataclysmic, those who emigrated to the United States rarely spoke of those years to their children.[14] Many adult children had knowledge gaps about their parents' and grandparents' pasts, particularly in regard to the war and its effects, although most had heard bits and pieces about their family's wartime whereabouts from parents who were young children during the war. Challenging stories told in a matter-of-fact way (e.g., about an uncle's dying, families having to flee bombs) left many respondents wondering about the intergenerational impact of the war on themselves and on their relationships with their parents. Despite its impact on modern Korean history and diaspora, there are few studies of the intergenerational impact of the Korean War on Korean Americans.[15] However, the generation that went abroad and those that are one generation removed from the war are beginning to document the effects of war via creative productions such as visual art, film, and creative writing.[16]

Those parents who did speak of the war experience usually did so in remembrance of family members lost during the period. Other parents relayed the trials of fleeing the war zone, living as refugees, and battling extreme poverty, hunger, and cold. Most often, however, experiences of war and its aftermath remain blank in the family record. According to Ramsay Liem, a noted Korean American psychologist, families whose ethnic group has lived through a collective trauma often experience intergenerational silence regarding that past:

> Silence has been found to be an important carrier of the unspeakable past, a medium harboring subliminal dread and fear, the object of projected assumptions and expectations, and a source of miscommunication among the generations.[17]

War survivors have understandably averted their gaze from past traumas. Immigrant parents were often reticent in sharing details of losses experienced during, and as a result of, the Korean War.

Kimberly, who came to the United States when she was about three years old, shared how she indirectly learned about her family history. "They wouldn't really tell me, but I would keep an open ear. Because you know parents talk. They're around friends." Adult children like Kimberly have had to work to connect the dots to understand their families' whereabouts during the war. Fred, who was American born, noticed a paucity of detail in his parents' accounts of the war; they have told him fragments with only an occasional sharpened memory of hardship, such as eating grass. Fred describes how his knowledge of the Korean War as an adult was largely based on external sources such as films, media, and books:

> I've got bits and pieces of it from my dad. My dad, he would just tell me they were oppressed. They were very poor. My dad had to eat grass to survive. He had to work two jobs, to just get by. But my mother's side, because they had some relationship established, some status, I didn't get the impression that they were poor or anything like that. But all my knowledge of the Korean War is through movies and media and history books. No first hand, or, obviously not first hand because it's my father, but the story that they did tell was very limited.

Similarly, David has fragments of information about what happened during the war:

> I know both of my parents were very young. My father vaguely remembers, but his older sisters told me stories of seeing charred bodies blown

up and so forth. But that's the extent, they weren't eyewitnesses, they don't recollect too much.

As a way to make sense of their parents' and families' histories, adult children of immigrants have been involved in gathering and uncovering stories. They also work to identify and understand how the tragic losses experienced by their parents as young children, as well as how their families survived in the post-war years, have impacted their lives and relationships in the United States. Vanessa, for example, shared how she has gained more interest in the last decade to learn more about her family's past and document the details. She jokes about how she did not pay attention to her parents when she was young, but now she is especially interested in learning about her maternal side of the family in South Korea and whom she has barely seen since her family immigrated to the United States:

> I don't know a whole lot about, even my parents' own life, because it wasn't common that they talked about their childhood, other than the fact, you know, when we're at the dinner table and we don't want to eat our food. And they say, "We had to go through garbage cans to just survive"—those kinds of stories, which you know as a kid, you're like—it's just the parents' way of trying to get you to eat.

Vanessa describes the loss of family members experienced on both sides as "brutal." Her maternal grandfather passed away when her mother was five, shot during the war because he was a police officer. Her grandmother, then pregnant with her third child, struggled to survive, and her mother had to discontinue her education at seventh grade. Post-war poverty truncated her mother's formal education, something by which her mother is still shamed: "Even to this day, . . . she'll remind us not to tell other people, you know, that she's only had a seventh grade education because of her pride and because of how much we emphasize education here." She also learned that her oldest paternal uncle was captured during the war and forced to serve in the North Korean army when the rest of her father's family fled to South Korea; they never saw him again. Their hopes of reunification were dashed in early 2000s when after decades of searching, they learned that the oldest uncle had passed away in the 1990s.

As Vanessa became more curious about her family history and her parents became more open with their children, she learned about the deaths, separations, poverty, and life disruptions of the "unspeakable past."

In their efforts to understand what happened to their families during the Korean War, many respondents also started to find compassion and empathy for their parents' "dysfunctional" ways of coping with life's difficulties, such as their inability to discuss the pains of life or even their striving for material and financial success. Jessica, whose family immigrated in the early 1970s, was told that the war reduced her family's circumstances to a whole new world of hardship. As South Korea's social system disintegrated, family members and fortunes were lost:

> My mom would tell me . . . her family had actually been well-to-do before the war and in the war they lost it all. You know? They just lost everything, and so they were struggling economically afterwards, and then she lost her oldest sister.

Connie had proactively asked her parents about her family's history during the Korean War, but it was a difficult subject. As she unearthed family and Korean history, she came to understand her parents more deeply and to recognize how the traumatic events of twentieth-century Korea shaped how they coped with difficulties. In her family, one cannot show vulnerability or sadness; in particular, her father valued strength and resented anyone in the family who felt self-pity. She attributes these characteristics to coping skills which he developed during the Korean War and which helped him survive this tumultuous period:

> He grew up in a war. He just doesn't think [self-pity] belongs in life because he wants his children to be strong and survive. . . . Because the kid that sits by the side of the road and cried didn't make it, right? The people who all, like, sat in their houses and cried probably didn't survive. . . . People who just said well, shit, I've got to get up and do it. I guess I'll cry tomorrow. They all survived. The ones who cried when they were hungry and you know, they missed the chance to raid an army—an overturned army truck—for food so they learned to just act before feeling so. . . . My mom and dad are both very emotional but they refuse to acknowledge a lot of their darkness.

Connie perceives her parents' need to be strong in difficult times as a learned coping style that emerged as a result of the Korean War and its aftermath, and one that has been modeled for and passed onto the next generation. Although she admires the resilience in her parents, she notes that the need to show strength also has had consequences for her own well-being. Growing up, she learned not to show vulnerability and to cope with life's difficulties by moving on without reflecting on the pain. She wished her parents had responded differently to the difficult times she encountered as a child:

> I wished I could have been able to tell my dad and still I can't do it today. "Dad, I don't feel well." And that doesn't have anything to do with being Korean but more about my relationship with him where he could say, "Oh, you don't feel well. Come sit next to me until you feel better." In my family, it's very cognitive and we're very strategic in terms of our thinking that if I do not feel bad and as soon as you feel bad you have to figure out how to not feel bad anymore. Instead of recognizing it as a process. I think that is half my parents' personality and another huge half of it is ramification of the war, where you didn't have time to feel bad. As soon as you felt bad, you got killed or you starved or something awful happened to you.

Connie describes how she still finds it difficult to just feel, process, and say out loud her negative emotions, and attributes this ongoing coping pattern to a combination of her parents' personality and the consequences of political, economic, and social upheavals of war. While Connie did not live through the war and the post-war years, she tries to use her understanding of Korean history by linking the historical to the personal to better understand her parents who did survive through the tumultuous years.

Kimberly, in her thirties, also reflects on the magnitude of her parents' trials, such as the impact of living through the Korean War and its aftermath. Kimberly has tried actively to understand her parents' lives as a way of putting in perspective personal traumas and resentment about parental neglect. She said that her parents did not talk much of their pasts, other than that "life was hard" and "it was hard to eat." She took Asian Studies and Asian American Studies classes in college and attended community events on the war to help her own understanding

of the Korean American experience and to uncover this tragic and cataclysmic chapter in her parents' lives. Kimberly now puts her childhood
in perspective as she remembers how her mother was always at work
and unable to be physically and emotionally available to her children.
She sees how cultural factors, historical trauma, and the situational
stresses of immigration shaped her family life in the United States.
Looking at her parents through her adult lens, she also finds ways to
forgive her "overwhelmed" parents for "never" being there for her in
childhood:

> I was sitting in my parents' shoes. Wow, it must have been hard for them
> to raise two kids, and try to make enough money to survive, being in a
> foreign country, and all the hardships they had to endure. It's no wonder
> they were gone. They were too busy doing other things. They were too
> overwhelmed. I know that they were working a lot, but because there was
> a lack of intimate connection with them, I always questioned why they
> were never there. . . . Being a mother myself, I am learning to understand
> children and parenthood—it's not just for Koreans but universally—we
> all kind of grow up and the culture is centered around parenting. We
> don't know how to raise our children. And they are vulnerable to being
> affected in a lot of negative ways. Because, my parents, my grandparents,
> were going through a lot of things during the Korean War, I think that
> must have affected them.

In adulthood, many children of immigrants noted how the legacy of
these traumas impacted their parents, resulting in particular, in emotional unavailability or disconnect from their own children's day-to-day
experiences. It is noteworthy that the respondents who learned about
twentieth-century Korean history tended to reassess the childhood
conflicts between themselves and their parents; rather than viewing the
conflict as one largely rooted in personality and cultural differences (for
example, "Korean" or Confucian authoritarian style versus more "Western" or "American" egalitarian style of parenting), respondents in their
adulthood explained their parents' shortcomings in terms of their having
endured war-inflicted trauma and loss. The ability to keep moving rather
than reflecting on the destruction, loss, and poverty that profoundly
shaped individuals and the nation was a way for many to cope.

Cathy, whose family immigrated in 1980, offers another example of explaining parents' behavior in the context of more recent Korean history. Cathy, who was thirteen years old when her family immigrated, shared that she did not have any conflicts with her parents until she went to college. She explains:

> It was when I was in college and I began to get more involved in political activities. And so they didn't like it. They were afraid of what would happen. Because my oldest brother in college was an activist in Korea and he got in trouble. So my parents got reminded of it. So it made them even more worried. . . . I actually talked to my sister. My sister and her husband got married during that year and so I was very close to my brother-in-law. So I talked to them and my brother-in-law would try to talk to my father. He would tell him that "it's okay, what she's doing" and stuff like that.

Her parents were intimately aware of what "political activity in college" meant in Korea during its post-war movement for democracy and labor rights—violent and sometimes deadly clashes between student demonstrators and police and military in full riot gear.[18] While Cathy asked her brother-in-law to reassure her parents that she would be all right, she also understood the reactions of her parents.

Many respondents have tried to understand the intergenerational impact of this war on their lives. As relationships with their parents shifted with age and life changes, and more English language resources on Korean history became available and accessible through films, books, and media sources, they may have turned to studies on the trauma of war and migration to understand how they might account for some difficult aspects of their upbringing and family dynamics. Many integrated and accepted that not only was life difficult in the United States for their parents as immigrants, but that what their parents and families experienced as young children during and after the Korean War was buried in silence for many decades as South Korea's militarized government pursued an ambitious and rapid economic development to achieve a "compressed modernity" at all costs.[19] By remembering and connecting the war and other elements of modern Korean history to their own upbringing, they have developed an empathetic and forgiving understanding of their parents' complexities, strengths, and limitations.

Recognizing Love: Parental Intentions

Many respondents discussed how when they were growing up, their parents did not express love through words, but through wanting the best for their children and financially providing to the best of their ability. For some parents, this required working long hours, going without vacations, avoiding purchases for themselves, and spending only on their children. Love for children may have been unspoken, but it was provided through such actions. Soomin, now in her thirties, observes that the sacrifices she saw her parents make made her feel loved:

> I think my family was typical. We were in a survivor mentality and we bonded because of it. I think when you grow up and watch your parents sacrifice so much for you, you feel loved. You know that they are sacrificing for you, and that this is a form of affection. It's not the same affection as American parents, but you know you're loved.

Respondents were very aware that many parents had immigrated to the United States to escape what they saw as limited economic opportunities and political instability of post-war South Korea and that the gamble did not always pay off in their favor; many parents were unable to utilize their pre-migration education, job experience, and social status and worked extremely hard in jobs they did not care for, often going without sick time or vacation. Migration also led to separation from family, kin, and social networks—another form of loss for the parents. As children came to recognize past hardships experienced by their parents, they also felt a need for giving back to them.

Respondents differed in their interpretation of what giving back meant. For some, giving back was about repayment, obligation, and duty. For others, it was a way to thank their parents for the support that they had provided while facing difficulties with limited English and work opportunities. And for yet others, giving back was just another form of the care that they had continually done for their parents. Respondents also discussed the need to give back to ensure that their immigrant parents would be comfortable in old age by providing financial and housing assistance as necessary. Thirty-year-old Roy, who immigrated when he was four years old, states:

It's not that we don't talk to them about it; it's a given that if they get old I take care of them. It's just the way it is. We don't really sit down and say, "Oh if I get older, you're going to take care of me." If my parents get older and they need to be taken care of, then they'll be taken care of. That's the way it is.

Almost all respondents discussed that they felt this need to give back to their parents, for their hardships and hard work, by providing care and support as their parents grow older.

Respondents noted that their immigrant parents sacrificed their lives for their families, especially to provide their children with opportunities for upward mobility in the United States. Respondents also expressed the desire to make sure that their parents receive financial, emotional, and physical care especially in old age. They vividly remember the difficulties their parents faced, and thus often want to reciprocate, especially when their parents become ill or needed twenty-four-hour care. Roger, whose parents immigrated when he was five years old, describes his feelings:

> I think it's because they sacrificed so much for us, and the fact that we came to the U.S. with very little, and to see where I am with my family, and to see where my brothers are with their families. It's just a real blessing, so, in that sense, we want to give back a lot.

Bob, who immigrated at the age of nine and is now in his thirties, also describes providing help to his parents as a form of love rather than of duty:

> We never think, "We owe them." We never said that as one of our motivations to help them. We just love our parents. Personally, to some extent, I really appreciate the sacrifices. I don't want to see it as a sacrifice, and maybe they don't either.

Scott, who immigrated at age thirteen in the late 1970s, and his siblings have been supporting their mother for many years. He explains that his desire to repay is not rooted in cultural tradition of filial piety or sense of obligation, but comes from having watched his widowed mother immigrate to the United States to raise him and his siblings. He calls his desire to give back as coming from the heart:

I wouldn't say that's an obligation. Duties? It's something that, it just comes out from our hearts that we feel, we have to. It's in our blood that we have to repay you know our mom. . . . Well, I've been helping her throughout my life, just repaying her back with all those stuff that she had helped us. I've been giving her money every month (laughing) for more than twenty years.

The motivation to give back to parents stems from not just from the care and sacrifices the parents made to during the respondents' childhoods, but also from the respondents' desire to make their parents' lives easier in old age and retirement. That also meant taking into consideration their parents' wishes and preferences in careers and dating and marriage decisions, even if they disagreed with or did not follow their parents' preferences.

Giving Back: Work, Love, and Marriage

As discussed above, parents' pasts may motivate children to make choices that would please them and bring a sense of security. Rather than viewing this as a form of delayed "individuation" or simply as an expression of a Korean cultural mandate, we can see this desire to take their parents' wishes into account as a form of "giving back" rooted in their shared experience as children of immigrants. So whether in terms of education, careers, dating partners, marital status, grandchildren, or relocation, respondents considered how decisions in these significant stages of life that serve as "conventional markers of adulthood" would impact their parents.[20] It must be underscored that many adult children did make job, career, dating, and marital choices with which the parents disagreed, sometimes vehemently. But even these choices were thoughtfully construed with their parents' needs and desires in mind. Although this type of decision-making could simply be attributed to a collectivist family value promoted in Korean and other Asian societies as well as their immigrant communities, it also can be viewed as a continuation of the emotion and other work that children of immigrants have done for their families since childhood in response to their parents' losses. That is, collectivist decision-making is also a result of a culture created by children of immigrants and demonstrates how linked lives operate as children come of age and immigrant parents grow older.

Work and Career Choices

Children of immigrants constantly receive the message in adolescence that the best way to respond to their immigrant parents' hardship and make their sacrifices worthwhile is to do well in school; the message is the same regardless of their parents' socioeconomic status, pre- and post-migration. Many said that their parents' work ethic provided a constructive model to follow as they strove for success in their own careers. Some felt that they needed to honor their parents' hard work with hard work in kind, by making full use of opportunities made possible by parental sacrifice. Many first-generation parents, especially those who experienced language and cultural barriers, believe that their children, with their U.S. degrees, accreditation, native English fluency, and cultural familiarity, would be able to break the occupational barriers that hindered their own careers. Those parents who were able to realize professional occupations but still faced language and cultural barriers also let their children know that they had high expectations for the second generation, who in turn faced parental and self-imposed expectations to be model children. As Yunjung, who was born in the United States, states:

> A lot of people came here, and their parents worked really hard to give them something that they never had. . . . Everything was given to us, we easily go to good colleges, and have opportunities in America, and speak perfect English, but not really thinking about the sacrifices our parents made, not that it's about repaying them necessarily with money, but with taking advantage of the opportunities we have, and just doing our best, and be successful within your own career . . . to take advantage of them, not to be fearful of taking risks, not to be lazy.

Many respondents did not agree with Yunjung that "everything" was given to them or that they "easily" went to good colleges, but most faced similar spoken or unspoken pressures from their parents to do their best and be successful within "safe" professional careers that relied on technical skills and licensing, or what Vivian Louie's Chinese American respondents deemed "Asian fields" such as medicine, engineering, computer science, and law.[21] Jessica, who came to the United States as a toddler, recalls a number of factors that led to her decision to become a physician. She says, "There wasn't direct overt pressure, but I felt a lot of pressure from Mom. . . . It was always constantly, you have to go to grad school or med school." Apart from this pressure, she characterizes her relationship with her parents as being overall "really good," and contextualizes this pressure with pre-migration stories about the Korean War and her parents' economic struggles both in Korea and United States: "I knew where they were coming from. I knew why they valued economic security so highly." Meanwhile, she admits that the pressure to excel did not just come from her parents: "I was already in a way pushing myself. So I was probably pushing myself as hard as anybody was pushing me." This negotiation took a number of years but Jessica managed to fulfill both her parents' dreams and her own; she did become a physician as her mother wanted and provides health care in vulnerable, underserved communities as Jessica herself desires.

While some like Jessica managed to fulfill the pressure to go into certain fields without compromising their goals, not all respondents followed educational and career paths that aligned with their own parents' expectations for specific careers and economic success, and many were adamant about pursuing their interests and choosing to go forward with their dreams. Partly to better understand his parents and what he referred to as the "Korean mentality," Dylan studied Korean history, politics, and philosophies, such as Confucianism, after he graduated from college. But he pursued his own career path in the arts and described parental influence on his career as "very little."

Richard, who immigrated as a child and is in his thirties now, notes that he went through a rebellious stage, but also observes that his parents "showed us a lot of love. . . . They were kind of hard on me in expectations, but they showed me so much sacrifice." He works as an administrator and jokingly observes that although his parents wanted him to become a doctor, "I had to decide for myself. They have supported me, and have not disowned me." Another respondent in his late forties describes how his mother's plans for his career did not square with his own talents and desires.

> My mom wanted me to become a doctor. Well, that career decision lasted through up to high school up to senior year and pretty much, it just went

down the hill afterwards. I don't know if that's something that was meant to be or not, but I got out of becoming a doctor and once again my other alternate dream was to become an artist, especially in the animation. But back then when I was growing up, people were saying that, "Hey, doctors and lawyers make a lot of money, and you become an artist and you're going to be poor and you won't have any money," and that was just something that everybody was telling me that I just couldn't pursue my career to become an artist.

In a parallel way, when Scott was a high school student in the 1980s, his parents persuaded him to consider a financially lucrative career but the love for cars that he developed led to a career and business in automotive services and repairs.

Studies of Korean and other Asian immigrant communities have explored how children's acquisitions of good education and financial prosperity in select professions are common components of their parents' achieving their American dream. Hence, immigrant parents may push children to choose more lucrative professions as a way to secure the futures of both generations (not to mention "bragging rights," as many respondents criticized). But many respondents also reported that while their parents told them to "study hard and do your best," they also told them to "do what makes you happy" and left career choices up to them. For example, Bob, who attended seminary after college, relays how his parents reacted when he told them he was considering becoming a pastor.

They never really pushed me towards high-earning careers like doctors or lawyers. Since they are Christian parents, they were like, "Do what glorifies God." When I told them I wanted to go to ministry and be a pastor, I think they were very hesitant but they never really voiced it. I think they started voicing these things in the last year or two, now that I'm wavering on that. Because obviously, they don't want me to suffer unnecessarily and were always concerned about that with the hardship of ministry life, pastor's life, stuff like that.

Ultimately, many respondents chose to work in a field about which they were passionate; they were graduate students, counselors/

therapists, physicians, teachers, professors, accountants, stay-at-home mothers, pastors, retail managers, engineers, bankers, graphic designers, writers, attorneys, business owners, business analysts, corporate managers and executives, and administrators. Even if respondents did not choose lucrative or "high-status" occupations, or chose an occupation with which parents were unfamiliar, most parents were supportive of the respondents once they graduated and started working. For example, Yunjung, whose parents wanted her to go to medical school, went to law school instead. Lauren's parents were confused when she told them she planned to become a social worker because they did not know what the job entailed; however, they became very satisfied and proud of her career choice, especially as they realized and utilized her vast knowledge and expertise of social services and programs.

Nonetheless, some at times felt guilty that they chose careers that may make it difficult for them to support their parents financially in their old age. Shelia, a teacher, discusses her expectations about supporting her parents as they become older:

> Definitely! On one hand, I think that I would love to do that for them. Of course! But I feel tremendous guilt because it goes back to the career I chose. If anything it has affected my ability to make money for them. I feel like I have made a very selfish choice. If I have, is that okay? Do I have the right to do that? It's a very difficult choice and they definitely expect that, my mom more so than my father. I think, not intentionally or selfishly or just trying to make me feel guilty, my mother would say, "When are you going to be taking care of me? I am already seventy years old. When are you guys going to take care of me?"

However, another type of support that Shelia's mother requests is that her children live near their parents, to take care of them in old age and illness. To that end, Shelia's parents, who used to live the East Coast near their own siblings, sold their business and moved to the West Coast be near their children. Conversely, several respondents chose to stay in California when offered jobs in other states because of their need to be close to their aging parents. Either way, it was important for children to consider geography and distance from their parents as they thought of providing care-giving support in the future.

Marriage and Children

After a lifetime of observing their immigrant parents' struggles and agreeing with them that education was crucial to their successful adaptation in the United States, respondents sought to give back to their parents through doing well in school and the workplace. In this life stage, they receive strong messages about another way to "give back"— through getting married (most preferably, to a heterosexual co-ethnic) and having grandchildren. Our respondent sample is split almost evenly between single and married: out of 133 reporting their marital status, sixty (44 percent) have never married, seventy-one (52 percent) are married, and three (2 percent) are divorced. Although some made (or were able to make) life-course choices around marriage and having children that matched their parents' wishes, many had to negotiate and debate with their parents. While these life-course expectations (not co-habitating with romantic partners, getting married and having children, in that order) are both verbalized and not verbalized by parents, making parentally expected choices is often perceived as a way of repaying parents for their sacrifices and contributing to their sense of establishment. Not surprisingly, many adult children, especially those respondents who are not married, reported feelings of burden, resentment, tension, and sometimes outright conflict as a result.

Most parents make heteronormative assumptions that their children are heterosexual and will marry, especially after finishing college and finding a job. Many single adult children also receive messages from parents to marry "right." Marrying right often means choosing a partner who is Korean and (at least) college-educated; Korean Christian parents may equally emphasize religious background. Karl, single and in his twenties, immigrated to the United States when he was ten years old. Although he has dated non-Koreans, he would prefer to date a Korean, and states that he is very aware what qualities his mother prefers in his future wife:

> My mom, she pushes it all the time. She flipped when I brought a Japanese girl home. She pushes it real hard. That hasn't changed over the years. She gave up on my brothers. My brothers are both dating Caucasians. . . . She gave up on them. The last hope is me.

Although Karl's mother had a strong preference that her sons date Koreans, she was especially upset when he dated someone of Japanese ancestry; other respondents noted that their parents and grandparents expressed the same sentiment, a legacy of Japanese colonialism (1910–1945) in Korean history. Karl is her last "hope" of having a Korean daughter-in-law, with whom she may be able to communicate in Korean and share the same cultural orientation in whole or in part. At the time of the interview, Karl was in fact dating a Korean woman who had lived in the United States for a few years.

Rhee and Yoo document the negotiations between Korean American parents and adult children that consistently center on love, dating and marriage.[22] They suggest that marrying another Korean or Korean American is highly prized, and that marrying outside the ethnic community is discouraged by parents because of the past historical memories associated with out-marriage and the Korean War and because of cultural unfamiliarity. Hence, co-ethnic intermarriage is valued, as well as being seen as a form of cultural capital for the parents within the Korean immigrant community. Nevertheless, many respondents were not married to co-ethnics: in fact, whereas 58 percent of our sample married co-ethnics, 42 percent married non-Koreans. Those who did not marry co-ethnics were most often married to European Americans, followed by other Asian Americans and Latinas/os. Among our respondents, women were more likely to outmarry (60 percent), but males were also out-marrying (40 percent).

Among the respondents were men like Young, who immigrated at the age of twelve and is married to another Korean American; his two sisters married non-Koreans. He describes his parents as "very open" and trusting of their children when it came to love and marriage: "They are very romantic in that they always emphasize love, marry somebody who you love, who loves you. My wife just happened to be Korean. That's probably my preference [more] than anything." But most respondents negotiated their love choices with their parents. Daryl, who also immigrated at age twelve, noted that his parents express their preference, but accept that Daryl will do as he wishes:

> In terms of dating and marriage I think they kept distance because in some ways they realize that they really don't have that much control.

I mean they would try to introduce me to their friends' daughters or whatever. Since I got married this year so now they're talking about, "You know, you should think about having kids," but they know that pushing hard doesn't—only thing that it does for me to is to push back harder.

The decisions to choose non-Korean partners were initially tense for others, but most parents accepted their children's partners, especially if and when grandchildren are born. Alice recalls her brother marrying a white woman and how her father had a terrible time accepting it: "My brother has two children, they love the grandkids, but they had asked him, promise me you won't marry her, but he did. So I don't know. I guess he's okay with it now."

As single adult children enter their thirties and forties, the pressure to marry intensifies and the pressure to marry a co-ethnic wanes. Lauren describes how her parents insisted she date and marry a Korean man when she was in her twenties but were less fixated on their future son-in-law's ethnicity when she turned thirty; ultimately her immigrant parents just wanted to see her married:

Before they just have be Korean, they have to be educated, affluent well off and on and on . . . but now they are like, well, Chinese is okay too. Then, any Asian guy and then it became: anybody is good. Just find a nice guy. Whatever. We don't care!

While Lauren laughed about the decreasing importance of finding a *Korean* husband, she also jokingly lamented that dating and getting married are not easy; finding the "right" person comes with the usual pitfalls, even if parents are no longer pressuring their adult children to find Korean partners. Most respondents say that their parents would prefer a Korean daughter- or son-in-law in order to lessen cultural and language gaps. Many of the single respondents who are in their thirties and forties and observing their parents getting older say that they are looking for someone who can help take care of their aging parents, whether by providing direct care or at the very least, understanding and supporting their desire to care for their parents. Charlie states,

I'm thinking, but that's going to play a huge factor in . . . the person who
I marry, whoever my wife is, because at the same time, yes, me being the
son, my role is to take care of my parents.

Lois, married to a non-Korean, explains that one of her criteria for a
partner was that he accepted that she would take care of her parents. In
fact, as the eldest daughter and the designated primary financial sup-
porter of her parents, she alludes to what Charlie notes above—the ideology that sons (and thereby daughters-in-laws) are obligated to take
care of parents—and expresses relief that her in-laws do not expect her
to take care of them in old age.

I was thirty-five when I got married and it was important to me to show
the person I was dating that I have this obligation and it was non-nego-
tiable. If you are going to date me, this is who I am and my family is
part of me. I think if I had married a Korean it would be more difficult
to be married to someone who I had to take care of the in-laws. I watch
Korean TV. There is a set of rules; there is a set of expectations of what an
in-law should be. I think I would be busier and crazier because I would
be taking care of two sets of parents.

While some struggle to date and/or to find a spouse with or without
their parents' approval, and while most hope to find someone their parents
would also like, those who identify as gay or lesbian wrestle with the realization that any of their choices for a prospective of life partner may not satisfy
their parents. Ryan, an Ivy League graduate who watched his parents sacrifice long hours so he could gain a good education, strove academically and
professionally in order to be able to "repay" his parents. However, when
Ryan came out as gay to his parents, they were adamantly against his sexual
orientation; the ethnic background of Ryan's partner generated much less
conflict compared to his gender and sexual orientation.

Well, I think if I was straight they would have strong preferences for me
to marry a Korean girl, you know, especially my mother. My father's less
strict about that kind of stuff, he actually, he's a little liberal. My sister married a white guy and, you know, they're okay with that. So I think that if I
was straight I think my mom would've been much more, strict about, you

know, wanting a Korean daughter-in-law or whatever but I'm gay. So it kind of throws it for a loop. . . . They don't want me to be with a guy period.

However, Ryan states that he cannot be guided by their expectations at the expense of his own happiness. Despite the conflict and tension around heteronormativity and marriage, Ryan tries to give back in other ways without denying his own identity and desires.

> I think the only way I feel obligated to repay them is to be concerned about their welfare and try to do the best that I can for myself. But the tricky thing about that is there has been a conflict about that. And so I don't feel like I need to repay them by doing something that they think I should do and then I don't really want to do. So then there lies a conflict and I won't repay them that way, if that makes any sense.

Patricia, an American-born queer woman in her twenties, had a painful and confrontational conversation with her father about her sexuality, in which her father threatened to disown her if she came out as a lesbian. She and her parents (father, step-mother, and mother) have not discussed her sexuality since, and meanwhile, her father has hired a Korean matchmaker to find her a co-ethnic husband. Patricia believes that her father is especially driven to find her a husband because her younger brother was married before the older sister. Although she describes the current situation as contentious, she refrains from bringing up her dating life so that she does not make it harder on her parents.[23]

In contrast, heterosexual respondents reported that their relationship with their parents improved after they got married and had children. For example, Jordan, the eldest of three children, fought less with her parents after she was married. In her parents' eyes, marriage marked both her independence and their own fulfillment of their "duty as a parent" to make sure their children were married and had kids; Jordan described this as a "very traditional part of them." She also shares, "So far they haven't said anything about raising my child. They love her to death. Maybe it's different because she's their grandchild as opposed to being their actual child."

The arrival of grandchildren—the third generation—provided an opportunity for the respondents to see their parents in a new role. Many tried to carve out a time for their children to spend time with their grandparents. While Young's parents had no racial or ethnic preferences for their children's spouses, they had not been so open in other areas. Young and his father fought constantly about school, and their relationship deteriorated in college, when his father laughed at the major that Young wanted to declare and tried to handpick both a university and a major for his son. Years later, Young confronted his father, who apologized for his actions. He shares how his parents have changed now that they are grandparents:

> They tell me that I'm strict, and I laugh. My dad would be like, "Why are you lecturing your kids?" and stuff like that. I just laugh. 'Cause I'm like, "Dad, do you remember how you treated me when I was growing up?" and I guess that's how grandparents become, they make corrections as they see their grandchildren. But, no, I think they're very . . . they have confidence in us.

Although Young mentions his immigrant father correcting his parenting style for being too strict, he also notes his father has confidence in his parenting style. However, other married respondents with children discussed how parenting brought on its own set of issues that they continually needed to navigate—including that of immigrant parents and in-laws providing unsolicited advice on a range of parenting issues and concerns. The respondents with children in their study also try to balance caring for young children as well as aging parents and in-laws, as explored in later chapters.

With conflicts over education and career choices behind most of them, respondents reveal that at this life stage, heteronormativity—dating, marriage, and having children—is not just an aspect of their personal lives, but a way to repay their parents and secure for their immigrant parents another type of sense of establishment and well-being. By and large, single heterosexual respondents want to find partners on their own terms; although many do take their parents' preferences (as well as their "nagging") into account when considering marriage, these preferences do not limit them (and as mentioned above, parents also reassess their preferences). Gay and lesbian respondents, on the other hand, must negotiate how their sexuality compromises their ability to be "good" sons or daughters, despite their efforts to be so in other ways. Single respondents do get and are mindful of the message (sometimes constantly and forcefully made) that their marrying and having children are important to their parents' sense of security, but it is to be seen how parents will respond as their queer children decide to get married and/or become parents. Indeed, although marriages and births of grandchildren in particular were celebratory occasions that often positively redefined intergenerational relations, adult children needed to continually navigate relationships with their immigrant parents and in-laws, especially if they received unsolicited advice about their own style of parenting, which often differed from their own upbringing.

Loving One's Self

Many respondents have dutifully followed their parents' instructions and in their own manner found ways to repay them in adulthood. They have also undergone an inward process of soul-searching, to identify who they were and what they really want, including choosing their own careers, whether and how to be partnered, and whether to have children or not. Even in considering different ways to raise their children, they often make choices in reference to their parents' wishes. Mindful of their parents' agendas but not defined by them, they find ways to care for their parents and themselves.

Growing up, the respondents used various ways of coping with the pressures of being part of an immigrant family, including attending a Korean church and talking to church staff, seeking out co-ethnic friends, or rebelling against their parents. Additionally, many respondents have utilized psychotherapy to put their upbringings into perspective, find their voice, and come to terms with their parents and past conflicts. For some, it was a way to identify pain, but many also learned how to be independent from their parents' imperatives. Some started to seek help in college, motivated by having personal space away from parents and family, as well as access to free or low-cost counseling sessions available to students. More female respondents than male respondents discussed their experience with psychotherapy, but all respondents found it beneficial.

Connie characterizes her relationship with her father as "very fiery." Although they were close, they also fought and screamed at each other constantly. As a result:

> I ended up going to therapy for ten years to work out my conflicts with my dad. But he didn't know because he's not supportive of that which

is fine, but now he is. He was pushing me in school and I would react. I didn't realize that I had to learn to manage the relationship and I would fall into certain, you know, sink holes each time.

Now in her thirties, Connie initially did not tell her father that she was in therapy because he was not "supportive," which is consistent with past studies that show that Korean immigrants tend to underutilize mental health services, including psychotherapy.[24] But years afterwards, he saw its value. Additionally, her parents perceived her marriage as an important milestone in her transition into adulthood. She observes, "Ever since I've been married it's gotten even easier. . . . They decided that I wasn't their primary responsibility anymore and all of a sudden the pressure was off. So, it's very easy."

Others used psychotherapy to cope with parental pressures related to academic and professional excellence. Sophia discusses how "achieving" meant earning love and how this affected her self-esteem:

> I was raised to believe that I had to earn the love of others through achievement. I am pretty driven now. I have accepted the fact that my father will never say he is proud of me, even if he is. I spent so much time as a teenager and undergrad in college thinking I was a loser, that I was an extreme underachiever.

She also observes that this low self-esteem led her to become suicidal in college. While her siblings had fulfilled her dad's wishes by attending Ivy League colleges, she felt unloved and unaccepted by her father who valued such achievements, and at the same time found that her white peers did not understand her family's dynamic completely. She had reached a low point in her life. She recalls that "When he yelled at me, he would sit me down at a table and scream at me, telling me I was stupid, I was nothing like him, that I was going to be a failure for life." Now in her forties, Sophia used psychotherapy to find her voice and self-acceptance apart from her father's conditional love.

Psychotherapy allowed many who were married to establish boundaries between their parents and themselves. Those who married co-ethnics experienced a stronger need to establish boundaries between their families of origin and the family they were creating. For these respondents, there was a strong need to please and respect two sets of Korean immigrant parents who expected much from their adult children. Nina, married to another Korean American, discusses the difficulties she and her husband face due to his mother's lack of respect for personal boundaries and privacy:

> A lot of the times, it can be a total struggle! My girlfriends—their mothers-in-law have keys to their houses and stuff. And I'm thinking: that's not going to happen! No! You call when you want to come over; you knock on the door. You're not having my keys. With some guys, this is normal. Yeah!

Nina further discusses how her Korean immigrant in-laws have never fully accepted her; they refused to attend the wedding, and treat her in ways that she experiences as spiteful and hateful. After psychotherapy, she came to realize that she should not take the attack personally:

> It was their own issue. It could have been anyone. It was not about me. It was about someone coming in and disrupting their family and [throwing] their dynamics and their relationship all off. It got to the point where my husband's relationship with his family really suffered—a lot. But he got to a point where he realized it was their issue. . . . It got to the point where it really interfered with our relationship. I'd gotten in a fight with his father, his parents. It was BAD. Super drama.

Through a marriage counselor, Nina and her husband took the steps to recognize that they needed assistance in navigating their relationships with their parents and their own. In addition, they were able to see the dynamics operating within their extended families and their need to come together as a couple and to establish boundaries with her in-laws who saw full access to their home as their parental right. Nina states how the counseling sessions provided that clarity:

> We explained to [the therapist] how Koreans mothers work and so forth, and she said, "In order for your relationship to work, you need to put your wife first. Your dad can take care of your mother and be her emotional support." My husband was the emotional support for his mother,

and he felt that responsibility. And that's what he learned, that's your father's role, and your role is to be there for your wife.

Some respondents sought psychotherapy because of their lifelong lack of communication with their parents. Natalie, whose family immigrated so that her father could attend seminary, had a "pretty good" relationship with her parents and strong support in her Korean American church as a teenager. She saw her parents as well-meaning, but not as an available source for support and advice. Alternatively, Natalie has found resources and other support systems to take care of her emotional needs:

> I think they are really good parents, but, they had a lot going on trying to make it. But on the other hand, they weren't like the parents you see on TV now. The prototypes that sit down and talk with their kids saying, "Tell me about all your problems." My mom tried to do that but I usually didn't go to her. If I had something that was bugging me I usually tried to deal with it by myself. That wasn't really good because you're too young. And then once I was in college if I felt like I was struggling, I wouldn't let my parents know I was going through a hard time or something but I would actually go to a counselor they had. They give student counseling services in school and that was really great to be able to turn to a professional if I needed that kind of extra support. And then I had friends, peers, your friends, your girlfriends.

Ji Hee's psychotherapy sessions also allowed her to confront her parents and communicate something painful. As a young adult, she went into therapy to treat her depression. She states,

> Throughout my twenties and my thirties, I was really depressed clinically, and I started drinking a lot and stuff, and so that's really what made me go to therapy. And I didn't go to figure out what was wrong with me. I just went because I wanted to not be so depressed. In the course of therapy, I realized the basis for all of my misery which hadn't been dealt with was when I was five years old, my parents left me and my sister in Korea for a year and half. And they came to America because they thought if they bring the kids, it'll be harder.

While Ji Hee's parents had good intentions in leaving their children in Korea, as a young child, Ji Hee thought she was abandoned. Moreover, this feeling was compounded because upon immigrating to the United States, her parents put their time into working and did not acknowledge what had happened. When Ji Hee finally confronted her parents, they were shocked and dismayed that the separation had affected her so traumatically. Ji Hee explains that more than hearing an apology, it was important for her to let them know what she was going through, and that she understood why her parents had to do what they did.

> Not in like a harsh way. I told them what was going on with me and I just laid it all out. And they were just totally shocked. Like they're not used to talking like that first of all, and then to hear their own daughter had gone through these years of depression and self-doubt and misery, and then realizing the source of it and all. My mom just kept crying and saying, "I'm so sorry, I'm so sorry." I'm not telling this to blame you. I'm not asking you to apologize but I need to tell you this just from my—I need to tell you, let you know what I'm going through and I realize, and that I don't blame you and you know, and that I understand your motivation and you did the best you could.

Although research has shown that Korean immigrants and their families underutilize psychotherapy and tend to turn to the church for help with stress and mental issues, for these respondents, psychotherapy provides a space for discussing better ways of coping with the past and present, gaining perspective, and finding their voices.[25] Many respondents disclosed how they as children of immigrants experience both external and internal conflicts within their family despite their desire to give back. It also indicates that our sample of children of Korean immigrants, especially women, seems to be open to using psychotherapy to resolve familial and personal issues and to benefit from seeking such services. They focus on the ability to set limits and not seek to please everyone. Caring for oneself also means accepting one's parents, with all of their nuances and limitations. As Sophia, recently diagnosed with early stage breast cancer, states:

> Currently, I am realizing my parents are who they are. They are aging and I'm scared. My father still smokes a lot of cigarettes each day. My

mom is borderline diabetic. They are in their late sixties. I try to give them polite encouragement to eat better and to stop smoking, but that doesn't work. I just have to accept them one hundred percent. This is part of taking care of yourself, too. Just accept and love your family.

Helen echoes similar realizations about learning the importance of self-care, knowing one's limitations, and not always caring for others around the clock. Helen shares that she works hard to balance her family life with her demanding job. But in the eyes of her mother-in-law who lives with them, Helen does not live up to the ideal Korean woman-hood of being a "sacrificial" wife, mother, and daughter-in-law because Helen and her husband view their respective careers and jobs as equally important. While she is grateful to her mother-in-law for all her help, she also laughs that she will not live up to the idealized image:

> I know my limits. I know there is no way I can be that Korean, you know? I am not a self-sacrificing person. I was a supportive person, but I don't sacrifice. There is a line. You know? When I sacrifice, it hurts me. And I let everyone know! I don't do it quietly. I have to make an announce-ment. I have to like signal to the entire world. I'm sacrificing! You'd bet-ter be grateful! You know?

While respondents are mindful of how they can give back to the immigrant generation, they are more aware of their need to find balance and care for themselves, and to accept situations that they cannot change. Overall, adult daughters were more likely to share how psychotherapy help them resolve past conflicts and restore communication with their parents, set boundaries between their parents and in-laws, and cope with the pressures and demands of the present.

Conclusion

Most respondents grew up with the strong and consistent message that they are the reason why their parents immigrated to the United States, and observed the losses and hardships that came with immigra-tion as their parents sought to achieve their "Korean American dream" of stability and establishment.[26] Therefore, as adult children of Korean immigrants come of age, they reflect on their parents' sacrifices, which serve as a source of motivation in their choices regarding careers, love and marital partners, and raising families.

Recovering family and Korean history, including that of the Korean War, and remembering their parent's pasts and hardships prior to immigration are ways for adult children to care for their parents, as are honoring the sacrifices their parents made and reciprocating for these sacrifices in their own life choices. But many also disclosed the conflict and turmoil that existed in their families and that they were not able to "do it all." Ultimately, despite their emotional connections to their immigrant parents' needs and past sacrifices, many have reached a major milestone in setting boundaries so that they can care for themselves, their parents, and other loved ones. This self-care may include gaining perspective on their upbringing by re-examining their pasts and working to improve their lives in terms of balance, health, and wellness. Finally, the narratives of respondents also show that many parents can change and adapt to their adult children's life choices and trajectories. The experience of immigration informs this sense of reciprocity and creates intergenerationally linked lives. The next chapter explores the role and continuity of culture and ethnicity in adult children of immigrants, how these respondents negotiate culture with regard to the previous generation, and ways that they reclaim and re-make it for the next generation.

3

Caring about Culture

I would get it in little bits, here and there, especially around
the holidays, like the Lunar New Year. I don't know what it
is in Korean, but kind of like Thanksgiving? We would go
to the cemetery and everybody would be there [laughs]. I
don't know what it is. Is it a holiday? Everybody is there.
My grandmother is buried in Forest Lawn. My dad makes
us go there. We always get in trouble because we don't go
there enough. He says, "If you don't go there for your grandmother, what will it be like when your mother and I pass
away? You're never going to visit us."
—Lauren

One significant practice of continuity and remembrance in Lauren's family is visiting her grandparents' graves on anniversaries and Korean holidays; her father worries that Lauren's generation (and beyond) will not
only neglect their grandparents but himself and his wife after they pass.
Lauren's father's sentiments echo concerns shared among many immigrants that their children born and/or raised in the United States will
forget the practice of remembering past generations. For many respondents, immigration creates separation not only from extended kin and
ethnic communities, but also sometimes from cultural traditions and
practices. Even though the immigrant generation may worry that such
cultural practices will disappear, children of immigrants do not forget
that they are intricately linked to the traditions and histories of their parents. This chapter explores these issues and considers, specifically, how

adult children of immigrants view their cultural identity; what aspects of culture and tradition adult children care about to continue for their own children and parents; and, when they do practice cultural traditions, how adult children negotiate "authenticity" (often meaning, as practiced in their own families) and remake those traditions on their own terms.

We begin this chapter with Lauren's observation, which humorously illustrates the conundrum of intergenerational relations, parental obligations, and cultural attachments as immigrant parents and adult children enter different life stages. Korean traditions, for many children of immigrants, are about continuing and commemorating family ties through cultural customs that have lost much of their vital context and meaning following decades of living in the United States. How adult children make sense of their own ethnic and cultural identity in relation to the practices associated with Korean and Korean American cultures often extends throughout a life-long journey, and links lives across generations. As articulated by the respondents, these practices are expressed in many different ways, including making and eating favorite foods, showing respect to elders, or following more elaborate cultural customs.

Like other children of immigrants, our respondents have varied experiences of familiarity with cultural rituals and their meanings and degrees of identification and attachment to their cultural heritage, as well as differing definitions of what it means to be Korean American. In addition to family, college plays a significant role in shaping and developing attitudes and identities, socially through friendships with both co-ethnics and other Asian Americans, and academically, especially in the post–civil rights era, with the availability of Asian and Asian American Studies courses, student organizations formed around race and ethnicity, and study abroad programs in a nation of parental origin.[1] Less well-documented is what elements of ethnic cultures persist and how they are practiced by the children of immigrants after college and into adulthood. This chapter examines the journey towards a formation of cultural and ethnic identity beyond the pivotal college years. It also examines the process of keeping, regenerating, and discontinuing cultural traditions, values, and practices. In particular, this chapter explores the work of women in continuing and remaking cultural traditions.

Ethnicity and Identity Formations

An ethnic group is generally defined by members who are set apart, by the group itself, and/or by outsiders and by their cultural character- istics.[2] Scholars such as Milton Gordon have defined ethnic groups as those broadly distinguished by "race, religion, or national origin," and Joane Nagel writes that ethnicity is constructed from "the material of language, religion, culture, appearance, ancestry, or regionality," while identity is determined by boundaries that establish one's belonging to a particular group.[3] Pyong Gap Min and Kyeyoung Park argue that ethnic identity emerges in young adulthood after remaining dormant in child- hood.[4] In their comparative study of second-generation Americans coming of age in New York City, Philip Kasinitz and his co-researchers define ethnic groups as expressing three aspects of difference among people—subjective identity, social networks, and historical accumula- tion of specific traits—even as individuals within a group experience each of these traits differently; although ethnic boundaries matter and shape identity, networks, and historical formations, group members do not experience and identify with ethnicity uniformly.[5] Despite these variations, making and remaking culture and ethnicity is a salient and vital part of everyday life for Americans of all generations and espe- cially for children of immigrants, who, in the process of negotiating their ethnicity, redefine what it means to be American.[6]

Recent studies show that having an appreciation for one's ethnicity and practicing cultural traditions are important to self-esteem and well- being among the children of immigrants.[7] In Asian American Studies, however, few texts have considered how parents transmit culture and ethnic identities to adult children. Mia Tuan's 1998 study on third- and later-generation Chinese and Japanese Americans deftly explores inter- generational racial and ethnic identity transmissions in which some respondents recalled parents choosing not to emphasize cultural prac- tices due to their own uncertainty about their origins and meanings. Others reported that their parents intentionally minimized aspects of cultural traditions in order to protect their children from racism in the form of backlashes against cultural expressions; parents and grandpar- ents may have faced this racism and wished to protect their children and grandchildren from similar experiences. Tuan's study shows that while third- and later-generation Asian Americans have some ethnic options, they are viewed as racial others and not as "real" Americans even after three generations.[8]

As children of immigrants come of age in contemporary American society, studying the racial and ethnic options of Americans of color remains significant; that is, while the dominant society debates how the United States will economically, politically, socially, and culturally incorporate contemporary immigrants, the continuing wave of largely nonwhite newcomers also calls attention to the question of how such racial, ethnic, and socioeconomic diversification will shape and/or hinder their transition into adulthood and belonging as new Americans.[9] Adult children in our sample are also working to recover or remember their pasts, cultural and historical; as children of immigrants, many have grown up with parents and other elders who see ethnic socialization as a significant aspect of parenting. Previous studies have found that in acculturating to life in the United States, many of these children lose language and culture over time.[10] In addition, shifts in socioeconomic mobility, residential patterns, and out-marriage rates among children of immigrants may appear to indicate that these Korean Americans have "lost" elements of their heritage in the process of assimilating into mainstream American life. Quite to the contrary, we find that the next generation of Korean Americans is reclaiming and remaking culture while also negotiating notions of authenticity and generational identity.

Culturally Korean? Language as a Marker of Identity

Language serves as an important marker of cultural difference for immigrant ethnic groups, both from the perspective of the in-group members and the dominant society.[11] For many Korean and other immigrants, the maintenance of homeland language is a way to preserve heritage and culture, as well as enabling communication with their children. However, studies show that children of immigrants quickly become English-fluent and often English-dominant.[12] Although the loss of the original language in the second and later generations is often seen as inevitable, many immigrant parents attempt to forestall or reverse the process by speaking to their children in the homeland language and enrolling them in afterschool, weekend, and/

or immersion language programs.[13] Throughout the United States and since the turn of the century, Korean immigrants also have established Korean language schools for their children in hopes that the language will be maintained and preserved.[14]

In an ethnic community composed mainly of first generation immigrants and their children, the majority of respondents felt that co-ethnics in the United States (and in Korea) often used their Korean language ability as a marker and gauge of their ethnicity. Across different immigrant communities, language ability has often been associated with identity and cultural authenticity, and those born and/or raised in the United States who are not fluent speakers are often criticized for their loss of their heritage language.[15] In her study of second-generation Chinese and Korean Americans, Nazli Kibria found that one way for them to deflect challenges to their identity as "authentic" Chinese or Koreans when visiting their parents' homeland was to display the ability to speak the language fluently.[16] Although her respondents exhibited various language abilities depending on geographic location, neighborhoods, and parents' insistence, "for some informants, childhood experiences of being condemned for their 'inadequate' Chinese or Korean language skills had been so powerful as to cast a deep and negative pallor on their general attitude, their feelings about being Korean or Chinese."[17]

The respondents in this study reported a wide range of Korean language ability, but those born in the United States were less likely to speak Korean as fluently as their peers who had spent a part of their childhoods in Korea; this trend is consistent with findings in other second-generation studies.[18] Some also read and write Korean fluently. For example, Helen, who immigrated as a child but moved back and forth between Korea and the United States due to her father's career, is fluent in both languages. Elizabeth, who came to the United States at age nine, said she "knows Korean fully." Kimberly who came at age three "didn't really learn to read and write Korean, until one day, my dad's friend sat down and decided to teach me for a few hours. I can read the phonetics of the Korean newspaper but I don't know what it means." Regina, who was born in the United States of parents who immigrated in the late 1970s, says she was taught Korean language "naturally and organically." But she was also curious about the language and actively sought help to improve her Korean. She learned the Korean alphabet from her grandmother, spoke Korean and English with her parents and her relatives, and asked them to spell out words that she did not know. "I would try to practice and send really poorly written cards. And that's how I wrote cards and letters, again very poorly, to my parents."

Depending on when their parents immigrated and where they settled, participants reported a wide variation in parental pressure or encouragement to learn the Korean language. Those with parents who spoke English fluently were more likely to communicate with them in English and less likely to speak Korean fluently. Those whose families were the only Koreans in town often felt more social pressure to become fluent in English as soon as possible, and thus had less incentive to learn or maintain Korean. Many respondents also said that their parents prioritized English fluency so that they could catch up in school.

Almost all agreed that co-ethnics use Korean language ability to gauge levels of attachment to and identification with Korean culture. This is especially the case as immigrant communities everywhere have become more transnational due to the communication and transportation developments which make it easier and more affordable to maintain social, cultural, political, and economic ties.[19] Those who did not learn Korean or lost their ability to speak it fluently recalled when co-ethnics (spanning different age groups and immigrant generations) challenged the authenticity of their ethnic identity or outright criticized their lack of cultural knowledge and ethnic identity. Many throughout their lives have felt social pressure to continually learn and maintain the language through classes or trips to Korea. Jeannie, who grew up in a white neighborhood, recalled being judged by Korean peers who immigrated later than she did:

> When I was in high school, more and more Asians came into the school district. I remember a group of Korean kids that came in. I'd been living there for years, so I had my [own] group of white friends. I was really offended when I heard one of them say, "Oh, she doesn't even speak Korean," because they heard me speak English, and they were all recent immigrants. It was like I was one of the white kids, almost. I remember feeling really offended by that.

Like Jeannie, many respondents shared incidents in which they were made to feel that that they were not Korean enough because of their lack of language ability. Mee Jin, born and raised in Southern California, observes, "I find that as I'm getting older, even if I'm in a Korean restaurant—because I don't know Korean and I can't order in Korean all the time, they look down on me." For Mee Jin—who had immigrant parents who spoke English fluently, grew up with a strong awareness of racialization as one of the few Asians in her hometown, and took Asian American Studies courses in college—her sense of Koreanness does not neatly overlap with language ability in the same way it does for some co-ethnics. She feels judged by co-ethnics who see lack of language ability as signaling her lack of interest in and attachment to Korean culture and identity.

Other respondents experienced similar encounters with co-ethnics who questioned their identity and attachment to culture because of their lack of Korean language ability. Lauren immigrated at the age of five and grew up in Los Angeles' Koreatown, learning Spanish with Latino peers. This is not surprising as Latinos have comprised a predominant residential population of Los Angeles Koreatown for decades, but yet it has not stopped co-ethnics from questioning her identity because she speaks Spanish and not Korean.[20] Significantly, Lauren is a social worker who is often assigned to Spanish-speaking clients due to her language ability. She does speak some Korean and is often asked to do some basic interpreting when the bilingual Korean staff member is not in the office. However, she struggles with using formal or honorific Korean grammatical structure (to signify social status and relationships between the speakers) and vocabulary appropriate to her age and profession, which elicits amused or baffled looks from the Korean-speaking clients. She notes, "People always ask me, 'You don't really look Korean, you speak Spanish, and what are you?' And I think, it doesn't really matter. Who cares?" But Lauren's comments alternate between acknowledging her own desire to improve her Korean, primarily to communicate with her grandparents, and refusing to let others judge her ethnic identity solely based on language ability.

> I want to be able to communicate, and I've thought about living in Korea for a year or so. I wanted to learn. Because growing up, my grandparents were here for a while, and they would say, "Aren't you ashamed of yourself? You speak Spanish and you can't speak Korean." And I would say, "Whatever!"

Although our respondents grew up in different regions of the United States, in diverse racial, ethnic, and socioeconomic neighborhoods, many are now residing in metropolitan areas with sizable Korean/Asian American communities that continue to serve as gateways for recently arrived immigrant co-ethnics and transnational populations. Many recalled sensing or hearing criticisms from newly arrived Korean immigrants, who judged their Koreanness on the basis of language ability and would sometimes blame the respondents' parents for "failing" to teach their children Korean. These criticisms stem from the assumption that the second generation should be bilingual, especially those who live in areas with continual immigration from Korea. Jordan, American-born and in her thirties, grew up in southern California in a predominantly European American community. Now living in a suburb with a large Korean population, her inability to speak Korean invites questions about her ethnicity from co-ethnics.

> People are curious about my background and why don't I speak Korean. They just were more outspoken about, "Well then, you can't be Korean—you must not be Korean. You must be Japanese or Chinese, because why wouldn't your parents teach you Korean?"

That second-generation respondents did not like being judged by their language ability did not mean that they dismissed the Korean language per se as being a significant part of one's heritage or identity. Many respondents who had stopped speaking Korean or did not learn it as children wished they could speak it as adults, for themselves and the next generation. Lyn, a twenty-eight-year-old who was born in the United States, discusses how her lack of fluency in Korean contributes to the loss of the language for the next generation:

> I don't speak Korean as well as my parents. If I have children, they'll definitely not be able to speak because I doubt that I'll speak Korean to them, you know? So I do feel kind of a sense of loss, like, they're losing some of that Koreanness. What I don't know, I can't pass on.

Some bilingual respondents echo this sentiment and are trying to find ways to maintain the language for the next generation. For example, Yunjung, raised in different cities in different U.S. regions where she and her sister were sometimes the "only minorities in school," maintained Korean through her parents' deliberate attempts in the home and in the community. Her family attended Korean immigrant churches and hosted a number of relatives in their home, including her grandparents who taught them Korean; she also remembers participating in family Bible studies conducted in Korean. Now, with only a few extended kin living nearby, Yunjung speaks Korean primarily with her parents. While language is not the only way she defines Koreanness, she reflects on the limited ability of her generation to teach Korean language, and thus at least partially Korean culture, to the next generation:

> We need to do our best to hold on to the Korean part of ourselves because I can see how. My sister has two kids, and a lot of my friends have children. We're already feeding them Korean food and stuff, but our generation is all fluent in English. It's so much harder to get the kids to talk, learn Korean, and they really won't have as much of a bicultural experience. I'm actually making more of an effort to improve my Korean too. It's something that could easily be overlooked, and I feel like if we don't make a deliberate effort, it'll be lost by our children's generation.

Yunjung learned Korean language, culture, and history through a number of ways, such as attending Korean language and Saturday cultural programs offered through the church in junior high school, as well as by watching Korean television dramas. However, she wonders whether nonimmigrant generations will be able to maintain Korean as a heritage language if English is clearly the dominant language for both parents and children. For now, she makes a "deliberate effort" to maintain her Korean language skills because she believes being bilingual is an important aspect of her bicultural experience. In the age of transnationalism and the rise of Korean popular culture in and beyond Asia, there may be more incentive and opportunities to learn or maintain the Korean language, although such opportunities still may vary by different U.S. communities.

Reclaiming Culture

Although the Korean language is seen as a major marker of culture, respondents cite complex and multiple ways of defining and understanding what it means to be Korean, as gathered from family members, co-ethnics, ethnic enclaves, ethnic organizations, college classes, popular culture, studying/living in South Korea, and/or mainstream American society. Most express how they identify as Korean American by drawing from a range of exposure to and familiarity and affinity with various traditions and experiences. In this way, our respondents' experiences echo previous studies of children of Korean immigrants coming of age in contemporary United States as immigration and racial/ethnic diversity continue to shift the political, social, cultural, and economic landscape of U.S. society. One study on this population observes that their "ability to select the best traits from their immigrant parents and their native-born peers yields distinct *second generation advantages*. Members of the second generation neither simply continue their parents' ways of doing things nor simply adopt native ways."[21] Although the journeys of self-discovery vary, respondents discussed feeling at home with being Korean American, coming to terms with bicultural upbringings and identities, and trying to glean these "best traits" from their families, kin, communities, and various segments of the dominant society.

Respondents remembered cultural misunderstandings between themselves and their immigrant parents, especially if they grew up in areas with few co-ethnics. But many chose to put the past in perspective and frame it in terms of positive gains of strength and cross-cultural wisdom. As adults, most choose to see their Korean American identity as fluid, open to change, and incorporating other types of differences, which they contrast with their parents' Korean-focused world. As Tom reflects:

> It's always a challenge. I wouldn't consider it a struggle, but it's something that we are aware of. Our differences from everybody else in our surroundings—it's becoming more of a non-issue for me. I definitely think that having two cultural influences is a very positive thing. It's one of those things that made our generation a little bit stronger, gave us the ability to adapt and understand other cultures and different people as well. I guess it could be a positive thing.

Several respondents note that their parents did not actively teach or transmit Korean culture to them; this was the especially the case for those who grew up with very few other Koreans and/or Asians in the vicinity.

As adults, some of them decided to pursue and learn about Korean culture and history on their own. Dylan's parents came to the United States as international students and the only value that they emphasized as "Korean" for their U.S.-born children was to earn straight A's in school. Now in his forties, Dylan (who did not earn straight A's as a student and therefore did not fulfill his parents' definition of Koreanness) sardonically recalls coming of age as a child of Korean immigrants in the racial milieu of 1960s and 1970s in a predominantly white small town:

> Being Korean—up until I was a sophomore in college—was tantamount to having a cleft palate, a clubbed foot, and a hunchback. That's what being Korean meant. Because there was no explanation. There was no reference that was relevant, accessible, or understandable. And then when I was a sophomore in college by pure serendipity I was taking a course in East Asian Studies, and I began to understand something about Asian culture, Korean culture, and then I began consciously to parse that out and . . . get a handle on it. I had the good fortune to do that. . . . I don't think many people do.

Dylan undertook an arduous and personal quest to discover what it means to be Korean American, partly to expand the content and definition of this identity beyond that of the "straight-A" student. Gerald, who was also born in the United States to parents who arrived prior to 1965 and who is now in his forties, similarly experienced being the first Asian and Korean kid in the neighborhood. Gerald's race marked him as a target of prejudice and bullying. As he says:

> You got to understand, when you grow up in a predominantly white neighborhood or environment and that's who you socialize with and mingle with . . . My mother did try to teach me and my grandparents tried - to teach me [Korean] but I did not want to learn. You got to remember, kids can be so cruel. I got picked on enough just for being Asian, I didn't want to learn how to speak it and give them more reason. But I regret that. . . . I can recall throughout my childhood even as a young adult saying to myself it isn't fair. It wasn't my choice to be Korean. I didn't choose to be this. I wanted to so badly to change my last name. I wanted to lose any identity of being Korean. I thought that the prejudice that went on was unfair and cruel. It was unjust.

Even respondents who did not grow up in such racially and ethnically isolated spaces made conscious choices as they came of age to pick, adopt, and sometimes remake aspects of their ethnic backgrounds and identities.

For example, Jeremy, who was born and grew up in Hawaii as an ethnic minority surrounded by Japanese, Samoan, Filipino, and Hawaiian peers, observes that he "didn't really experience the Korean culture. Besides just living [it] through family and relatives, I don't think I ever really got to experience the culture." Jeremy identifies ethnicity as integral to who he is even as he philosophizes that he could never fully understand his heritage and his family's cultural worldviews. Noting different aspects of his cultural inheritance that he learned from family and friends and chose to emphasize, he also stresses that his ethnicity helps him to frame "the only life I know how to live."

> I guess with my parents, I learned how to respect my older sisters. And then with friends, just how to deal with the social aspect. I never really got a chance to learn, I guess just stories about Japan and Korea being invaded but nothing into detail. My parents celebrate Korean New Year. We celebrate almost every holiday. We probably wouldn't have either. It's funny, it seems as the years go by, these things, these holidays and events don't seem as celebrated as much. How can you hate your culture? This is the person you were born into. It's the only life I know how to live, and again there's parts of the culture that I like and understand and there are some parts I don't. I'm glad I'm able to differentiate between the two and make the best decision for myself.

As he discusses his lack of familiarity with Korean history ("just stories about Japan and Korea being invaded but nothing into detail") and waning cultural observations ("these holidays and events don't seem as celebrated as much"), Jeremy seems to exemplify what many respondents have felt in their work to reclaim their culture. There are gaps in his knowledge in terms of culture and family history, and many Korean traditions are no longer observed in the same way as in years past; but despite these losses and changes, he still feels profoundly connected to his culture.

In adulthood, many respondents like Jeremy pay less attention to co-ethnic definitions and assessments of their Koreanness and feel connected through their heritage despite "imperfect" or spotty knowledge of its content. Many describe an internal sense of connection to Korean culture and values as an inseparable aspect of who they are. Joy, who is American-born and in her thirties, grew up in southern California. Her parents, who came to the United States to study, speak English fluently, and she is unapologetic about not learning the Korean language as a child. Compared to other self-identified Koreans, she views herself as becoming "more American," especially in her post-college years.

> If someone just wants to know my ethnic background I would say Korean because it would explain a lot towards my physical features or what not. But I think I'm more American than Korean, especially when I compare myself to people who would describe themselves as Korean. I think I'm everything—the way I think, the language I speak, where I live—American. That's changed; in college I would have been a lot more like, "go Korea!" I'm not really that Korean anymore.

Compared to more recently arrived Korean immigrants in her community, and partly as a result of her family's early immigration and adaptation process, Joy feels that she is not "really that Korean anymore." Yet, Joy notes that Koreanness still strongly informs the way she relates to her parents, even though she describes them as "not that Korean, either." While Joy is careful to clarify that filial piety and taking care of one's family are not unique to Koreans, she considers her attitudes toward her parents and co-ethnic parents-in-law as grounded in ethnicity and culture.

> The whole filial piety thing is big. This is where I am kind of Koreanized. I do see myself taking care of my parents or my husband's parents and making it a priority to see them on a regular basis so they can see their grandchildren. We go out of our ways to show respect to them. We visit a lot—both sides. If emergencies come up, like take them to the airport, water their lawn; when my mom was away I would go and cook meals for my dad even though he never asked. I don't know if that is necessarily Koreanized, but I feel like that is part of who I am as a Korean.

Although language is often seen as a marker of one's affinity to the Korean culture, for Joy, culture is much more embedded in the behavior of care and respect for elder family members.

As these respondents illustrate, ethnic identity is complex and cannot be reduced to linguistic ability. Rather, it involves an interplay between one's knowledge of, affiliation with, and familiarity with culture, and, simultaneously, the social construction of racial and ethnic identities by group members and outsiders. Like Joy, Julian notes how being Korean American goes beyond knowing the language. While he acknowledges that he fits internally and externally ascribed (cultural and racialized) markers, Julian feels that to be culturally Korean involves interactions with and attitudes toward family, especially following Confucian ideals about relationships with and respect and care for elders:

> How I interact with my parents, how I interact with my parents-in-law, responsibility, in terms of taking care of my parents financially. I think that's a very Confucian thing in terms of responsibility to family. Let's say, for my wife's side of the family, I'm not blood related to them, but if there's some sort of happening or tragedy or difficulty, I'm obligated to get involved, right? So I think that's a Confucian thing.

For Julian and Joy, Koreanness is transmitted through interactions that determine their social relations, and are defined by roles and responsibilities that emphasize obligation, respect, and responsibility to the older generation.

Many have started to define being Korean by emphasizing what they want to pass on to their children. Almost all respondents define respect for elders as a tradition they hoped to transmit. Joon-ho, who immigrated at age twelve and is now in his forties, is less concerned about his children speaking Korean. Rather, he hopes that the value of respecting elders will continually be passed on to generations to come. Like many other children of immigrants, he and his spouse choose to uphold aspects of their heritage that matter to them:

> I still don't see the necessity of having to teach them Korean, but I told them, I said, "If you guys want to learn it, then learn it." My wife and I, we decided that we don't think it's that necessary. If my daughter comes to be an age where she feels like, "I want to learn it," then I think she can pick it up because she has that basis. We don't force them to go to Korean school or things like that. Again, basic cherry picker. There are certain

things that I'm very stern about. I like the Korean etiquette of respecting elders and things like that. It's something that I really respect.

Like Joon-ho, Soomin also immigrated as a child to the United States. Asked what aspects of Korean traditions and culture she would pass on to her young children, Soomin echoes Joon-ho, but adds that these Korean traditions are simultaneously reinforced through families and social institutions such as the immigrant church:

I mean, for Koreans—the number one value is filial piety. Growing up, that's just expected, right? And it's reinforced, especially at church activities. You're always taking care of the elderly. You make sure that they have a seat. You don't go in front of them. You bring them food first before you eat. You serve them first. All those things.

While such examples of respecting elders exist in other cultures, they are integral aspects of mainstream Korean cultural tradition as shaped by Confucianism. Of the many traditions that comprise Korean culture, respecting one's elders is seen by many Korean Americans as the most positive, and the least controversial, custom of Confucianism, which emphasizes hierarchical social relations.[22]

At the same time, when asked what aspects of their parents' marriage they would not replicate in their own marriage, most respondents replied that they did not like to see inequality and unequal division of household labor and that they were especially bothered by how the majority of the housework and childrearing fell on mothers or the wives, who often worked full-time outside the home. While some respondents attributed this unequal division of labor to Korean culture, others noted that the intersections of ethnicity, gender, and generational differences need to be taken into account; women take on the "second shift" across different cultures, economies, and societies.[23] For example, Regina, whose parents immigrated in the late 1970s, historically and socially contextualizes her critique of gendered division of labor:

When I was younger and going to Korea as a kid, my grandmother didn't want any boys in the kitchen. She didn't think it was a place for boys, so I think it was just part of the culture. It wasn't just that women felt that they had to be in the kitchen, and it wasn't considered as "Oh, this is unfair." That was just the way the culture worked. However my parents' generation, since they both work full-time jobs, I think that is unfair. But, I also don't think that it's just a Korean American issue, or an Asian American issue. I think that generation, maybe between the forties and the fifties, that generation just overall, even in non-Asian American families the household responsibilities tend to fall on the women. I think it's safe to say that although a lot of that has changed now, there are still a lot of households like that.

Regina shares that she still has a "lot of interest in Korean culture and Korean history." Like Korean language, Korean culture came to her "organically and naturally." She notes that "We grew up on Korean food. We grew up not wearing shoes in the house. We'd celebrate certain Korean traditions and my grandparents lived nearby so I saw them regularly growing up." But she also took an active interest in learning Korean history from her relatives, as well as finding out details about pre-migration life on both sides of her family to supplement what she learned in high school and college. In college, she purposefully studied Korean history after hearing about the Korean War for the first time in her high school U.S. history class. Regina did not have children at the time of the interview, but hoped that her children would have more classroom and extra-curricular opportunities to learn about different cultures, Korean and otherwise:

> I'm really optimistic because I think in the future, that there will be a lot more classes and a lot more options for kids to learn about more different cultures, and more different heritages. I want my children, whether or not they're fully ethnically Korean, to learn at least something whether I'm teaching them or they're learning it at the school.

What cultural traditions do children of Korean immigrants follow in their adulthood, and what practices do they hope to pass on to the next generation? The next section examines the "cherry picking" of Korean culture as respondents discuss how they revitalize and rework Korean holidays, customs, and rituals in adulthood, and especially for their children and aging parents.

Remaking Culture: Connecting through Korean Holiday and Ritual Observations

For most respondents, memories of cultural practices revolve around eating and the celebration of holidays and traditional ceremonies. In addition to eating Korean food regularly, almost all respondents remember their mothers and other female relatives making special Korean dishes to serve at family gatherings during particular holidays or milestones. Several respondents remembered celebrating Korean holidays with their families as children, most especially *Seollal*, New Year's Day, and *Chuseok*, a harvest celebration or Korean Thanksgiving.[24] Recalling the importance of food on these occasions, many respondents saw sharing favorite Korean foods with their children as a way of reclaiming culture, as is observing the tradition of celebrating first (*dol*), sixtieth (*hwangap*), and seventieth (*chilsoon*) birthdays. In general, though, gender remains an important factor in passing on these traditions. Among respondents, it was women more often than men who discussed being the key to transmitting cultural ceremonies to the next generation.

Past Cultural Celebrations in Immigrant Families

Many respondents remember New Year's Day as the one most celebrated in their families. Nina, a Korean American in her thirties who grew up in a predominantly European American town in southern California, continues to observe New Year's Day (the only Korean holiday her family celebrated) with *saebae*, the tradition of visiting and bowing to elders to welcome the New Year. Many respondents recall celebrating New Year with their kin. Caron, who lived with her mother, and then her father and stepmother after her parents' divorce, recalls that for New Year's Day, grandparents, aunts, uncles and cousins gathered together; she also notes that her stepmother had made *mandoo* (dumplings) for the recent New Year. *Tteok guk*, or rice cake soup, is another traditional dish; it symbolizes turning one year older at the beginning of the New Year, rather than on one's birthday.

Herb, in his twenties, was born and raised in different suburbs of Los Angeles and attended Korean school as a child, but like other respondents, he did not retain much of what he learned of language, history, or culture. It was not until his grandfather moved to the United States that he considered Korean language to be a necessary aspect of his Korean identity; as he laughs, "I think I was in early junior high. I couldn't speak Korean very well to him, and I realized this, and he got really mad. I thought, 'Oh, I shouldn't have ditched Korean school.'" Although his parents also emphasized education, Herb's primary sense of Korean identity is rooted in his parents' instructions for and modeling of how to behave around elders both at home and at family gatherings and holidays. He states:

> Like in New Year's, you do the whole bowing thing; when you meet your elder you always *in-sah* [greet]. Family gatherings and stuff, just day to day stuff with my family. How to talk to your elders, a lot of elder stuff, like respect and things like that, that's a huge thing. Education, constantly emphasized. . . . In terms of history, I wasn't taught much. Identity and culture had more, from my parents and our regular practices.

David grew up in Los Angeles' Koreatown and identifies as second generation. For his parents, both Korean and American holidays were primarily seen as reasons for getting together with family without incorporating cultural practices, such as bowing or specific games traditionally associated with the holidays. David comments:

> My parents, though first generation, they don't try to do the whole cultural thing as much. Although we meet on New Year's Day, Chuseok— full moon, I don't know what it's called, Full Moon Festival or whatever it is, Korean Thanksgiving, Independence Day—not really, probably New Year and Chuseok, those two. Thanksgiving is not a Korean thing. If there is an occasion, they want us to meet. We don't really do the whole cultural thing like play *yut-nor-ee* [a traditional game played on New Year's Day] or anything like that or do the whole bowing thing. We used to, but not as much these days.[25]

For most respondents, New Year's Day family gatherings adapted and became simpler—reduced to the elements of special foods, bowing, and sometimes gifts—as relatives moved away, and they themselves grew older. Herb remembers a childhood marked by elaborate New Year's

Days and a multiday funeral to mark the passing of his grandfather, as well as birthdays and other extended family gatherings. Many reported that New Year's gatherings have become more festive as they (and/or siblings) have had children, who are dressed in *hanbok* (traditional Korean clothing) to bow to and greet their grandparents and other elders.

However, culture is not just recreated by immigrant families; the observation of Korean New Year's Day has been reformed multiple times by the South Korean government since liberation, and especially throughout the politically tumultuous 1980s. While New Year's Day was one of the most commonly cited examples of Korean culture and ritual among our respondents, it is notable that families tend to celebrate New Year's Day on January 1, rather than according to the lunar calendar as in contemporary South Korea.[26] Since all of the families in the study immigrated to the United States before 1989 when the South Korean government restored the official New Year celebration to the lunar calendar, they (and their Korean American contemporaries) are more likely to observe the holiday on January 1, not simply because this is when it is observed in the United States, but because observing it on this date was part of a "modernization" policy instituted by the Japanese colonial government in 1898.[27] In fact, the South Korean government has adopted different policies on how to observe and celebrate the New Year as a public holiday, changing the calendar from solar to lunar and the number of public holiday observances from one day to four.[28] South Koreans and more recent Korean immigrants celebrate Lunar New Year, something that many of our respondents, who are children of old-time arrivals, still view as "Chinese" New Year. While New Year's Day remains one of the most popular ways for our respondents to connect to and reclaim Korean culture with nostalgia, it is also nevertheless an overlooked example of how state policies, a continuous immigration, and transnationalism have quietly altered notions of cultural "authenticity" for the adult children of immigrants.

Welcoming the New Generation: Baek-il and Dol

Respondents discussed various ways they were transmitting culture with the next generation, whether it be through food, Korean language school, or sharing family histories. Other customs that many respondents find meaningful, especially in middle adulthood, are *baek-il* and *dol*. *Baek-il* observes the one-hundredth day after a baby is born and *dol* marks the first birthday, two important milestones due to high mortality rates in much of Korean history. On these occasions, the family and guests come together to share special ceremonial foods and wish the baby continued health and longevity. These rituals can link the generations together in the United States, and serve as a reminder how kin is continued and expanded after the loss and disruption of migration.

Respondents also mention holding or attending *doljanchi* (first-birthday parties) for their own children, nephews, nieces, and friends' children. In South Korea and the Korean diaspora, *doljanchi* ranges from intimate gatherings at home to large and lavish affairs held at restaurants and banquet facilities for families and friends.[29] Observed *dol* traditions include dressing the birthday girl or boy in *hanbok*, arranging foods such as rice cakes and fruits in a traditional display, and featuring the practice of *dol-jabi* to predict the child's fortune and future. In *doljabi*, several objects are placed on a table before the child, and the first item that she or he grabs is said to predict her or his future.[30] It is important to note that this is a significant cultural ritual for immigrant grandparents; anthropologist Soo-Young Chin observes that "although the child is the focus of the celebration, it is the grandparents who are seated at the table of honor and given credit for the generativity of the family."[31] Simple or elaborate, small or big, *dol* parties have become more significant for this generation of Korean Americans as they come of age and have children. In honor of the past and their ancestors, and sometimes influenced by the latest *doljanchi* trends in South Korea and the transnational community in the United States, they rediscover and restage Hundredth Day celebrations and first birthday parties from old fuzzy, pre-emigrant or early immigrant life family photos.[32] However, because grandparents, especially the paternal grandparents, are viewed as the ones seated at the "table of honor," *dol* parties can also be stressful events fraught with disagreements and conflicting points of view.

Whitney, an American-born mother in her thirties and a business executive, had her first child after finishing graduate school. She planned her *dol* by herself as an outdoor picnic and celebrated this Korean tradition in a casual venue that she wanted for her daughter's birthday. This created conflict with her in-laws, whom she describes as more traditional than her own parents:

> My mother-in-law adamantly was opposed to everything for Rebecca's
> *dol* because it wasn't traditional enough. She called it a pseudo-*doljanchi*.
> I had the fruit. But it was outdoors. I rented tables and chairs. Everyone
> loved it except my mother-in-law. She said that she was allergic to the
> sun, except she plays golf! I followed [the tradition of providing] fruit
> towers, but didn't follow *tteok*. I did do *doljabi*.

Whitney's mother-in-law made a fuss that she had deviated from tradition by not having a banquet held indoors. As her way of negotiating
the older generations' demands for authenticity, which were not only
about rituals but also concerned class-appropriateness, Whitney hired
a Korean American event coordinator, who staged a trendy baby décor
and theme for her second child's party that featured catered American
food with *tteok* (Korean rice cakes) as decoration, dessert, and party
gifts. Although she spent more on a party than she had budgeted, she
did this to make sure it was "traditional" (albeit with the updated and
modern diasporic twist) enough to her in-laws' liking. Whitney also felt
the pressure to please her in-laws because this child was the first boy in
his generation on her husband's side. In order to avoid conflict, Whitney gave her mother-in-law more control in the planning of this event.
She reflects on how she negotiated different family members' sentiments
and wishes surrounding the first birthday party, including her in-laws'
delight at the birth of a grandson, and her own desire to celebrate the
arrival of a healthy baby after many years of trying:

> My husband would rather save up money [for our children] to go to
> college. But for me, it is a celebration of life—I fully respect it—just do
> not be so extravagant. I also wanted it to be fun for our friends' kids. I
> wanted to respect Wes's parents without giving ourselves up entirely. We
> spent more money on Henry's. Wes's mom was calling me every other
> day. If Henry had been a girl they would not have invited as many peo-
> ple. My dad wanted to do it in our backyard!

With help from her mother and aunt, Whitney planned her first child's
dol as she liked—as a low-key affair with some Korean elements.
Although Whitney was against stereotypical extravagant *dol* parties and
disagreed with her in-law's preferential attitude toward the grandson

and male heir, she let her more traditional mother-in-law have more say in planning her grandson's *dol.* But since she herself could not put on the event with her full-time job, she hired an event planner (who specializes in *dol* and children's birthday parties) to decorate the *dol-janchi* as her mother-in-law wanted. Her mother-in-law's wishes dominated over other family members' wishes, including those of her own son. Although Henry's *dol* can be read as an example of increasing "marketization of personal life"—and of American, not just Korean, life—it is also a way in which Whitney and her husband give back to their parents—rather, specifically to his parents, since hers wanted a backyard gathering.[33] Moreover, because Whitney and her husband do not live near his parents and siblings and have limited contact with them, allowing his parents to plan the first birthday party was a way for Whitney to negotiate ethnic traditions and in-law relations.

To incorporate the "proper" cultural elements in *doljanchi,* some middle-class professional Korean American women like Whitney hire event coordinators, who tend to be recent immigrants in their twenties and thirties, also middle class, and are hired for their modern aesthetics and familiarity with Korean *dol* customs. Hannah, a mother of twins in her thirties, also ended up hiring an event coordinator when her work schedule became hectic and her mother was busy caring full-time for her grandchildren. With the help of the event coordinator, they had a *doljanchi* for almost 250 guests. The celebration involved a combination of tradition, the influence of her social circle (her family was invited to many of her Korean American friends' *dol* parties, and she felt obligated to reciprocate), and observing the wishes of her mother and in-laws. Hannah says, "It meant a lot because we went through so much [trying to conceive]. Even though we grew up here, those things have been ingrained in us and it would have felt not complete if we didn't do something like that." Hannah and Whitney, who are both married to co-ethnics, illustrate how adult children of immigrants do not simply replicate tradition but also must negotiate generational expectations, traditional meanings, social reciprocations, and their own hectic work schedules. Their husbands helped with some aspects of the event planning, but not with the "cultural" aspects of *dol,* for which they utilized their financial resources and access to the ethnic/transnational *doljanchi* event-planning industry in the greater Los Angeles area.

Other *dol* parties described by our respondents were much smaller in size and scale. For those married to non-Koreans, negotiations around tradition are further worked out by celebrating their spouse's family traditions as well. In the spirit of cooperation, these celebrations are sometimes modified to "fit" with their blended families. Jessica, whose husband is Chinese American, recalls her child's *baek-il*:

> We kind of combined this with the Chinese Red Egg and Ginger Party. Except that it just ended up being a Red Egg and Ginger Party instead, a traditional Chinese banquet at a nearby restaurant. The timing (at about two to three months) is similar to the Hundredth Day, so we just figured one celebration was enough.

However, she celebrated her son's first birthday in a modified Korean style, which adopted some traditional elements and still retained the celebratory meaning for her mother and for herself:

> My mom helped to prepare the dinner and the stacks of fruit. We got a traditional Korean rice cake that said *dol* in Korean. We did that activity where you put out the string, pen, money, book, etc., and see which the baby picks (he picked the book). My mom and I planned it. Maybe forty to fifty people attended the party, which was held at my mother-in-law's house. The event was meaningful for me, since it's one of the few traditional Korean celebrations we still hold, and the only time [my child's] worn a *hanbok*. I have pictures from my own *dol*, and it was meaningful to think of so many generations who'd celebrated in a similar way in the past.

Others who are married to non-Koreans also echo similar ideas about the blending of multiple cultural traditions. Angie, married to an Asian American of a different ethnicity, had three first birthday parties for her son Isaac, even though she only found out about the first birthday ritual through her mother:

> One with my family at a Korean restaurant—traditional and formal with family—my parents insisted. I couldn't care less. Then, we had a very low-key barbecue with my husband's family, who is very private. Three parties that year—how spoiled is Isaac? I also had a third *dol* party

with my two friends. Our three children were born within weeks of each other. One was [a] white American woman married to a Korean man, and one was a Korean woman married to a non-Korean.

Interestingly, prior to her mother's telling her, Angie only had vague memories of her own *dol* through pictures and did not quite understand the significance of *doljabi*. Yet, because she had had one at the insistence of her mother, Angie relayed what she had learned about the meaning of *dol* to her friends who were interracially married. As a result, the three intermarried friends decided to host a joint first-birthday party for their mixed-heritage Korean American children—a *dol* without the particular rituals. While this last party clearly indicates how adult children of Korean immigrants can exercise their "ethnic options," and choose, discard, and modify cultural traditions as they wish, Angie's decision to accommodate the different expectations and personal preferences of both sides of her blended family also illustrates the important role that grandchildren and first-birthday events—regardless of specific content and formats—play in honoring both the grandparents and the first generation.[34] Whether held at restaurants or in backyards, these rites of passage are meaningful to multiple generations of Korean Americans, who, as adult children, negotiate ethnic, transnational, gender, and class influences to reclaim cultural traditions.

Celebrating Longevity: Hwangap and Chilsoon

As demonstrated in previous chapters, adult children recognize their parental sacrifices and find ways to give back. For some respondents, cultural practices and passages are ways to celebrate their parents' milestones, including *hwangap* (sixtieth) and *chilsoon* (seventieth) birthday celebrations. According to anthropologist Soo-young Chin, *hwangap* marks the fifth completion of the twelve-year lunar cycle, a significant occurrence during times of shorter life expectancies; *hwangap* has traditionally marked a person's entrance into old age and the transition to retirement, both in the family (where the person is no longer the head of the household) and society (where work and other examples of participation in public life are no longer central).[35] Chin also observes that meanings and forms for *hwangap* and similar "late life rituals change to meet the differing and changing environments" in both South Korea and in the United States due to migration and urbanization.[36]

As their parents age, respondents attach significance and meaning to celebrating their parents' sixtieth and seventieth birthdays, although according to our respondents, the meaning of these milestones has been somewhat altered: given longer life expectancies and economic situations, most of their parents do not retire at age sixty, and many are still working after age seventy. Just as significantly, due to the changes in adulthood in contemporary societies, adult children may still be finishing their education, getting established in their careers, and may not have children by the time a parent becomes sixty years old. For both the immigrant parents and their children in the United States, age sixty-five is considered a much more important "late life" milestone because it signals the eligibility to receive Social Security (for most) and Medicare, which relieves financial burdens for both generations. Sixtieth and seventieth birthday parties remain significant symbolic rituals that serve to retain cultural traditions and maintain family ties, but are no longer tied to formal retirements.

Depending on the requests of their immigrant parents and the financial situations of the adult children, some sixtieth and seventieth birthday parties are major affairs with a long guest list, while others are smaller, more intimate and individualized affairs, celebrated through family dinners, gifts, and special trips. Adult daughters are usually the key organizers of these birthday celebrations. For example, Soomin's oldest sister arranged the *hwangap* celebration for their mother, which was held at the church with over a hundred guests (all the children split the cost of the dinner). Their mother's seventieth birthday party was smaller and held at a restaurant, but again her daughters organized the event, invited guests, and paid for the festivities.

In contrast to daughters, who plan, organize, and help pay for the celebrations, adult sons are more likely to contribute financially to these events and gifts. Bob, in his thirties, was financially unable to provide a sixtieth party for his father, but mentions that when his father turned seventy, both he and his sister were working and in better financial situations. They planned and saved up for their father's dream seventieth birthday gift: a family trip to Hawaii. His older sister planned and made the trip with their parents, while Bob helped pay for the vacation. While Bob discusses the importance of filial piety in his gift to his parents, he does not stress having greater responsibility as the son of the family, or following the traditional patriarchal system. Rather, he acknowledges and is grateful that his older sister, who is financially more secure and more established in her career, has provided much of the financial assistance, care-giving, and other acts of filial piety. At the same time, he and his sister have wondered how family dynamics will change if both siblings bring other people into their household through marriage. Meanwhile, practices of filial piety and attachment and maintenance of rites of passage like that of *hwangap* are filtered through the social and economic realities of which child can provide more support, which is sometimes determined more by age rather than by gender.

Albert, now in his thirties and married with children, was finishing his education the year his father turned sixty. Albert and his girlfriend at the time (now wife) lived within driving distance from his parents, so they drove down and went to dinner. He explains that in contrast to his wife's parents, his parents did not view the *hwangap* celebration as a big deal and did not request a lavish affair. However, Albert also observes that he did not give much thought to these rituals because he was still finishing his education and did not have an income at the time of his father's *hwangap*, for which children are responsible for covering all the expenses.

> When I was finally working, I actually bought my parents both really nice watches. I just felt like it was an expression that they've been patient for a very long time, and supporting me for a very long time, and I think I guess it maybe have been a little more egocentric in that way. It was more about my timeline than theirs. I think they're not that demanding and I guess one could say I could probably try harder, but they didn't seem like they wanted that much out of it. We grew up with just the four of us. I don't have extended family in the United States, so I think the most we wanted was to just have time together with the whole family.

Albert learned about *hwangap* through his wife and her parents' higher expectations around what children should do for their parents who turn sixty.

Hwangap, which often functions as a big family reunion, is also important for Angie's family. Angie is the oldest of three children in her family; all three siblings are married with children. She recalls that when her parents turned sixty, the children took them out to dinner and "got them a nice big gift." This *hwangap* was a small, family event. However, they are planning do "something huge" for her father's upcoming *chilsoon*. Although the children will split the costs for the parents and their respective families, Angie will be the main organizer of the *chilsoon* gift—a family vacation that serves as a reunion, since the siblings live in different states—whether her "workaholic" father wants it or not.

> We're all flying to Hawaii and do that there, which should be interesting . . . because my dad's the stubborn sort and he doesn't exactly like the life, so we're sort of forcing it on him [laughs]. . . . "You'll love it dad, trust us [laughing]." He just likes to work, so we're forcing him to take time off.

In Angie's family's case, the trip is in honor of a cultural ritual and ethnic tradition, but also supports Chin's argument that the "focus of late life rituals is on family solidarity and support."[37] It is also a significant financial and time commitment for the family members, and serves the dual purpose of reaffirming ethnic rituals and being a family reunion.

Gracie, a stay-at-home mother, lives in California while her parents live in another state, so she and her sister also celebrated her parents' sixtieth and seventieth birthdays through family trips in far-away locations. Gracie recalls,

> Each vacation was a week and included my mom and dad, and my family and my sister's family. My husband doesn't get a whole lot of vacation, and we have to spend some of it every year visiting my parents and his at their homes, so I can be pretty selfish about the rest of our vacation time. . . . My mom once suggested that we have a whole family vacation every year or every other year, and I wasn't excited about that idea at all. But for those special birthdays, there was no argument— my sister and I planned the vacations, and paid for them when my mom would allow us to.

These vacations can also be stressful since family members may sometimes experience conflicts during extended periods of enforced closeness. Even though she loves her parents, Gracie finds these trips challenging because she and her sister get into fights; however, she could not avoid these late life rituals because of their significance. Like many of our respondents, Gracie, her parents, and her siblings live in diverse states across the country, and vacations like this provide few, infrequent opportunities for geographically scattered families to get together or to splurge on special trips of a lifetime.

The clear pattern that emerges from the practice of these Korean rites of passages is the gendered and matrilineal nature of who plans, organizes, and carries out these special occasions in families, regardless of how "traditional" or transformed these celebrations are among adult children of immigrants. The women plan *baek-il* and *doljanchi*, usually with the help of their mothers, aunts, female friends, female cousins, and sometimes, female Korean American event planners. Despite the value of filial piety and the focus on eldest sons and their responsibilities in the patriarchal and gendered hierarchy of the Confucian family system, among our respondents, daughters are in fact more prominent in planning and organizing *hwangap* and *chilsoon*. They are also more likely to keep in contact with their parents and ask their wishes and preferences. If there are no daughters, then daughters-in-law are the next most likely person to rally and coordinate all spouses, siblings, and in-laws to plan these milestones. Helen, as her parents' eldest child, and as the daughter-in-law who has been married into her husband's family the longest, has been in charge of all the parties to mark sixty and above milestone birthdays for both sides of the families. She quips, "I planned it all. I called and made arrangements. My sister-in-law helped with the last one. We would talk, and my sister-in-law would call. It was easier for me bossing the nieces and nephews because I married into the family first." Erin, in her forties, is the only daughter in her family; as the one who lives geographically closest to her parents and is emotionally closest to them, she has helped plan five parties for her parents and in-laws, with more to come. Erin shares that

> The seventieth parties were great because aside from the tradition, it was a celebration planned and paid by the children. It was especially meaningful when we celebrated my father-in-law's seventieth because he was really sick during that time.

Like Bob, Erin also attributes the different levels of involvement to the financial status of the siblings at the time of the milestone birthday. Her parents planned and paid for their own *hwangap* parties with their families and friends. For *chilsoon* parties, Erin first asked the parents and in-laws how they wished to celebrate, including details of the dinner, trip, gift, and so on, and then all the children planned and paid for the celebration.

As they enter middle adulthood, our respondents find themselves reviving, learning, and reforming old Korean traditions. *Baek-il* and *dol* celebrations, preserved as old photographs from their childhoods, take on new significance and are revived in an ethnic, immigrant, and transnational context as our respondents welcome the next generation and introduce these new family members to previous generations. As they celebrate the birth of their children, nephews, nieces, and friends' children, our respondents find themselves buying or renting *hanbok* for their children and arranging simple to elaborate birthday parties featuring traditional rice cakes, *doljabi* with traditional or modified fortune-telling objects, or beautiful decorations and food inspired by both American and South Korean trends. Regardless of the form, these parties serve the purpose of introducing the third generation to the immigrant generation, while reconnecting the 1.5 or second generation to their childhood experiences of similar traditional events.

Similarly, as aging immigrant parents hit milestone birthdays—sixtieth, sixty-fifth, and seventieth—our respondents negotiate the cultural significance of these birthdays with regard to their own life stages, and financial means, and other ability to go on family trips. Due to the growing life expectancy of the first generation, on the one hand, and the length of time required for the next generation to finish higher education and additional education or work training, on the other, sixtieth birthdays tend to be relatively low-key celebrations. However, by the time the parent turns seventy, many of our respondents are better positioned financially and thus can do something more elaborate—and their parents expect celebrations from their children.

Another influence on the type of sixtieth birthday celebration is whether our respondents (or at least one offspring in the family) are married and have children. Traditional *hwangap* honors the older adult's retirement and transition to passing the "head of the household" role to the next generation; the heteronormative expectations around this life cycle and stage transition are that the next generation have married well, settled down, and had children.[38]

In the families of our respondents, if the sixtieth birthday celebration consists of a party with a large number of guests, the seventieth celebration tends to be a smaller intimate event. But in general, parents and the adult children plan family trips, which preserve the meaning of the ritual while updating its traditional forms and elements. Called *hyodo gwangang* (filial tourism), trips (especially trips abroad) are becoming the present of choice for the baby boomer generation who have grown up in the affluence of contemporary South Korea, where adult children arrange, book, and pay for their parents' tour packages. Korean Americans also tend to give gifts of travel, especially in honor of immigrant parents who did not travel much due to lack of vacation time and/or financial constraints.[39]

Conclusion

For many respondents, their experience of Korean culture during their adolescence and young adulthood was often related to the Korean language, which is generally the external marker by which first generation and transnational co-ethnics judge other Korean Americans' connection to culture. At the same time, those who do not speak Korean fluently challenge how language fluency is used as *the* salient marker of ethnicity; they claim this focus provides a limited perspective of what it means to be Korean American. In adulthood, many respondents are reclaiming their cultural heritage in new, different ways that go beyond the Korean language. In previous research on Asian Americans, studies show that fourth-generation individuals are the most likely to feel impelled to gain back what they have lost culturally, while the second and third generation are focused on "assimilating."[40] By contrast, the respondents in this study work to transmit aspects of their Korean American culture to their children. In the current post–civil rights era, with its climate of greater tolerance for ethnicity in public spaces, these respondents are actively reclaiming their culture in new ways, especially as they and their parents enter new stages of life. Many who did not grow up with Korean culture have sought it out in their adulthood in various different ways. Adult children of Korean immigrants find themselves remaking culture especially around rites of passage as their parents age, and in recognition of children's first one hundred days or first birthdays when they have children of their own. Increases in the availability of transnational information and communication, as well as increased capabilities to travel, have also encouraged the process of reclaiming and adapting Korean culture in Korean American contexts. As our respondents describe, the differing ways of observing milestone birthdays serve as an excellent example of how individuals, families, and societies respond to and reclaim their culture by interpreting it in new ways that provide them meaning.

These respondents do this consciously as they are reintroduced to, or actively seek out, life-change rites of passage and their meanings; this process rekindles a connection to ethnicity and culture that goes beyond just knowing the Korean language. Respondents who reclaimed and remade cultural traditions such as New Year's Day or *dol* or *hwangap* were in a way remembering and connecting multiple generations together, while also reclaiming culture for the third generation. Women—in particular daughters, daughters-in-law, and their maternal kin—lead this cultural resurgence; they revitalize and rework cultural expressions, practices, and the meanings of "traditions" among adult children of immigrants. Cultural productions were just one way in which adult children of Korean immigrants expressed, reclaimed and remade culture. Couched in this framework of reclaiming and reframing culture, the next chapter explores how adult children of Korean immigrants work to be present for aging parents.

4

Gender at Work

Bonnie is naturally a caretaker-type of personality, and I
think that I was drawn to that for a variety of reasons. So,
then, she naturally plays that caretaker role for her parents
and my parents. We have a running joke that she is the
Director of Parental Affairs. When I was in residency, I was
difficult to reach because of my work schedule and time
zone [differences]; my wife would broker the middle role
and spend time talking to my mother. She is a natural in the
role. I don't think she loves it. I think she [would] love for it
to be a shared responsibility, but she's naturally better at that
than I am.
—Albert

Albert, a married father of young children, is very appreciative of his
wife, Bonnie, who runs their household and takes care of both her and
his parents. Without her labor and attention to their extended families, he would not be able to devote the amount of time he does to his
work. Albert attributes her willingness to take on this role to her innate
"caretaker-type of personality," suggesting she is "naturally better" at
such tasks as staying in regular contact with both sets of parents, while
acknowledging that she would prefer that he share in the care-work
responsibilities for their respective families. Later in the interview, he
discloses that he can be most supportive of his parents by providing for
them financially now and in the near future. While Albert uses individual situations and personal characteristics to explain the division
of care-work responsibilities in their household, his admiration of and

appreciation for his wife's work in the family domain strongly adhere to long-held "traditional" values about women's roles. Research shows that the majority of care-givers to older family members tend to be women despite changes in women's economic participation and demographic patterns, as well as shifting cultural expectations regarding women's roles in recent decades.[1]

Past research on relationships between aging parents and their adult children shows that children often provide support prior to the stage when parents become frail and are incapable of caring for themselves.[2] This support comes in diverse forms, including emotional (e.g., visiting, checking in through telephone calls), financial (e.g., paying bills, providing allowance), and tangible (e.g., providing transportation, helping with household chores).[3] Studies have also documented the gendered patterns of parental care-giving and shown that daughters are three times more likely than sons to provide assistance to parents.[4] While sons do care for their parents and take on many of the responsibilities, studies have also found that married heterosexual men—like Albert above—rely on their wives to assist them or provide much of the help with older parents.[5] As wives, daughters, and/or daughters-in-law, women do more of what is known as "kin work": that is, maintaining and developing close ties with and among family members.[6] This chapter explores how, when, and who among the respondents step in and negotiate current and future care for aging parents while they are relatively healthy and independent; in connection to these factors, this chapter also examines the intersections of ethnicity, culture, and gender that shape care-giving expectations, attitudes, and practices.

Transition into Older Adulthood: "Being There" for Parents

As parents age, they experience retirement, changes in their marriage and/or marital status, "empty nest" syndrome, reduction in income, loss of family members, friends, and loved ones, and other milestones and transitions in the life course. Studies of older adults and Korean American families have indicated that the support of their adult children takes various forms including emotional, financial, informational, linguistic, and other tangible means.[7] As explored in earlier chapters, the lives of Korean immigrants and their children continue to be linked as parents use the well-being of their children to measure their own survival, success, and attainment of their immigrant hopes and dreams. For adult children, former expectations around doing well in school or not getting into trouble give way to new and different ways of "being there" for their parents along life-course transitions.

The Confucian concept of *hyo*, or filial piety, "exemplified by the expression of responsibility, respect, sacrifice, and family harmony," is a core cultural value that historically has regulated intergenerational attitudes and behaviors in Korea and many other East and Southeast Asian societies.[8] According to Confucianism and the primogeniture system, after the father retires from public life, the eldest son becomes the official head of the household. As the only or the primary inheritor of family assets, the eldest son becomes legally responsible for the care of aging parents and younger siblings. In South Korea, public institutions and national family laws have reinforced the patriarchal family system and gender inequalities in norms and practice, despite equality guaranteed before the law in the national constitution.[9] However, the rapid industrialization and modernization of post-war South Korea have changed family structures such that they are more nuclear and smaller in household size, while fertility rates are declining and participation of women in the workforce, especially of married women with children, is rising.[10] Moreover, the women's movement, which challenged and pressured the national government for decades, has effected multiple revisions of the family law code, including the abolition of the long standing head-of-family system in 2005.[11] In the United States, Korean immigrants and their adult children are also rethinking and redefining traditions and ideals around gendered care and responsibility and intergenerational interdependency as they balance family resources and local and national programs, services, and structures.

Respondents share a range of different ways they try to be there for their parents. To the extent of their ability, many respondents provide financial resources such as allowances, mortgage payments, gifts, gift cards, and trips to retired parents, especially those on fixed incomes. Among those whose parents that have retired, most report that their parents rely on Social Security for post-retirement income. They also provide other types of tangible support, such as performing household chores, planning finances, giving rides, providing computer/technical assistance, translating, and interpreting, and accompanying parents to appointments.

Respondents also help their parents navigate aging and manage relationships and bonds with other family members. In a study of Italian Americans in Northern California in the 1980s, anthropologist Micaela di Leonardo defines this type of work as the *work of kinship*, a third type of work that women do in addition to (1) household work and childcare and (2) work in the labor market. Di Leonardo writes that this work of maintaining ties and connections with other family members is invisible but essential in creating connections across generations; it takes "time, intention, and skill," and it is also largely women's work.[12] Men are less likely to do work to maintain kinship networks across households, and they are less likely to provide this type of care work across generations.[13] According to di Leonardo, the unpaid nature of the work of kinship and its critical role in nurturing and maintaining family networks form an important intersection in which it is possible to view women's lives and the family from both "labor" and "network" perspectives within feminist research.[14] Considering the work of maintaining kinship ties and caring for generations in terms of intersections of race, gender, and class also illuminates how such values and work are not limited to particular ethnic/cultural communities, even though respondents may characterize them as commonly practiced in their ethnic groups.[15] The women in this study are also more likely than the men to report that they call, visit, and listen to their parents, offer encouragement, and show appreciation. This chapter focuses on respondents' worries, challenges, and strategies in dealing with aging parents who are in relatively good health but are experiencing various life-course changes and losses. Moreover, it also explores the gendered nature of the work of caring for Korean immigrant parents.

Adult Daughters and Emotion Work

The majority of our respondents report that while their parents are in generally good health, they have observed changes and transitions as their parents adjust to older adulthood, and retirement. Some parents welcome the opportunity to rest and take vacations for the first time in decades while others worry about their future finances. Some struggle with losing their income and/or jobs, which had brought identity and purpose or kept them busy. While some parents keep busy taking up leisure activities, meeting with friends, babysitting grandchildren, and/or volunteering at church, some respondents share that their parents feel the boredom and loneliness of empty-nest syndrome. While both male and female respondents express their desire or feeling of duty to take care of parents, a gendered difference emerges when they discuss types of care-giving. Daughters are more likely to be aware of the emotional changes their parents are experiencing, and more likely to discuss ways in which they have tried to address those changes and maintain ties to their parents; in other words, daughters are more likely to do emotion work. Sons go into less detail about specific changes in their parents' lives, but do discuss the pressure they face to be financially responsible for their parents. Among married respondents, males are more likely to say that they rely on their spouse to do the actual emotion work while female respondents do the emotion work themselves in negotiation with and support from their spouses.

Regardless of marital status, daughters tend to express a greater feeling of closeness to their natal families. Married adult sons, on the other hand, especially those with children, are less likely to state that they feel emotionally close to their natal family. Female respondents are more likely to make phone calls and face-to-face visits than their male counterparts. Julian, a second-generation Korean American in his thirties and the eldest son in his family, states:

> From the time I was eighteen, I've been pretty detached from my parents. I don't call them on the phone or anything like that and though my mother was more involved in my early life, as an adult I [have] come to really respect my father even though I don't have that affectionate close relationship with my parents. My mother wishes she could, but I don't want one with her [laughter]. I mean, I love my mom but I am just detached from her.

Some female respondents report that the sons in their families exhibit this similar sense of detachment towards their parents. Some remark that their brothers or husbands are "clueless," "unreliable," or "unaware" when it comes to the changing needs of their aging parents and parents-in-law. For their part, many male respondents say that they rely on family members to remind them to check in with their parents. Albert discusses how others, including his own parents, need to remind him to keep in touch more often as they get older:

My parents say it very directly actually: "You know, your dad is going to Korea for a while; can you call your mom weekly just to let her know that you care about her?" And they do it that way where they tell me to do things for the other parent while they're gone. And you know, it's been an ongoing theme. I feel like, they probably think I'm a little too distant or aloof.

In fact, in the families of our respondents with sons and daughters, both the parents and the adult children assume that a daughter will end up caring for the parents, rather than the son and his wife as dictated by the traditional patriarchal family system in Korea. This assumption reflects the social patterns in both U.S. and South Korean societies, in which women have served as the primary care-givers to elderly within the family—a situation that has required them to balance time for themselves and/or children, quit their own jobs or reduce hours and shift to part-time work, and sacrifice their own financial stability.[16] For instance, Sabrina's parents used to own a business but sold it when her father was diagnosed with cancer. Although his cancer has been in remission, he has been too weak to return to work full-time, and her parents have been living off their meager savings for many years. Although Sabrina was glad that they sold their business because the work was so physically hard on them, she was especially concerned because she, her parents, and her brother were all financially strapped at the time. It was significant that she and her parents seemed to excuse her brother from primary care-work duties even though "he's the son," due to his financial condition ansd responsibility to *his* own wife and child. In contrast, Sabrina, who was not married at the time of the interview, had limited her recent job search to working no more than an hour's drive away from her parents because everyone expected her to take care of them.

Soomin, who is in her early forties, makes the critical observation that compared to her sisters, her brother rarely spends time with their mother. She states,

My sisters and I are friends, and we get along, and we talk to each other and spend time with each other. My brother just did not feel the same way. He was never very close with us. Sons are useless!

Soomin lived outside California for many years due to school and work but returned to be near her family as her mother experienced different health issues related to aging. Other daughters also respond to the changing needs of aging parents, even as they feel a similar sense of ambivalence as that expressed by Soomin regarding sons.

Sometimes, daughters' changing relationships with one or both parents affected their responses. Chelsea, in her forties, discusses how her parents' expectations of her changed over the years. Growing up, Chelsea felt a lot of pressure do well in school and go to a "name-brand college," and that was the extent of the relationship and communication between her and her parents. Now that they are older, their expectations of her involve emotional, financial, and other kinds of support. While Chelsea has provided such support, she has done so begrudgingly—especially for her father, who she feels does not deserve his children's help or support in his old age. Chelsea shares:

> I was thinking, as you're getting older and older, they have certain expectations. Like especially like birthdays and like all these holidays, Mother's Day, Father's Day—they always expect something. Even though they don't deserve it, like they have bad relationships with their kids and so forth, they still expect that. . . . The sad thing is, like, I'm close to my mom but I'm not that close to my dad and he's never really done anything for us.
>
> I don't really feel like it at times but then when they expect it and they need it, it's just hard to say no. Especially, you know, at their age, they're feeling kind of lonely and vulnerable at times and as you get older and older, it seems like they get emotionally more attached to their kids and they expect more from them.

Despite her negative feelings toward her father, Chelsea still sees her parents bimonthly and speaks with them on the phone because she does not want them to feel alone. She also provides the kin work for her in-laws, especially her mother-in-law, whom she compares to her father, describing both as "hands-off" parents who did not spend very much time with their children when they were younger. As a result, Chelsea, not her husband, is the one who remembers birthdays and holidays, buys cards and gifts, and calls her mother-in-law. While her husband and his siblings spend time with their father, they do not provide such emotional support for their mother. Despite her ambivalence, Chelsea provides emotional and social support for her father to whom she feels no attachment, and for her mother-in-law, to whom her husband feels no attachment. And while Chelsea does care work for her in-laws, her husband does not spend time with or provide support for her parents, though he does spend time with his own father. Following a similar gender role split, Chelsea's own brother does not spend time with their parents. But in exchange for this clearly gendered division of care work, Chelsea does receive intergenerational support; Chelsea and her mother share a close bond, and both her mother and mother-in-law have provided childcare. Her case illustrates that care work and providing different kinds of intergenerational support are not cultural norms or given, but actions developed because of the various needs among generations. It also highlights how—despite the emphasis on the duties of first-born sons that many respondents cited as one stressed in traditional Korean culture—daughters and daughters-in-law actively provide care-giving within their families, albeit with ambivalent feelings in some cases.

Emotion Work: Managing Parents' Relations

Much of family emotion-work literature focuses on managing emotions of individuals, rather than on managing relationships. However, studies have shown that not only do women comfort and nurture individuals within a family, they are also involved in relationship work as well, which entails managing and encouraging emotional bonds among family members.[17] For example, Brenda Seery and M. Sue Crowley's study on relationships between fathers and their children found that mothers are key to enhancing these relationships, with strategies such as encouraging positive father-children activities and relations, praising fathers for fathering, and, when father and children are unhappy with each other, mediating between them and seeking ways to redress angry and hurt feelings.[18] The women in this study are also the key relationship managers for their aging parents; they express the intention to be present and available for their parents as they age. These women help manage and mediate their parents' relationships with themselves, their spouses, and siblings. They are emotionally present for aging mothers who care-giving for ill fathers. Adult children whose parents are

divorced and/or widowed often regularly check in on the single or sur-
viving parent who is often living by him- or herself. Although all of our
respondents do such relationship management in order to mediate and
encourage relationships among family members, some express ambivalence about their roles and responsibilities.

One of the first issues daughters discuss is how they notice one or
both parents wrestling with the physical and emotional consequences
of aging, such as getting tired easily, wishing to drive less, or feeling
lonely, and then how they try to help, working to manage their parents' emotions by offering a listening ear, advice, or working to calm
an agitated, anxious, or upset parent. Connie's parents, who are in their
seventies, retired out of state after selling their California home for a
profit. Connie worries about them experiencing loneliness and being
challenged to make new friends after moving to a new city in old age.
She regularly visits her parents to check on and be with them because
of her concerns regarding their loneliness—"because they spent nearly
thirty years in Los Angeles before moving out of state, where they have
no network of friends." Although her visits with her parents might consist of sitting in front of the TV or going out, and might be less focused
on deep discussions, she believes her frequent visits and mere presence
are helpful to her parents.

Others discuss how they observe and try to manage strain and
changes in their parents' marriages. Bickering between parents often
draws adult children into the middle to referee differences and disagreements, and even separations and divorces. Adult daughters mention how they support their parents, especially mothers, through marriage difficulties or through the loss of a spouse. Adult sons mention
sisters or wives (if they are married) providing emotional support for
their mothers. Chelsea talks about the time her mother declared she
wanted a divorce, and her father responded with despondency. For six
months, her mother talked daily with Chelsea. She states:

> She needed someone that was a sounding board. She had no one else to
> talk with that would give her perspective. My father has always been a
> controlling man and my mother had pent-up anger. They were not on
> speaking terms. . . . I was trying to help my mom by listening to her and
> giving her advice to come out of her shell.

Chelsea's mother hesitated to divorce due to fear of disapproval from other Koreans in her community who view divorce as taboo, and relied heavily on Chelsea to help her through the crisis of separation. Chelsea showed her mother how to put her foot down and set limits on her father's demands, and how to seek happiness on her own terms. "I taught her she had the strength to stand up for herself," she said. Chelsea worked to empower her mother, who decided to return to her husband with greater strength and control in the relationship.

Sophia, whose father's temper often turns into violent displays of anger, continues to be there for her parents by visiting them often and managing their marital as well as intergenerational relations. Sophia reveals how, for decades, she has been trying to manage her father's anger and protect her mother from his abuse. She shares this example:

> The biggest thing I have done to ameliorate my parents' marriage is to travel back home from California with my kids. My father hates to travel. So, even when my kids were newborns and traveling was heinous, I made the trips so that they could enjoy their grandkids. My sister and I would worry that my parents were going to fight too much, that our father would go back to beating mom during the cold, dark, winter months, and we'd stagger our trips home so they would enjoy grandkids and not get too bored and angry.

Sophia has felt the pull of her siblings and mother to be there for her father and has responded by making travel plans to spend winters with them or to call at the cost of her own health and well-being. She states:

> I still do that, every year, I travel to them and they rarely travel here. I was diagnosed with breast cancer last month. I am having a bilateral mastectomy in a couple days and my mom and sister call me and say, "You should call dad; he's really worried about you." It's warped, I know.

Even though Sophia wryly describes her situation as "warped," she does not give up her role as the relationship manager and nor will her family let her do so.

Gracie, a second generation Korean American in her forties, is also striving to be present for her parents who live outside of California, and particularly for her mother, the main care-giver for her father who has Alzheimer's disease. Her fiercely independent mother does not like to ask for help from her daughter; Gracie feels the only kind of support she can provide is emotional care, through weekly calls to her mother. Although Gracie does provide this support, she dreads the actual conversations that she finds to be one-sided. She feels conflicted because her mother does not ask about her or the grandchildren. Gracie's comment below illustrates the ambivalence that she experiences while doing relationship management and trying to be present for her mother:

> As much as I love my mom, I think she's totally crazy. And, because she's a very social and active person, being cooped up with my dad in the house all the time makes her even crazier. And she loves to talk—does she ever! Because her world is now limited to the house and my dad and his helper, the talk is often redundant and—there is no real gentle way to say this—quite boring. Also, she's never been a great listener, but with all that she's going through it's gotten worse, rather than better. She would rather recount to me for the millionth time how my dad made a one-word joke than hear what her grandchildren are doing. It's fine, and I try not to force stories about them anymore, but sometimes I wish she'd be more interested in them. I also wish I could be more interested in her stories, but I just do my best to listen and try to sound interested.

While many provide emotional support to mothers who are experiencing troubles in their marriage or caring for ill fathers, several respondents discuss what it is like to care for a divorced aging parent or recently widowed parent. Caring for a parent without a partner often means that adult children take on aspects of that role. Cindy's seventy-one-year-old mother recently became a widow, and although her mother is healthy, self-sufficient, and financially secure for the time being, Cindy, in her forties, is concerned about her mother living alone. She began to call and check in with her mother daily after a particular incident:

> It is of concern to us that she lives alone and so I've developed a habit of calling her each day to make sure that she is okay. This was triggered by an incident one day when she got locked out of her house in an enclosed

courtyard. The door closed behind her and she had no way to get out of the courtyard. She yelled for help but it was a long time before a neighbor heard her and was able to unlock the door for her.

According to Cindy, her mother wants to remain independent and does not want to burden her own children because of her experience as the primary care-giver for her husband and mother-in-law (before they passed away) and as the full-time caretaker of their family business throughout that time. Cindy and her brother have a strained relationship with their paternal relatives who did not help with care-giving duties and relied on Cindy's family (on her mother, the daughter-in-law) to do everything. At the time of the interview, Cindy and her brother were helping with complex paperwork and financial planning, but they saw their mother taking care of things on her own or relying on her church friends for day-to-day support. Conscious of how difficult it was for her mother to be the main breadwinner and the main care-giver to her sick husband and mother-in-law, Cindy tries to provide emotional support, and she and her brother are planning her long-term care. Cindy observes the lessons she and her brother learned from taking care of her father and grandmother and how much they appreciate their mother's work:

> Having shared this experience [taking care of their elderly grandmother] with my brother, when it comes time to be more actively involved in taking care of our mom, I think my brother and I will be better able to share the duties. It's easy to help my mom because she is very appreciative of whatever assistance we provide. Her needs are manageable and reasonable and so she makes it easy for us to care for her. I think that this is not the case for all families. I am aware of many of my friends who are caring for aging parents who are much less self-sufficient than my mom and whose parents are also very difficult to get along with.

Due to her mother's easygoing qualities, their close relationship, and shared care-giving experiences for other family members in the past, Cindy is confident that her brother will support and split care-giving responsibilities in the future. While she provides emotional work, Cindy does not feel that she is doing it alone as "the daughter" of the family.

Emotion Work: Worrying about the Future

Several respondents refer to traditional patriarchal and patrilineal expectations that sons (and daughters-in-law) are responsible for living with and taking care of elderly parents. Elder sons, for example, mention that they are expected to take care of their parents according to Confucian and/or Korean cultural traditions that stressed patriarchal responsibility. However, daughters also say that it is their duty to care for their parents, and expect that they will be part of this care work despite the patriarchal norm. The discussion of how care can be provided and what they feel they could provide also differs by gender. While sons' responses revolve around duty or expectations, daughters tend to discuss in detail their aging parents' current and future needs and anticipate challenges that will have to be met. More often, daughters are looked upon within the household as the ones who will become the primary care-givers when the time comes. Compared with sons, daughters express more concerns and worries about the details of their parents' lives and possible future impairments.

Both sons and daughters worry about their parents' futures. For example, Ryan's parents live in southern California and he lives in northern California. At the time of the interview, Ryan was drafting estate plans and a living trust for his parents who had recently recovered from a financial setback. When asked whether the family talks about who would take care of the parents in old age or illness, Ryan says:

> I haven't thought about it enough. I do think about it periodically and it's actually a conversation I have to have with my sister on how to deal with that. I don't know how we're going to take care of them when they get really old. And then one difficult view is when one passes away, what are we going to do with the other.

Because their baby boomer parents are healthy and financially secure, Ryan and his sister have not been confronted with the need to take care of ill or disabled parents along with their responsibilities to their own families, jobs, and other commitments. However, the fact that Ryan worked on their estate planning and living trust indicates how adult children help their parents prepare for the future.

Among respondents, daughters are much more concerned about providing not only emotional support but also future financial support. Daughters discuss how they have had to think about their parents' aging process and the "what ifs" before their parents have broached the subject. Parents' language barriers often hasten respondents' thinking about care-giving issues as parents approach old age. The majority of respondents report that their parents can speak English adequately, but do not read and write English fluently. Generally, fathers can speak, write, and read English better than mothers; 10 percent of mothers cannot speak English compared to 5 percent of fathers. While some parents are English-fluent, and most immigrant parents have been able to take care of themselves for decades with limited English fluency, the combination of entering older adulthood (with its attendant need to access and understand documents related to aging issues such as Medicare, Social Security, and senior apartments) and the rise of technology (including the shift to internet and/or electronic health records, which make it difficult for some older adults to access information and assistance) contribute to the respondents' need to research, translate documents, fill out applications, and speak with service representatives on behalf of their parents.

Adult daughters who live far from their parents worry about fulfilling their parents' needs and think of different ways to spend more time or find ways to relocate parents closer. For Vanessa, in her thirties, the geographic distance from her parents was a dilemma she did not foresee when she and her sisters moved away from their home state and settled in different parts of California. The geographic separation from their parents who need more care as they grow older worries her and her sisters, and they have sought ways to close the distance. Their main solution is to persuade their parents to relocate near them:

> I never really grew up thinking that we would be scattered all over the place because family was always important to us. And then I moved to California and I was like, I'm never moving back because of the weather, and also because my career was here, and then I met my husband. It just worked out that my [middle] sister followed me down here a year after I moved out here and stayed, and then my younger sister. So, now our

goal is to get our parents down here . . . if there's a large Korean community and they want to be closer to their daughters. It is important for us to have them down here, so we're going to hopefully move them down here.

Vanessa and her sisters have a tacit agreement to coordinate caring for their parents, each doing what she can through visiting, managing medical appointments, handling the details of red tape, planning their parents' move to California, and/or providing financial assistance. She does not see this work as a burden and she is grateful that she belongs to a family in which the children step up without hesitation to provide intergenerational support. She is also fortunate in having siblings—notably, two sisters—who are willing and able to contribute in complementary ways to meet their parents' needs. As Vanessa describes:

> You knew you would eventually be responsible for your parents' well-being when they got older. And in fact, my sisters and I are fortunate and very blessed to have been born in this family because we all agreed that our parents are the core of our lives and our futures still. When my mom came down with the severe depression, because she was lonely, we decided together, let's move them down and we'll alternate. . . . I mean, for a while there, my sister would take care of all their financial needs, I would take care of all their day-to-day kind of operation stuff. I actually go home quite often, so that I can take care of stuff like that, where I can go through their mail. And then my younger sister, because now she's got two kids, would make their doctor's appointments. My sisters and I don't see that as a burden. We want to take care of my parents.

Like Vanessa and her sisters, whose mother battled depression at the time of the interview, other daughters extrapolate future concerns about their parents' general health, often providing a sounding board to their aging parents about their lives. Alice shares her worries about her mother's health, but sees it as a universal concern of "other adult children":

I'm worried about my mom's health. She has two sisters with diabetes, and she's a prime candidate for that. She's kind of chubby and she never exercises. I do worry about her health. I guess I have all the other worries as other adult children. My mother is sixty-five. I do wish she would exercise and take care of herself better. My dad, physically, he's in great shape.

Angela shares concerns about her parents' physical, mental, and emotional well-being. She discusses how her father still harbors dissatisfaction about how life has turned out in the United States. Rather than enjoying his "golden years," he is eaten away by his belief that he did not meet educational and financial goals he had set up for himself. One of Angela's goals is to reassure her parents that they should be satisfied with their lives by remembering how they were able to raise and provide for their children in the United States:

> Because they are at an age where there are a lot of worries, our goal is for them to feel satisfied that they raised three children to be pretty good and they are doing fairly well and they provided an opportunity to do that. My dad doesn't feel satisfied, he still feels like he didn't earn enough money as he could've, he didn't have the education he wanted, he is in many ways, dissatisfied. . . . He is not very satisfied. My mom has concerns but she still is more satisfied than my dad with the ways things turned out. Just trying to relay to my mom and dad, that things are really good and have a peace of mind and relax and enjoy your life now, and I'm not sure if that's an easy thing to do.

Angela's retired parents are in their seventies and they are living on a combination of Social Security, an allowance from their children, and "a tiny savings." Her parents live in southern California and Angela and her siblings live in southern and northern California. At the time of the interview, her parents were generally healthy and lived in a retirement community with many Korean friends nearby. She observes that in this community, her parents and other Korean older adults rely on each other; she notes, "It's funny; they are stubbornly independent, they don't want money from kids. They don't want to burden kids in any way." But she nevertheless thinks about the future and worries how she and her siblings can best meet their parents' needs while taking care of their own young children. Angela adds,

My siblings and I think about this a lot right now. My mom is six years younger but she seems to have a lot more physical and psychological ailments than my dad. In general, we kind of wonder, in the next five years or so, what would we do for long term care, what would we do—should we put them in our house or a skilled nursing [facility]? These are all questions we worry about as we get older. I mean, we are in this generation in which you are taking care of both your parents and your young ones.

Although Sabrina explains that she is "forever indebted to her parents" for immigrating to the United States, and sacrificing their own comfort and opportunities for those of their children, she wishes she did not have to be so responsible for taking care of her financially strapped parents. Sabrina predicts that she would become the main care-giver because she is financially better off than her older brother. She is close to her mother but not to her father, who was physically and emotionally abusive to her and her mother. Sabrina, in fact, is gratified that she will not have to depend on her children for her own survival because she will be financially and culturally independent.

They don't say that care-giving is an expectation, but I don't see how they could survive. As much I'd like to take care of them, I'm not really thrilled that I have to do it. It's more like if I have to do it, but I wish things were different. I wish my parents were well off. I wish they had their own life and financial independence. I wish we were more acclimated more to the American culture. In that kind of sense, I'm thinking this is something that has to end with me. I know I'm not the only one in the States who has parents like this. I think our generation got stuck with the short end of the stick. I'm actually kind of thrilled that I'm financially independent and that my kids won't have to worry about me.

Yet, intergenerational support flows in both directions. At the time of the interview, Sabrina shared that her brother and his wife were counting on Sabrina's retired mother (not father) to provide childcare, since the couple works full-time. Thus, childcare provided by Sabrina's mother will give crucial assistance to her brother's household, and, in the future, Sabrina may receive similar childcare support from her mother so that she does not feel "stuck with the short end of the stick" in providing intergenerational support.

Negotiating and Coordinating Support for Parents

As the daughters discuss the type of care work they do for their own parents and sometimes their in-laws, sons reveal how essential their sisters and/or wives are in supporting their aging parents; sisters and wives often provide emotional support and other types of kin work for both sides of the family. Although daughters do the majority of care work, both sons and daughters must negotiate with their spouses regarding care work for their parents and their spouses' parents.

Some male respondents feel pressure as the oldest or the only son to take primary responsibility for their parents, but most do not have to fulfill this expectation. Rather, following stereotypical gender norms, many foresee their main role as providing financial assistance while planning to "share" care responsibilities with their siblings. For example, Bob and Herb, two unmarried men in their twenties and thirties, project that they will take care of their parents along with their siblings. Herb, a second-generation Korean American, discusses how this duty to care for his parents arises from cultural expectations communicated by his relatives.

> Yes, I do feel a sense of obligation. The obligation comes from both the Korean cultural expectation as well as myself. But the Korean cultural expectation comes from my extended family, like my cousins. They are just reminding me to do that.

At the time of the interview, both Herb and Bob lived with their parents and adult siblings, and viewed co-residence as culturally appropriate and mutually beneficial; they (and their siblings) also get along well with their parents. They predict that they will live near their parents in their old age, if not with them. They do not discuss how their future spouses might affect this plan.

The effect of marriage is particularly striking for the male respondents. Many married male respondents observe that they make decisions about care-giving arrangements for their own parents with their partners' input. Regardless of birth order, married male respondents mention their spouses, and how any care-giving decisions, especially ones that involved living near or co-residing with parents, would have to be made with the consent of their partner. One such respondent is Peter, whose parents live in another state. According to Peter, his parents have a closer relationship with his younger brother, who lives in the same state as they. Meanwhile, Peter's wife, Sue, and his mother do not get along, and Sue has reservations about living with or near her in-laws. Finally, Peter and Sue get along much better with Sue's own aging parents, who only live about thirty miles from them. Therefore, Peter cautiously offers that his "option . . . at the very least" is to contribute financially and weigh all the factors that complicate expectations and logistics regarding sons, filial piety, and aging parents. Peter shares:

> To be honest with you, I don't know what would happen if they need care. I don't know if I can move there, and I know they don't want to move here. I would love it if I can take care of them if we were closer together. I'm not sure how that would work, and I know Sue wouldn't want to do that. . . . Ideally I would like to be physically there to take care of them, but practically speaking, I don't think that would be possible. The only option is making sure, that they are financially well taken care of, and at the very least, I want to do that.

Peter does feel a sense of responsibility towards his parents, but his responses indicate that he and his wife are geographically and emotionally distant from his parents, and closer in both respects to her parents. Therefore, Peter sees financial support as the most practical way to help his brother, the designated primary care-giver. Women like his wife, Sue, play a critical role in determining the quality of intergenerational relationships and care-giving expectations and planning for the future. Indeed, this is true of the women in the study, who often feel responsible to provide care to their parents, regardless of marital status or birth order. But even though the women feel the urge to care, it is usually unmarried daughters or married daughters without children who provide the most primary support to their parents. Married females with children often feel torn by the competing demands of caring for kids and parents and often do not have the capacity to care for their in-laws over their parents following patriarchal protocols of filial piety.

Although women facilitate kin work among siblings, this work is not free from tensions. For women who marry a co-ethnic, their in-laws may have expectations of care work, especially from the daughters-in-law. Nina, a second-generation Korean American in her thirties, has "always been close to her folks" and jokingly describes herself as "a very nagging worrisome daughter" who talks with her parents daily. It is Nina, for example, who reminds her brothers and sisters-in-law to call their parents when they go out of town as a sign of respect. In contrast, she has had a difficult relationship with her parents-in-law who want a more "traditional Korean" daughter-in-law than herself—specifically, someone who speaks Korean more fluently. Nina predicts that her parents will live with her and not her older brothers as they get older or sick, but adds, "I don't have a great relationship with my in-laws. . . . Yeah, I don't really want them to live with us [laughs]. If my husband wants to stay married to me! Just kidding." One conflict between Nina and her in-laws involved Nina refusing to give her mother-in-law a set of house keys, which would allow her to visit her son's home any time, unannounced. At the time of the interview, her parents and parents-in-law were all healthy and financially secure. Although Nina continues to work on her relationship with her in-laws and does see them regularly, her own close and easy relationship with her parents and the contrasting difficult relationship with her in-laws has shaped her care-giving attitudes and expectations for the present and the future. Nina has designated herself as the main care-giver of the natal family; she has also prioritized her own parents over her in-laws in terms of providing care and support in the future, and she expects her husband to support her plans. Like Nina, many adult children of Korean immigrants have redefined ideologies of filial piety and care-work responsibilities. They do not adhere to traditional gender norms and expectations; often, neither do their parents. Respondents often point to the quality of the relationship between the parents and various siblings to explain why a certain sibling would be the primary care-giver. Married male respondents, like Peter and Nina's husband, consult their wives and together create the boundaries regarding the type of care-giving they are willing and able to provide for their in-laws and own parents. Daughters tend to describe their emotional bonds with their parents and are more willing to consider co-residency, even as they wonder how they are going to juggle their responsibilities as daughters, sisters, wives, and mothers. Peter and Nina's discussions also highlight the changing roles and influence of daughters and daughters-in-law in Korean immigrant families, as well as lessening degrees of adherence to the Confucian system, which has traditionally emphasized the patrilineal family over the matrilineal family in terms of support and kin interaction.

Female respondents who are married and have children worry about their own capacity to juggle multiple responsibilities for work, their spouses, their children, and their aging parents. Female respondents with young children express the most concern about how they will manage care work in the near future. While unmarried women or women without children also assume they will take care of their parents, they are less likely to go into details about what it would be like to juggle care for aging parents, spouses/partners, and children.

Joyce and her two older brothers had discussed how they were going to take care of their parents and how they would split financial and other responsibilities. Unlike Nina, who sees herself as the willing care coordinator for her parents, Joyce, who works full-time outside the home, wrestles with what the reality will be like for herself, her husband, and children and parents in their old age. Joyce says,

> I think that when the time comes—when they do become elderly to the point where they have to be taken care of by us—it's going to be very challenging, extremely challenging, especially with your children. I think about it a lot. I think about what impact it's going to have on my children, what impact it's going to have on the quality of life of my husband, and, if my mother will be happy.

Nancy, a mother of a young child, also describes these worries about future frailty and the impact it could have on her and her family. She and her siblings discussed—once with their father but mostly without him—how they would provide future support to him and their stepmother. They agree that if he decides to live with one of the children, the others would cover their living expenses. So far, their father is unsure about his future living arrangement—in Korea, in the United States, with one of his children, or independently in a retirement community.

The relationship between him and his children has been strained in recent years due to a family business venture that went sour ("My dad is great at many things, but his strong suit is not business-savvy. . . . It was a very stressful ten years in the relationship between my siblings and him"). Because she got out of the family business early to focus on her own job, Nancy believes that her relationship with her father is more intact; as a result, she is the one who mediates between her father and her siblings whose relationships are "hard and awful." She describes the sense of duty that they had toward her father:

> My dad would say things like "When you guys grow up, I wonder who I should go live with, whoever has the most comfortable home or who-ever has the most food in their fridge?" And then later on, he would say things like "Well, whoever has the most kids, I'll go live with them because that'll make me happy." You know, so that was always an expec-tation that "I will live with one of you, and you will care for me, I just haven't picked who." I think a lot of our decision to pay for my dad's living expenses on a monthly basis right now is out of that sense of duty, because it's not out of our relationship—you know what I mean—it's not because we're so incredibly close to him but more of our duty and obliga-tion. And you know, for whatever Americans will say about it, I think it has its good role, and I think it's fine to do things out of obligation and duty because there is obligation and duty and we're not just responsible for ourselves. So here I go up on my soapbox, but I do think we have obligation to pay respect to our elders. And for me, specifically to my dad through the years that he loved me and raised me, you know? And he did it then, maybe if it's not an intimate relationship right now, I have an obligation and I want to do that for him.

Nancy recalls how difficult her family's life was in the United States: in addition to their mother's illness and passing away, the family experi-enced extreme financial hardship as they started—and ended—a num-ber of different businesses and jobs. When she was growing up, she saw her father as a "kind of role model . . . he could do no wrong in my book," but through her adult eyes, she recognizes that he suffers from depression after dealing with years of a "lot of different kinds of stresses." While she and her siblings will take care of him and their stepmother out of sense of duty, Nancy's desire to take care of him is also deeply rooted in remembering the struggles and sacrifices of her parents, and how they loved and raised their children to the best of their abilities.

Yet, Nancy wonders what would happen if her father becomes ill like her mother, whose debilitating illness required around-the-clock care until she passed away. Nancy and other family members took care of her mother for years before she died, and she would like to do the same for her father, but is conflicted between the desire to take care of him and the worries about how it might affect her spouse and children. Nancy reflects,

And that's when I'll have to ask myself how much is caring for my dad costing my family, you know—how much is it costing my husband, and my relationship? How much of a toll is it taking on my kids? And I won't know that until he comes to live with us, and I'll see how much it's taking a toll. And then we'll have to have a harder conversation if it's just not working. But I want to try that first, because it hurts me to think about other people caring for my dad, if I'm able to do it. I just don't trust other people to provide the same level of care and love, you know. So we'll see.

Relationships between parents and children change throughout the life course as children grow up and view, through their adult lenses, how fallible and frail their parents can be. Nancy appreciates and sympathizes with her father for how he and their mother provided for their young children, and his financial, personal, and other struggles over his lifetime. But his continued lack of business acumen, tendency to rely on his children (but not relinquish his paternal authority), and lack of verbal communication over the years, have eroded the relationship between him and his adult children. The link that remains is the sense of duty and obligation, which Nancy defines as a useful and important societal value, but one that she contrasts with the sense of love and closeness that bonded the rest of the family to her mother during her illness. Still, Nancy wants her father to have the same level of care that the family provided for her mother, and continues to think about the ways to do this in the midst her own ambivalence and questions about how different care-giving arrangements may affect her siblings and her own household.

"We Are His Retirement Plan"

Daughters expect themselves, and are expected by others, to provide more emotional work, and adult sons expect themselves, and are expected by others, to provide more financial support. But most respondents in the study amicably negotiate and divide current care-work responsibilities with their siblings. Siblings split duties evenly, by their ability, availability, or desirability. For example, Nancy and her siblings pool their resources to be their father's "retirement plan":

> All he has is Social Security, just a few hundred dollars a month. And he has Medicare now, and that takes care of the health and dental. But really we're his retirement account—his kids. So we supplement a few hundred dollars, probably comes to $1500, something like that, to just make it comfortable enough. So we are his retirement plan.

Many parents are self-sufficient, healthy, and financially prepared for retirement. Other parents, like Nancy's, are not financially ready to retire, or may need some assistance from their children. Many respondents feel compelled to financially support their parents, at least partially, so they can enjoy the comforts of life that they may have missed in earlier life stages. This financial support takes a variety of forms, including paying the mortgage, providing a monthly allowance, and bestowing vacations and other gifts. Joyce, a 1.5-generation Korean American and mother of two children, exclaims: "Part of it is feeling like, my God, you spent all your money on us! You know? I mean, I think they're fine, but they don't have pensions. They have some money saved up, but really nothing."

Many adult children feel a strong sense of responsibility to financially provide for their parents, especially insofar as half of the respondents report that their parents do not have any retirement savings. In response to their aging parents' financial vulnerability, many adult children start to offer various kinds of tangible support. Joyce's parents have no retirement funds but refuse to accept money from their children; consequently, Joyce and her siblings, who have become financially secure, give non-cash gifts of financial support, such as paying their parents' property tax as a Christmas present, and giving gift certificates to grocery stores. Joyce clarifies:

It's not like we're paying them for anything, but we want to make sure they're comfortable. . . . They won't accept the cash, but, you know like a $500 gift certificate to Safeway, so they can buy food and, you know, stuff like that.

Helen, a 1.5-generation Korean American in her forties, lives far from her own parents. She and her siblings collectively send money to their retired father, who was paying off business debts at the time of the interview. She comments,

I send my father allowance every other month. It's not a lot but $300 every other month. My sister and I, we take turns. And then I know my brother gives him allowance too, so it's like the two together and then he can have monthly expense.

Helen also discusses the support she receives from her in-laws. She is one of the few study respondents who lives with her in-laws, who retired with little savings and, following traditional Korean customs, had expected to live with one of their children in old age. Helen's case is different, however, because her in-laws moved into *her* home, though only after the eldest son with whom they had lived previously became divorced. Even though Helen, who works full-time outside the home, and her mother-in-law often have different, if not clashing, beliefs on appropriate roles and behaviors of women, wives, and daughters-in-law, they provide critical support for each other. Helen notes:

My in-laws are definitely very crucial to our family. My mother-in-law cooks. My father-in-law does a lot of minor chores around the house. They cover for the nanny after she goes home. I mean, in so many ways, they fill in the holes. Otherwise we would have had to pay for, or our lives would be much more crazy. So, oh yeah. Even though I have issues with my mother-in-law, I am so grateful that she doesn't complain and she does it so willingly. Of course, she does it willingly for her son, not for me. But I should stop being so picky [laughs].

Elizabeth, in her thirties, lives with her parents and a younger sibling. Her self-employed father and her mother, who has held different part-time jobs, owned a home but otherwise did not save for retirement.

During the real estate boom of the mid-2000s, her father bought a larger home for investment purposes. Elizabeth pays for the mortgage and car insurance for all family members while her parents cover food and other expenses. Elizabeth shares:

> I am concerned that it's becoming imminent that my dad is going to retire, and if he does, how am I going to support my parents? That is a pretty big concern. Hopefully, my brother will get a job soon, and he can help out.

At the time of a follow-up interview, Elizabeth's father had retired due to health reasons, and she and her brother continue to pool their financial resources with their parents. Her father's desire to move to a larger and more expensive home as an investment would not have been financially feasible without their decision to live with them and help cover the expenses.

In addition to worry, some express anger that their parents did not save for their own retirement. Ji Hee, for example, describes how her parents have failed to save for retirement while they were working. She realizes that her parents spent their limited income on her and her siblings—especially on college tuition—but that does not keep her from feeling angry that her parents did not plan for their own future. This lack of a safety net has shifted their post-retirement financial burden onto Ji Hee's shoulders, who feels it acutely:

> They used the money I gave them to pay their car payment but my parents live very frugally. They were able to subsist on the fixed income they have from Social Security every month. . . . The thing is, what makes me angry is all these years that they worked, they put us through school and they took care of us. Yet, they never saved for themselves. They never saved. They don't have any kind of retirement. Nothing. They live month to month on Social Security. It makes me really angry and they didn't have [the] common sense to put something away. Given that, I am really responsible for them.

Julian's father, an engineer, worked for about thirty years at the same company; then he was let go due to the company's financial difficulties, and his 401k retirement plan lost about two-thirds of its value in the mid-to-late 2000s. Julian and his brother, who live in different states from their parents, pay their mortgage. As Julian says:

> Actually, my brother and I arranged for them to purchase a condominium. No, not a retirement home, just a townhouse or condo, and I basically provided an arrangement for them to purchase a property and apply a minimum of that 401k savings to a down payment, and my brother and I are basically paying half of the mortgage each on their house so they can live there forever.

He jokes that while his mother (not his father) expects her children to take care of them in their old age, his parents moving in with him would be an "impossibility." He could not see them living in the same house, and if necessary, he would hire a care-giver for his parents. Julian explains the pressure to take care of his parents as being a result of a generational and age difference:

> I think for the first generation mindset, it's like a given. . . . They have taken care of their children, they have taken care of their parents too and it's just a way of life, part of what is right. It's [an] unspoken rule, kind of. And so I certainly feel that pressure, I think. . . . Man, if I didn't have to take care of my parents, I would be wealthy [laughter]. You know what I mean, that's like a selfish type of thinking that as a human being, you think about it—wow, you know, my life could be different. But my parents wouldn't think that way if they were taking care of us, or taking care of their parents, for example. Well, I think that's my parents; they are a little older.

The financial support did require sacrifice on his and his brother's part. While Julian makes fun of his self-interest, he contrasts his attitude with that of his parents, who he feels would provide the same financial support without labeling it a sacrifice. Julian reiterates that he and his wife could not provide the type of hands-on care that his mother wanted in her old age, but the current arrangement worked while his parents were still healthy and beginning to dip into their retirement fund. Citing the lack of an "affectionate close relationship," Julian provides the financial assistance in response to the pressure he feels to provide for his parents. What is also noteworthy is that he observes that his wife would go and take care of her parents if the need ever arose because she "is much closer with her side of the family." For Julian, providing *some* sort of care for their parents is based on cultural expectations that may not always align with the quality and closeness of such relations.

Charlie, an only child in his twenties, currently lives with parents and gives them money, usually a few hundred dollars at a time, whenever they need it. He gets along well with his parents, and especially with his mother, and cites love, obligation, culture, and gender as shapers of his attitudes, expectations, and practices around care-giving.

> With Korean culture, you know, I think we have always been raised that, as the first child, it's your responsibility to take care of your parents, especially for the guy. Being the only child is definitely a heavier burden. A lot more comes out of my shoulder because of that but definitely I definitely understand my responsibility to really support my family—my parents—especially in the case that they need me. There's always satisfaction and care but also there's a sense of obligation as well. They're my parents and I love them, I do what I can; but I don't think you could ever forget there's always going to be a sense of burden, you know? Having to do all that and what helps me to justify is what they've done for me. . . . [I]t's a payback kind of thing.

Charlie attributes his sense of responsibility to a value and norm related to being a "first child" and a "guy" in Korean culture (Elizabeth, in an earlier discussion, mentions the same responsibility as the first-born and a daughter). As an only child, however, he has no siblings with whom to share this combination of satisfaction, care, and burden. Charlie worries about what might happen when his parents need help with both finances and more hands-on care. His father works in construction, and his mother works in the garment industry. Although his parents are healthy, his father's construction work had slowed at the time of the interview, foreshadowing his parents' future need for financial assistance. Charlie also remembers how his parents bought a home during a housing bubble and lost it when his father's work slowed down during the recession of the early 1990s. Charlie explains that at this time, he is "not carrying a full load. . . . They're giving me food to eat, they're giving me a house to live in, they give me all that so when you measure all that up, they're still giving me more than what I'm giving them." But his parents' lack of retirement funds and their precarious finances make him worry about how he could support them on his own. He especially worries how he could provide both financial and more hands-on care when it becomes necessary in the future.

> Once their health becomes an issue where they need to go to a doctor or whatever, usually when you have siblings, you guys can rotate or take turns and sacrifice in that way. But if my mom or they need to go to the hospital or my dad needs to go, you know, maybe in one sense they can take care of each other, but you know, there's really going to be no one to do it except for me to really fall back on. And then at that point, it's going to affect my job and how am I supposed to do and it definitely will be difficult in every way; that's a huge concern, you know? They don't have any retirement plan; they have nothing to fall back on, so it's tough right now—let's see how that goes.

Complications of Being There for Parents

Despite expectations and best intentions, time constraints, family and work obligations, and/or geographic distances curtail how much respondents can do to support their parents. Those who work and/or have children discuss how they juggle already full schedules to make room for their parents' growing needs. Moreover, if they live in a city or state far from their parents' homes, they face additional travel time and expenses, and the usual obstacles and interferences that distance imposes on spending time together. Two-thirds of respondents lived in the same state as their parents. Of those in California, a majority lived within thirty minutes of their parents. Although many resided near or within the same state as their parents, one-third of our respondents had parents who lived outside California.

Most respondents call their parents at least once a week. Their conversations often consist of updates about grandchildren or inquiries about how their parents are doing and reflecting on their activities during the week. Adult children use telephone calls to help bridge the distance and provide emotional support for their parents amidst their often packed and hectic lives. This is a prolific and enjoyable time for most of our respondents and their families as they welcome and celebrate milestones such as graduation, career advancement, marriages, grandchildren, retirements, and sixtieth and seventieth birthdays. Such milestones also mark the undeniable process of aging; some observe that their retired parents have increasing health issues and are not as mobile. Respondents discuss how busy they are, how they wish they had more time, and how they try to be there for their parents.

Jeff lives about forty miles away from his parents in the greater Los Angeles area. Although this seems like a relatively short distance, he does not see his parents as often as he would like. His parents, who are in their late seventies, are in good health but do not drive. Jeff wishes he could provide more support and companionship to his parents. Although he realizes that time is of essence as his parents are getting older, he finds it difficult to spend time with his own wife and children.

> I want to go see them more often, and just be with them, spend more time with them or go on a trip with them, but that's kind of hard with our busy, daily life. It's very hard for me to get vacation at the same time as my wife, and go on vacation with my parents, grandparents for our kids. It's really hard, but it's something that I want to do.

Mee Jin, a second-generation Korean American in her late twenties, manages an upscale retail store about fifty miles from her home. She moved back to live with her mother after her father passed away from cancer. Her hours are so consumed by work that it is difficult for her to spend time with her mother even though they live in the same house.

> I feel a sense that I owe her a lot and at the same time I don't even think it's monetary. I think she wants me to pay her back in time but I can't do that right now . . . being able to pay her back, because it's so difficult 'cause I can't spend that time with her. I have to come home from work and finish a project or finish a presentation or work on a review. I don't have time to spend with her and that's the hardest thing for me.

Having the desires and best intentions does not mean that there are no tensions, frustrations, or even angry episodes when respondents and their parents do spend time or live together; parents and adult children have their own ways of doing things. Respondents had to work to maintain their own health which sometimes meant setting limits on what they could handle in terms of care work for their parents. In Soomin's family's case, one of her sisters moved in with their mother. This arrangement has helped all the siblings feel at ease that someone has been looking out for their aging mother. But living with their mother for several years took a toll on the sister. As Soomin notes, their mother can be difficult:

> Yeah, I'm concerned that my mom will be alone. But, she's very difficult to live with. She's very stubborn. She has very particular taste—you know, she wants to live how she wants to live. It's not exactly how my sister wants to live. I mean, the house is a mess. She brings all kinds of things that her friends and church people give her. Like, the refrigerator's a mess—she won't let anybody throw away anything. A part of it is, when people give—it's like showing interest to them. They don't want to throw it away. They bring it, but you can't really eat it all by yourself, or throw it away. And then it rots and that drives my sister crazy.

Cindy discusses how tensions and misunderstandings between older immigrant parents and their adult children are common. She thinks that many Korean immigrant parents feel they are "entitled" to their adult children's attention, respect, and care while the adult children are overwhelmed with working, raising children, and trying to maintain their own lives. She states that many parents do not know how to communicate with their adult children and also may feel that their needs outweigh their children's needs; these two factors complicate relations between the two generations.

> They demand respect without giving respect. They don't make an effort to understand their children or have an open dialogue and so misunderstandings and resentments get in the way of their relationships. I am very grateful that my mom is more "modern" and that she makes great efforts to try to communicate with me and my brother. This doesn't mean that we don't have misunderstandings but in the end, we always try to work them out. Because of the language and cultural barriers, sometimes it's possible to walk away from a conversation with a totally different

understanding and it's not until later that we realize that we both heard something else. But in the end, we love each other and so we make an effort to try to communicate that to each other.

Conclusion

Research has shown that care-giving and relationship management in families is highly gendered.[19] Growing up Korean American, our respondents were socialized to view taking care of elders and especially aging parents as a core ethnic and cultural value; in particular, many men have been socialized to understand that in Korean culture, elder sons are responsible for taking care of parents (and their younger and female siblings) based on systems of Confucianism, primogeniture, and patriarchy. Growing up as children of immigrants, our respondents also view care-giving as a form of "giving back" to their parents for their struggles and sacrifices in the United States, but they may also feel ambivalently about fulfilling these expectations. The interviews indicate that daughters, not sons, often act as the glue in the family, performing kin work for parents, siblings, spouses, and in-laws. Daughters, regardless of marital status, take on the task of checking in with parents, while adult sons and daughters collectively share the task of financially supporting their parents. Female respondents keep in contact with and support their natal parents and their parents-in-law. While unmarried respondents discuss how they would support or have supported their parents, married male respondents share how they consult their spouses when it comes to planning and arranging care-giving. They also mention that their wives take care of their natal parents. Although this can be viewed as male respondents' slacking and pushing care-giving responsibility onto their wives or sisters, it is clear that many male respondents respect their wives' wishes and boundaries, as well as gender role views, about kinship work and care-giving. That is, the male respondents do not adhere to traditional patriarchy norms, and they do not expect their wives to take on the role of traditional daughters-in-law. They share their responsibilities with their siblings, especially sisters.

In the United States, daughters are the primary care-givers to older persons, whereas in South Korea, daughters-in-law (especially those

married to eldest sons) are the most common care-givers to older disabled family members. But as rapid industrialization has changed the
cohabitation patterns of the multigenerational family and relationship
dynamics between mothers-in-law and daughters-in-law, Korean society
is increasingly viewing all children, sons and daughters, as responsible
for supporting elderly parents.[20] Another study finds that as the traditional male-breadwinner model declines and the number of dual-earner
families rises in contemporary South Korea, more married couples are
relying on and utilizing both patrilineal and matrilineal kin to provide
intergenerational support such as childcare.[21] Among our respondents,
filial piety is not emphasized only on the patrilineal side; daughters
emerge as the main coordinators and providers of current and future
kinship work, as well as planning and providing care-giving, which
includes financial help. Female respondents remain close with their
birth families and coordinate care and support for parents with siblings
and partners, who in turn typically rely on daughters and sisters. While
one study of never-married Chinese American and Japanese American women (ranging from ages thirty-three to eighty) finds that eldest
daughters in particular feel great pressure to sacrifice themselves to take
care of their parents and siblings, the daughters in this study, reflecting changing social differences and attitudes towards daughters, do not
express a similar sense of disadvantage or unfair expectations based on
gender and birth order.[22] However, they may still express ambivalence
including feeling frustrated, irritated, and angry about the quality of
their relationships with their parents or their ability to juggle limited
time and finances; sometimes, their push to take care of their parents
supplants their own needs and takes an emotional or physical toll.

Regardless of gender and birth order, respondents wrestle with the
complications of trying to be there for their parents, and coping with
competing demands that make it difficult to spend as much time with
their parents as they feel they should. Most respondents who have siblings coordinate with each other to contribute different aspects of support such as face-to-face visits, telephone conversations, and allowances, but it is the daughters who are more likely to spearhead such
collective efforts.

The analysis of responses shows that despite the normative Korean
familial system being articulated as a patriarchal one, in actual

expectations and practices, daughters tend to be the ones maintaining multigenerational Korean American families. Though daughters may find meaning in this work, they may also need to set limits on what they can handle, as it affects their own families and their own physical and mental well-being. For both daughters and sons, some level of filial piety is important not only to meet cultural expectations, but also to protect the future well-being of their parents. Many realize that substantial health issues for their parents might be waiting just around the corner and are unsure what roles they would be willing and able to take on. They assume, however, that one way or another they will provide some type of support. The next chapter explores the narratives of adult children whose parents have faced serious chronic or life-threatening illnesses, and how they navigate cultural expectations and roles as well as structural barriers in the U.S. health care system.

5

In the Midst of Caring for Ill Parents

He had cancer but because he didn't have health insurance
we didn't know. I graduated [from college] and I came down,
back to L.A., in December. Nobody told me he was sick.
Nobody. I think he didn't even know how sick he was—he
thought he had indigestion. He had liver cancer but nobody
knew. When I came down he was getting worse and worse
but he didn't have insurance so I took him to the L.A.
County hospital. . . . By the time they admitted him, 80 percent of his liver was cancerous so there was no way that he
could live. So they told us, your dad has three to six months
to live, so go home and wait for him to die.
—Michelle

By the time Michelle's uninsured father finally decided to seek medical help, his liver cancer was in its advanced stage. Her mother quit
her job to become his full-time care-giver, and suddenly, her parents,
who had owned a string of small businesses over the years and had
two children in college, had no savings and no income. Devastatingly,
Michelle's father passed away just one month after diagnosis. For the
next few years, the sisters coordinated with each other to ensure that
their mother would not be alone. Michelle turned down an out-of-state
job offer to live with her mother while her sister finished college, who
then returned home to live with their mother so that Michelle could go
to graduate school.

Michelle and her sister are part of the growing cohort of adult children who—in their case, suddenly and unexpectedly—encounter

care-giving responsibility for their parents. According to the 2010 census, the older population (that is, over the age of sixty-five) in the United States numbered about 40.3 million, the largest in the nation's history; between 2000 and 2010, this age group grew 15.1 percent, compared to 9.7 percent of the general population.[1] While most older adults in the United States are healthy and independent, they are also making the transition into a life stage which can be marked by chronic conditions, sudden illnesses, and decline. Moreover, they are living longer. According to the 2010 U.S. census examination of ten-year age groups of older adults, the fastest population growth occurred in the 85–94 age group, which increased by 29.9 percent since 2000.[2] Aging adults and their families begin a challenging journey as they learn about the informational maze and responsibilities of care-giving. Spouses, adult children, siblings and others must dedicate substantial time and resources to the family member's care, which is a physically, emotionally, and financially involved task. One national poll in 2007 found that 31 percent of baby boomers with living parents provide financial or personal care assistance for at least one parent, and a 2009 study by the National Care-giving Alliance and the American Association of Retired Persons found that about 26.8 percent of their respondents served as unpaid care-givers to one or more adults; one third of those care-givers took care of a parent.[3] The 2009 study also found that between 2004 and 2009, care-givers of adults not residing in a nursing home were more likely to receive help from another unpaid care-giver. As the general population ages, and in greater numbers, informal, unpaid care-givers provide a critical component of the health care system and services for older adults in the United States. And although husbands, sons, and other male relatives are taking on more of the burden, studies indicate that women comprise about 75 to 80 percent of care-givers and are more likely to provide more labor-intensive and consistent levels of domestic help and to change and/or reduce work schedules and hours to accommodate care-giving responsibilities, as well as experience greater negative physical, emotional, and social health consequences.[4] Scholars suggest that as family sizes dwindle and more women are in the paid workforce in the United States, both boys and girls should be socialized to become care-givers from an early age, thereby including both genders as care-givers in supporting families in the future.[5]

Recent studies of Korean American elders indicate that the care of chronically ill or frail older adults falls mainly on adult children or spouses.[6] A 2009 study by the National Care-Giving Alliance found that Asian Americans (of Japanese, Korean, Chinese, Filipino, Vietnamese, and Asian Indian ethnic backgrounds) were more likely than any other racial or ethnic group to be caring for a parent who was old and frail or suffering from dementia,[7] and were more likely to be juggling work and care-giving responsibilities for aging parents.[8] Compared to other racial or ethnic groups of this so-called "sandwich generation," who often take care of both older and younger family members, Asian American respondents were most likely to say they had adjusted their lives to accommodate family responsibilities.[9] However, despite providing the most care to their aging relatives, Asian Americans also expressed the most guilt that they were not providing enough care, with foreign-born respondents expressing more guilt compared to their U.S.-born counterparts (81 percent to 47 percent), and greater agreement with the statement that their children should care for them in their old age.[10] Most studies of Asian American elders examine the experiences of baby boomer immigrants in the role of care-givers. Little is known of the care-giving practices and challenges of the adult children of immigrants.[11]

As discussed earlier, respondents have managed their filial duties and roles in different ways at various life stages. The expectations they have for themselves shift from helping out their parents at work, brokering between their parents and the dominant society, and pursuing academic and professional achievements to choosing romantic and life partners whom their parents approve, and then having (grand)children.[12] Although these aspirations and expectations are not explicitly "Korean" or limited to Korean Americans only, respondents nevertheless describe them as values and goals important to their Korean immigrant parents, and address those desires and expectations in a variety of ways, ranging from fulfillment to active resistance. Care-giving is viewed as an extension of filial duties as parents enter retirement. The lives of Korean immigrants and their adult children continue to be linked as many parents face challenges that include language barriers, prejudice and discrimination, lack of information regarding illness, health, and health care services, and difficulties interacting with health care providers and institutions. Furthermore, Korean Americans continue to exhibit one of the highest rates of lack of insurance due to high rates of self-employment.[13] Life-course theorists have hypothesized that socio-economically based inequalities are exacerbated in old age, due to lifelong accumulated disadvantages and lack of protective resources, such as health care access and health education information.[14] Social factors such as immigration, class, and race ultimately impact health and intensify the difficulties of aging.[15]

For anyone diagnosed with a chronic illness, understanding medications, adjusting to symptoms, and making changes to one's lifestyle to effectively manage the condition are both crucial and complex. Poorly managed chronic health issues can lead to increased mortality and morbidity.[16] According to a "double jeopardy" theoretical model, both race and class have an impact on health.[17] Aging Korean immigrants also face additional difficulties due to living on limited incomes, functioning with limited English skills, and struggling with navigating health care services. Some develop chronic health conditions that worsen in old age due to the lack of preventive screenings in their younger years, or like Michelle's father, because medical appointments have been postponed on account of being uninsured and the high costs of out-of- pocket health services. Studies have documented that older Asian Americans face bias and discrimination in health care settings, often experiencing gaps in treatment, such as missing needed cancer screenings and services for diabetics.[18] Studies also indicate that older adults with limited English proficiency have worse access to health care and report lower emotional well-being than older adults who only speak English.[19] Caring for an ill parent involves gaining access to care and advocating for best possible care, while helping them understand their diagnoses. While caring for elderly parents is challenging for anyone, adult children of aging immigrants also navigate through the multiple and intersecting jeopardies of race, socioeconomic status, and limited English proficiency as they are thrust into the role of supporting, educating, and advocating on their parents' behalf.

This chapter focuses on those respondents who have begun caring for ill parents, and in so doing have entered another stage of their intergenerationally linked lives. Some respondents recount their experiences as their parents were dying and the role they and other family members took to support them, while other respondents describe helping parents who have developed chronic health problems and need aid accessing health care. These respondents also struggle to find ways to care for themselves and balance their lives as they embark on the emotional, physical, and financial work of caring for aging and ill parents from near and afar.

Working to Get Accessible, Equitable, and Quality Health Care

The majority of respondents describe their fathers' and mothers' health as good to excellent, but approximately 15 percent of the sample report that their parents' health is poor to fair. These respondents help one or both parents navigate the health care system more effectively by assisting them in accessing healthcare and insurance (such as Medicare) and acting as translators and advocates.

Numerous studies on racial and ethnic groups and health care indicate that Korean immigrants, particularly in urban metropolitan areas where they live in concentrated numbers, lack access to health coverage and care. Among racial and ethnic groups in the United States, Korean Americans demonstrate one of the highest propensities to start their own business, concentrating in retail and service businesses.[20] In 2000, approximately 20 percent of Korean Americans were self-employed, double the rate of self-employment in the total U.S. population.[21] Many immigrants also work in co-ethnic-owned small businesses that may not provide health insurance and other benefits. Ethnic and immigrant entrepreneurship is often touted as an example of successful adaptation and economic self-sufficiency of communities, but this high self-employment rate may be one reason why Korean Americans consistently demonstrate the lowest rates of health insurance coverage among racial and ethnic groups in the United States.[22] Recent health care debates have highlighted this problem, and while lack of health insurance is not endemic to one group, high rates of ethnic entrepreneurship may come at a cost to the health and well-being of Korean American entrepreneurs, families, employees, and communities.

Several respondents note that taking care of their parents began with helping them access health care. About 80 percent of the respondents' parents have some form of health insurance largely due to Medicare; parents under age sixty-five are more likely to lack insurance. One way that some respondents and their siblings take care of their parents is to pay, in whole or part, their health insurance costs. For example, for a while Jacob helped pay his mother's health insurance premiums, which came to about $800 a month. She had chronic health issues, including hepatitis, and carried private insurance due to the complexity of her condition. Because of skyrocketing costs, Jacob's mother dropped her health insurance the year before she became eligible for Medicare. Although her decision provided much relief for Jacob, for whom paying her insurance was a real financial burden, it is unclear how they would have managed if she had had medical emergencies during her uninsured year.

Respondents also help family members cope with and manage their illnesses, search for information on the Internet, and communicate diagnoses and necessary treatments from doctors to family members. Some respondents encounter an uphill battle while educating and encouraging their parents to change unhealthy behaviors and manage chronic illnesses. For years, Jacob has tried to get his mother to change her diet in order to relieve chronic stomach problems. He shares:

> I keep badgering her—you have to eat more fiber, and stuff like that. . . . It seems like she never listens to me. She always listens to her friends. That's what she keeps saying—"My friends say this and that" and then, something would happen and then I tell her, "I told you! You listen to your friends. I looked it up and then, you know, I told you this is how it is." My mother then would respond, "Why did you waste your time doing this and that?"

On the other hand, adult children also work to ensure that their parents are heard and treated with kindness and respect in various health care settings. Recent studies support the view that such advocacy may be critical for older adults, and especially for those who belong to racial and ethnic minorities, are immigrants, and/or have limited English proficiency. Those with chronic illnesses often experience being discredited and ignored by those around them, including health care providers.[23] A national study by Quyen Ngo-Metzger, Anna Legedza, and Russell Phillips finds that Asian Americans are more likely to state that their doctor did not listen to them, did not understand their background, and did not adequately inform them about major medical decisions. They also report access to fewer services, exams, and counseling and to lesser quality of patient care compared to white Americans.[24] Asian American respondents are more likely to attribute these poor doctor-patient relations to their race and limited English ability, and believe they would be treated with more respect by their doctor if they were white.[25] In another study that compares Asian American and white Medicare recipients in major metropolitan areas, Ernest L. Moy, Linda Greenberg, and Amanda E. Borsky also find that compared to their white peers, Asian American older adults receive poorer care and are less likely to be offered important cancer screenings and diabetic services.[26]

Immigrant parents' vulnerability to being ignored or neglected by health care providers stimulates many kinds of advocacy by adult children. In earlier chapters, we discussed how adult children of immigrants become a form of social capital for their parents in that their socioeconomic attainments, English fluency, and adaptation to and familiarity with the dominant society all assist the family in their survival and long-term adaptation in the United States. Many respondents continue to use such skills to ensure quality care for their parents. For some, this may involve defending the parent's dignity and insisting that the parent deserves common courtesy and respect. Patrick, in his twenties, recalls what happened when his mother was diagnosed with cancer. He had accompanied her to a medical appointment and noticed with dismay that the doctor preferred to discuss matters with him in a way that discounted his mother's intelligence and humiliated her.

> I remember this one doctor, this white male doctor, acting like she doesn't know what's going on. She would say something and then he looks at me and ask me the same question and . . . it was just so degrading. Just because it's like, my mom is telling you the exact same words. . . . I was really icy towards him and I was just like, as my mom just said, you know? She said the same exact thing.

Similarly, Andrew believes that his mother has been overlooked within the health care system due to her limited English proficiency. Outraged by the bureaucracy and complexity of the system, he expounds on how a request to consult a specialist turned into a months-long odyssey of mounting frustrations, and how he decided to ensure that his mother would finally be seen by a neurologist. Andrew shares:

I've actually used my documentary experience to advocate for my mom with the health care system. It took her, like, almost four, five months to see a neurologist. I got fed up with this so I brought my video camera. That particular morning, she was scheduled to see a neurologist but again she was rerouted to another floor. I had my camera on my shoulder. And I said I just want to document my mom's health care . . . to make sure she sees somebody because her health condition is degenerating. So they did two things. They called the sheriff and two, they found two new neurologists on that same day and they spent forty minutes with her and she got the best care . . . but they also called the sheriff, so it was a little sacrifice for me.

Vanessa, who is in her thirties, also shares how caring and advocating for her mother who lived in another state was not an easy task:

Working with the American health system has been kind of tragic! I can't even tell you how many incidents I've had with the dentist office or her primary care physician or her vision doctor. . . . I've always found myself battling with these doctors and trying to get them to coordinate her health care. Now specifically, now with her severe depression and working with her psychiatrist, the flood of doctors that she's seeing—it's become a real tragedy because I don't think she's getting the care that she needs because of the language. I've had to make several trips [out-of-state], just to deal with her doctors.

Vanessa expresses her frustration that, particularly due to language barriers, she needed to be a constant advocate on her mother's behalf to secure and coordinate the necessary quality of care from the health care system.

Soomin has had similar experiences helping navigate care for her seventy-nine-year-old mother who has been hospitalized multiple times due to internal bleeding, a broken bone, and fainting. Her mother speaks limited English, and although she lives in Los Angeles' Koreatown and has Korean-speaking physicians, she inevitably encounters health care providers at the hospitals who speak only English. Soomin comments:

It's the hospital staff. They speak English. If you're not there 24/7, it's very, very inconvenient, even for the little things that she does. It's not a—it's not an important decision that you need to discuss with your doctor or someone fluent in English, but anything that's a minor communication, such as even getting water, you know? There could be a Korean-speaking staff, but a lot of times there aren't, so you need to be there the whole time.

Soomin and her sisters, who live throughout the greater Los Angeles metropolitan area, have rotated staying with their mother during her hospital stays. Soomin, a mother of young children who works in the private sector, feels that she and her sisters need to be their elderly mother's advocate to explain her symptoms and medical history even with Korean-speaking physicians. She states:

> In terms of being able to express what she is going through to the doctor—you have to be able to explain your symptoms really well, to be able to get the right medicine, pain-killer, whatever. She wouldn't be able to articulate, which would make it hard for the doctors to understand causes and find out. . . . Let's say she has an interpreter who takes care of her, but if you don't know the history, it's hard to explain. It's very complicated to explain the symptoms, how you're feeling and all that. You have to know the person and the history. For example, she might say, "My leg hurts." And the doctor will ask, "When did it start hurting?" And she doesn't remember, but you might remember because you know the history. So, there's that continuous knowledge that's required and also, to be able to articulate that in English.

Lois, in her mid-forties, lives in the Bay area while her parents live in southern California. She takes care of her parents' health by advocating and translating for them, and this has included delivering bad news from their doctor. Her parents owned a small business and were uninsured for most of their lives in the United States. They did not have access to regular preventative health screenings and often ignored symptoms that warranted a doctor's attention; in one instance, although her mother was experiencing ongoing menstrual bleeding, she refused to see the doctor because she was uninsured. When her mother was diagnosed with stage-four cervical cancer with Lois standing at her side, she had to interpret the terrible news. She vividly remembers what that was like:

> I remember just standing there; my mom's lying on the exam table saying, "What did she just say?" And I just lost all words. I couldn't even

remember—my mind went totally blank. I'm sure it took me like five minutes to come up with words. I remember saying, "Mom, you've got to hold on. I have to think of the words." And then of course, I found the word "cancer" but I obviously didn't know the word for cervical cancer.

Lois, who works full-time and is married, was flying down at least twice a month on the weekends to take care of her mother, whose cancer was in remission at the time of the interview.

Cindy, whose father passed away from late-stage cancer, remembers taking care of him by translating in health care situations and dealing with his HMO. Even though her father spoke and understood English fairly fluently, he did not have a Korean-speaking physician, and Cindy noted that he would not ask questions during appointments and would come away from them with a "different understanding of what the doctor said," which she attributed to his culturally influenced attitude and behavior. Additionally, she observes,

> Korean translators were not easily available and even when it was apparent that he didn't understand something, it was usually up to me to try to explain it to him using my limited Korean. . . . While I consider myself conversationally fluent in Korean, I don't know a lot of medical terms so when I try to explain things I was reduced to using childish words to try to describe a process or a procedure. In the end, I think what needed to be communicated was accomplished but it was sometimes a very frustrating process.

If her father had to wait for weeks to schedule a procedure that the physician ordered, Cindy would call the HMO on his behalf and try to get an earlier appointment.

> As is typical with HMOs, it's easy to be overlooked if you don't follow up. The more you can advocate for yourself, or have someone advocate for you, the better the system works for you. For example, his doctor would say you need this test and then he would call for an appointment for the test but the appointment center would tell him that the next available appointment isn't for three months. Then, I would call and ask to speak with someone else, explain the situation and find an opening for the appointment sooner, either by getting an earlier date or finding an

opening at another location. Other times, there might be a difference of opinion on what is needed and, on several occasions, I did call and speak with Member Services and obtained more services for my dad than he would have received on his own.

Carrie, in her thirties, cared for her father after he was diagnosed with a diabetic coma. He was uninsured and had no known health conditions prior to his hospitalization at age sixty-four. Carrie, who had just graduated from pharmacy school, was thrust into the role of caring for her father due to her health care background. There was also no one else, since Carrie did not want to worry her younger sister who was still a student. Carrie translated the gravity of the condition to her father, who was more distraught by his failing business than by his deteriorating health.

Multiple organs were failing, said the doctors. They were just waiting for his labs to look better before deciding what to do. They said he would have to go to a nursing home; he would no longer be the same. I explained to my dad that he needed to get better and to let the doctors do what they had to do. I explained to my dad the best way possible without making it too scary. I said his organs were not functioning well, especially his kidney. My dad did not understand. He was psychologically distraught.

Carrie advocated for her father, going to the hospital twice a day to get the best possible care for him and facilitated discussions between him and the doctors. She translated the medical procedures, for example, when the nurses would put in the catheter. Carrie's father passed away just a few months after diagnosis and hospitalization. She served as his interpreter and advocate during the crisis that shook the family, and provided emotional labor and financial support for the rest of her family.

Adjusting to Illness, Loss, and Role-Reversals

Previous chapters show that respondents' parents encouraged and expected their children to pursue educational and professional achievements as expressions of filial duty; their schooling, jobs, and other life milestones such as marriage could, however, result in respondents living in different parts of the state or the country from their parents and/

or siblings. Under the circumstances, if a parent became ill, respondents have found ways to coordinate care-giving tasks with siblings (if they have any) while taking care of their own families. They also wrestle with preserving their parents' independence while trying to address the physical, emotional, and/or social tolls of the illness. Respondents who live near their parents discussed tasks such as accompanying their parents to their medical appointments and procedures, while those who live hundreds or thousands of miles away discussed the challenges of caring from afar and providing emotional support despite the geographic distance. This is especially a pressing concern for respondents with single, divorced, or widowed parents.

Cindy, whose father passed away after a three-year battle with late-stage cancer, recalls the losses that she felt and the role reversals that occurred as he dealt with the diagnosis and the subsequent treatments. Her mother ran their family's small business while caring for him full-time; Cindy and her brother, who both lived near their parents, were in charge of accompanying their father to appointments, translating medical information, and relieving their mother at the hospital. In contrast to her usual ways of setting personal goals for herself and striving to achieve them, Cindy felt helpless for the first time in her life: "There was very little that I could do to help my father." Cindy and her brother sought second opinions and best treatment options since their father had health insurance; they also tried to gather and translate information, as well as advocate for their father within the HMO system. Cindy discusses how her father's illness created a role reversal in her family:

> As my father's health deteriorated, he became more child-like and our roles became more reversed. Growing up and even as an adult, he was always the typical Asian male head of household who was the ultimate "boss" of his family and also his business. But, he didn't have much of a relationship with me and my brother as adults and as his illness progressed and he became weaker, I could see that outside of his role as father, husband, and business owner, he was unsure of himself and how he could relate to us.

Cindy wonders if her father had lived longer, would they have developed a more intimate relationship? Cindy and her brother are much closer to their mother, who took care of not only of her sick husband but also her elderly mother-in-law before they passed away, and says she wants to go into a retirement home or assisted living facility so that she does not burden her own children with care-giving. But in Cindy's perspective, "both my brother and I are better prepared to handle taking care of our mother because of what we've all experienced in taking care of our father and grandmother." The care-giving experience and loss strengthened the siblings' relationship with their mother, and reinforced their resolution to take care of her in the future with the support of their spouses.

Andrew lives in the Bay area while his widowed mother continues to live in the Los Angeles area, where she is part of an active, closely knit church community. He jokes that "the Confucianist part of me has already asked her to stay with us. . . . So has my brother and my sister but, of course, she's fiercely independent and she doesn't [want to] burden anyone, you know?" After his mother developed a chronic pain in her leg, the siblings started to visit more often and take her to doctor's appointments or on shopping trips for groceries and other items she may need. Andrew discusses feeling helpless as his mother grows older—especially when his mother tries to minimize or conceal from him her increasing physical pain—and how much he relies on his wife to take care of his mother and to deal with his helplessness.

> Emotionally, it's hard to see your mom aging. I think you can go in either of two ways. One is, drop everything, go there and just do everything for her. That's one impulse. The other is to distance yourself and let my wife take care of it or . . . be more stoic or philosophical or distract yourself. I don't want to go in either direction. I want to stay with the pain but I don't want to be overwhelmed. . . . I've got to be rational without. avoiding the pain that's there. I think the most painful part is just seeing your mother in pain.

Hyunsook, who is single and in her thirties, also lives in northern California while her parents live in southern California. Her father has struggled with medical issues for decades; her mother, his main caregiver, is beginning to experience her own health issues due to aging, and Hyunsook worries that while her mother could take care of her father when he needed help, her father would not be able to take care of her mother if she became ill.

My dad has always had one issue or another with his health. And several years ago—many years ago at this point—he had a really serious surgery. So I went down there for a few days and helped take care of him. But living in northern California, and my parents being in southern California, in the back of my mind I always know that something is going to happen at some point, and I have to be prepared for it. I have to be ready at any given notice. . . . I'm sure other people think about . . . regular Americans or mainstream Americans think about that, too, so in that sense, it's not too different that I am choosing to live my own life and not take on those really hard-core Korean traditions. But it's something that I think about a lot, *a lot*, with my friends and with my family as well.

As a teenager, Hyunsook paid little attention to her father's health issues because her mother, the primary care-giver, did not ask for help from the children. But now, with her mother becoming older and more frail, she worries that "if my father were to get sick, my mom takes care of him, but if my mom were to get sick he can't take care of her." She is more acutely aware of her mother's aging process after moving up north for work, and is bracing herself for impending care-giving responsibility from afar. She explains that the fact that both she and her sister live away from her parents increases her consciousness that she has to be "ready at a moment's notice" to take a few days off from work or take other, more permanent measures as unexpected situations arise. While she believes that any "regular" or "mainstream" Americans would feel the same way about filial duties, it is noteworthy that she makes a distinction that reveals her view of Korean culture: If she were "hard-core" Korean, she says, she would already be in southern California near her parents and not "choosing to live" her own life.

Elaine, in her forties, grew up in southern California and has lived in northern California since college. After her father began to experience illness and her brother moved to another state for work, her parents decided to move up north to be closer to one of their children after they retired from owning a string of small businesses. Resembling many in their age cohort, Elaine's parents wished to live in proximity to, but not with, their adult children, and they chose to live near a daughter. Elaine's realization that her parents were becoming more dependent on her is a common theme that respondents express around aging and family relations.

It's very different now. Well it's same and it's different. I'm still close to them but they are more dependent on me. . . . They are dependent on me financially, they are dependent on me for—you know, they have a lot of needs—like the Internet. . . . My dad's pretty ill, so I have to take him to the doctor, and go with him to medical appointments, stuff like that.

Yet, Elaine notes that her parents do not rely on their children entirely; while they are more dependent on her for some things, her mother is still the daily care-giver for her father. If her father were to pass away from his illness, Elaine wants her mother to move in with her but thinks her mother would prefer to move into an apartment complex for senior citizens. Elaine admits that "I haven't really talked about it. It would depend so much on the particular situation, what level she was functioning." Her mother is, in fact, relatively healthy, and she is more autonomous than her father. But like Hyunsook, Elaine views herself as the next care-giver in line should her mother's health decline.

Other respondents share how difficult it was to become aware of their parents' increasing dependence and illness. Connie, in her late thirties, described her relationship with her mother, a retired nurse, as "easy" and the relationship with her strong-willed father, an engineer turned small-business owner, as very close but difficult. She jokes, "Even though [my father] and I are close, we literally go, 'Okay, Dad, half an hour's up. We're going to start fighting. So why don't you go watch some TV?' and he says, 'Okay.'" Connie and her sibling live several hundred miles away from their parents, who eased into retirement by selling their home at the height of the California real estate bubble and moving into a lower-priced senior housing community. Her father's heart attack was the shocking reminder that her parents, now in their seventies, have aged. She recalls that

My brother and I had distinctly different reactions to my father's heart attack. I think for me seeing my dad vulnerable was toughest since he was such a strong figure in our household. . . . I wasn't so surprised at my dad's sudden change in health as I was disturbed by his frailty.

Gracie, a Bay area transplant, who was born and raised in the Midwest where her parents still live, discusses the difficulty of trying to support her parents from afar. Her still "youthful and vivacious" mother is a full-time care-giver to her father who has Alzheimer's disease. She describes watching him change with each visit and clinging to the memories of how her dad once was, for herself and her children:

> Just before he got pretty sick, he insisted on not coloring his hair any more. So it was a pretty big shock—one visit he was him, and the next visit, his hair was entirely white. It changed his appearance a lot. With the Alzheimer's, he's not really there anymore. I see the physical aging a lot more, and then there's this kind of distance where I don't really see it as my dad aging, I see this older guy who is not really my dad anymore. He's my dad, but he's lost somewhere in there, so at the same time he's not my dad. . . . I struggle with holding onto that memory and that part of him, because I don't want him to get lost and replaced with this him that's only kind of him.

Family members may have expected to live close to each other and provide different types of support as parents age, but, given necessary moves, it is not easy to uproot lives. Gracie's parents do not want to leave their community and home for over forty years. Meanwhile, Gracie wants to live in the Bay area to raise her children, and does not see herself moving back near her parents.

> Because I can't physically be "there" for my parents, I do try to support my mom emotionally. It's really hard to do, because my mom is fiercely independent, and not only has trouble asking for help but even has trouble accepting help when it is offered unsolicited. And the best thing I can do for her is to let her do things her way.

Other ways in which Gracie tries to care for her parents include calling her mother once a week, and whenever she is able to visit, running errands for them, fixing things around the house, and going to medical appointments with them. Gracie shares that both she and her sister, who lives a day's drive from their parents, "try to help out, and sometimes if there's something we think needs to be done, we try to divvy up the work according to who is better suited to it." At the same time, the sisters often argue over how to support their parents. Overall, Gracie's responses reveal that despite her desires and a lifetime of close relationships with her parents, care-giving is difficult to coordinate from afar as aging parents wish to remain independent in their own homes and not burden their children, while adult children follow their own life trajectories. She is both thankful and heartbroken for her parents:

> Mostly my dad's disease just makes me so sad. He worked really hard his entire life to provide for his family. . . . My mom did the same, and was looking so forward to my dad's retirement, so that they could finally enjoy themselves. They saved all their money for us and saved for their retirement so that they'd never have to ask us for anything. They had plans to travel and enjoy each other. They never got to do any of this. My dad's disease is so progressed, and my mom is tethered to my dad. . . . My mom will never put him in a nursing home until she's nearly killed herself taking care of him. There are so many things I wish I could do for them. It breaks my heart.

In this stage of linked lives, respondents learn to deal with new responsibilities of care-giving, including the emotional difficulty of watching their previously self-sufficient parents struggle with illness, declining health, or death, sometimes from hundreds or thousands of miles away. Respondents also wrestle with how to support the care-giver parent. As the above discussions underscore, many tensions and challenges surface as respondents and aging parents try to make sense of cultural expectations, traditional family support arrangements, and competing responsibilities such as work and having young children.

Work and Division of Responsibilities among Siblings: Closeness and Tension

Carrie decided there was "no one else" who could take care of her father and she acts accordingly. But like Michelle and her sister who try to support their unexpectedly widowed mother, most respondents who have ill parents negotiate care-giving responsibilities with siblings. Usually, one sibling will take the lead and coordinate efforts so that each sibling can provide financial, practical, and/or emotional care according to his or her ability and availability. Most often, the older (or oldest) sibling in a family is the one to coordinate care, but those older siblings who have children may delegate coordination to siblings without children or to those who are most available.

For example, Scott, in his forties, is the youngest of his siblings. He has remained in the Bay area so that he can remain geographically close to his mother; he also gives her a monthly allowance and drives her to medical appointments. However, when asked about elder care plans for the future (she is in her late eighties and in good health), he replies, "I'm the youngest child in the family, and my oldest brother who's in his sixties right now—he's actually the man that actually discusses this matter with my older sisters about elder care issues." Andrew, an eldest son, explains how his siblings and wife are the key to taking care of their widowed aging mother who suffers from a chronic illness:

> I'd like to adopt and modify a Confucianist approach to helping our parents. I mean, we have to be pragmatic, more realistic. So, whoever is more available, . . . we need to sort of take turns and I think, luckily, all our siblings, we sort of get along with each other so we always talk about our parents, our mom, and we're always thanking each other for chipping in and things like that. Of course, you never feel like you do enough, you know?

But in other cases, the challenges of taking care of ill parents can take a toll on siblings' individual well-being and their relationship with each other. Lois, an eldest daughter with no children, explains how she and her sisters divided up responsibilities.

> We have by our personality, divided up the work, but I predominantly take care of all the health care issues, all their financial issues, and every-thing. I almost had to give this up because my life was just getting too stressful. I even had, like, a little timer set up in my calendar at work to call in refills for the prescriptions. After I'd called in, I would say, "Dad, I called in refills for Mom's drugs. You can go pick it up this afternoon."

While Lois took on medical advocacy and financial support for her parents, her sisters help with day-to-day tasks. When her mother needed round-the-clock care, her younger sister was the one who got up to take her mother to the bathroom, bathe, and clean her, giving the kinds of assistance Lois could not provide from a distance. However, as the eldest, Lois states she feels pressure from the rest of the family to be the strong, responsible one. As she was growing up, Lois's parents told their daughters that family members would have to take care of each other, and because "we don't have sons," the sisters would be responsible for taking care of their parents. Despite this projection of her family being a tight unit, Lois feels that she carries the heaviest load as the eldest: Her parents "have this image that I will take care of everything"— and it seems that her sisters do also. She has learned to turn to her husband for comfort, but not to her sisters, to whom she refrains from complaining in order to manage their emotions and their relationships.

> Yeah, and I just sort of cried on my husband's shoulders and you know, I tried crying with my sisters. I have realized, though, it's not very helpful because my sisters feel so hopeless and guilty, and I didn't mean to impart guilt on them. My whole point is just to vent and have somebody to vent to that could understand all the nuances that I'm going through, but what I end up with is just making them feeling guilty and not being helpful to me so I've just sort of given up on that.

Although siblings work together to meet different needs of parents, disagreements about how to take care of them can arise and result in misunderstandings and tensions. Gracie, whose parents live out of the state, explains what happened between her and her sister:

> I had visited my dad earlier, and was a bit depressed by the way he was sometimes just left to sit by himself. I could see why they would just leave him, because he's pretty unresponsive, but he would just sit at the kitchen table after breakfast and fidget with the potholder or the tablecloth. So I got a few little toys (brainteaser type things) for him to keep his hands busy with. I didn't by any means expect him to do the puzzles, but they come with such pleasing shapes, colors and textures I thought he could just hold them in his hands and touch them.

Disagreements about their intentions, exacerbated by their father's illness, have resulted in sharp exchanges between the sisters.

My sister was feeling so defensive and angry. She kind of took it out on me, and at one point told me, "You can't make him better—trying to do those brain teasers is not going to make him better." That *really* ticked me off. She not only had no idea of what I was doing, but was completely unaware of the hypocrisy of her statement. The entire thing blew over, but I'm not sure I ever forgave her for that. We have entirely different ways of looking at the world, of dealing with things.

In some cases, siblings and other relatives voiced their opinions and more, about who could and should "step it up" for their parents, which proved to be an emotionally intense, exhausting, and conflict-filled process. Janet, in her forties, lives in California and the rest of her family lives in another state. Her mother suffered a major illness that was misdiagnosed by the first physician and hospital. Thinking she was going to die, her mother checked herself out of the hospital against the doctor's advice and returned home, where she needed round-the-clock care. Her other siblings and even cousins, who lived nearby, had to take care of her mother, who refused medical treatment and eventually, her siblings called Janet and asked her to help out. Janet, who was worried about her mother's health but explains that her mother has a "difficult personality," went out to support them. Although her siblings were glad that Janet could take care of her, Janet knew that she needed to care for herself, too. Thus, she sought solace in spirituality during her mother's hospitalization and recovery—first for her mother's health, and then increasingly for the resolution of their painful family conflicts. Janet describes her brush with martyrdom: she did all she did to be a "good daughter," and she faced the need to protect herself emotionally from her mother's behavior when her good intentions were not enough.

> Well, I prayed a lot. I actually would go into the hospital chapel and pray that Mom's health would improve. But then her health did improve, and I found myself praying for forgiveness of all this ugly interpersonal stuff that was coming up between us. I started out with good intentions, to take care of myself emotionally, but I felt like she was treating me with con-tempt, telling me, what's the use of you? I did all this stuff— organized her medication, got her to dialysis, prayed my heart out, helped her through the holidays, took her to church and to parties, did all the errands . . . and

the better she got, the worse I felt. . . . I was trying to show her I'm a good daughter while at the same time, protect myself from feeling abused.

Janet's mother made a recovery from her illness and eventually stabilized. Janet made several more visits, each lasting about three to four weeks at a time to take care of her mother. Although her interactions with her mother were emotionally difficult, her worst experience involved her aunt.

> My aunt came over for Thanksgiving and Christmas and the aunt got it in her head that she was going to force me to move back home and be a full-time servant to Mom. And she decided well, it's her job because she's the oldest sister. And there was this point where she was pestering me in my face and I said, "Well, I'm going walk out of the room now." She followed me and started yelling. She grabbed me and slammed me against the wall. . . . Now my mom is like in the room while this is happening saying nothing. . . . It's horrible. And my dad who can barely think coherently, came into the room, heard the commotion. He came in, he was like "No, no, no, stop. Don't do that." He was very concerned.

Her aunt's extreme actions were based on her belief that as the only unmarried child, Janet should move back and take care of her mother, and her aunt had the authority to make this demand because she was the eldest aunt. However, Janet saw her aunt's "controlling" behavior as a personality characteristic and not due to Korean culture or traditions. Her sister, who lived nearby and had the closest relationship with their mother, became the primary caretaker of their mother's affairs and health and not Janet's brother, the eldest son in the family (again, demonstrating selective enforcement of "cultural" gender and birth order norms). Janet was glad that her mother was learning about in-home services available through Medicare and becoming more independent from her children.

Balancing Act: Caring for Parents, Others, and Self

Even though Janet had a difficult relationship with her mother, she returned to help her siblings take care of her and in her own words, "show her that I'm a good daughter." Respondents often attributed their desire to be good sons and daughters to growing up and watching their immigrant parents struggle in the United States, as well as having internalized values that define Koreanness as being there for one's family. Many respondents also referred to their parents' lifelong sacrifices as motivating tool, whether their parents had or had not achieved stability and other life satisfaction in the United States. Studies of Korean American and other Asian American children of immigrants conducted in the respondents' twenties demonstrated that they idealistically looked to the future as one in which they will show their gratitude to their parents, including caring for them in their old age.[27] However, realities clash with this idealism, as caring for frail and disabled elderly parents is a difficult task that can lead to increased distress and overburdening.[28] Realities also include geographic separation, financial limitations, and competing demands for time from work, family, and other obligations. Moreover as they dealt with difficulties and losses that their parent(s) faced, respondents described feeling a range of complex and conflicting emotions, from anguish to guilt to resentment. Respondents discussed the many ways that they tried to cope. Those married with children most often noted the need for balance and ensuring that caregiving of a parent not take over the other care-taking duties. Elaine discussed the strain of caring for her aging parents in addition to working for a living and meeting daily responsibilities to husband and young children. She stated how she was attempting to balance these multiple demands:

> It's really trying to balance everything . . . doing a good enough job as a mom, and doing my job here at work. That's a big sort of daily concern, it's a juggling act. . . . It's more daily stress. Concern? . . . For the family, my parents and Mike's parents, how long will that be sustained?

Others found different ways to cope with the changes in their parents including finding humor, meaning, or support from close friends. One way that Gracie coped with her father's progressing Alzheimer's was to keep his memory alive by recounting stories about him to her children. Gracie describes how she also uses humor to get through the pain of this loss.

> I sometimes cry. I often make off-color jokes and laugh. When my husband went through difficulties some years ago, we learned that anything, if you take it seriously all the time, can make you cry endlessly. So we

laughed about it. We would make such completely inappropriate jokes that it would have made anyone listening to us curl their toes. I do the same with my dad's illness. It's not meant to be a sign of disrespect; it's just a way to do something other than crying.

Respondents who experienced care-taking in their twenties recounted how they worked to stay connected but also coped by continuing to live out their life goals and dreams. For example, Patrick's mother was diagnosed with cancer in his senior year of college. Since he attended a university about one hundred miles from his family, Patrick described how he tried to be there for his family by phone while trying to finish his studies, partly because his younger sister who lived at home would disappear and not answer their phone calls. As a result of her absence, his parents called him daily; his father, who owned a store, would tell him about how stressed he was at work about the business and his safety, even though he had never had such conversations with Patrick prior to the health crisis. His mother would tell him about her physical condition and the pain she experienced.

> I was really also stressed out about completing my thesis because it was this monkey on my back. . . . Then I started feeling really stifled because my parents were constantly confiding in me. I don't know what to do with all of that and, I started really wishing that there were boundaries but I didn't know how to create those boundaries because I just felt so terrible, you know? So I actually started seeing a therapist.

His mother had a successful surgery to remove the cancer, but she developed other debilitating chronic pain. Patrick and his father took turns taking her to different physicians in northern and southern California because no one could diagnose her illness. Patrick also spent the year helping his father at the store and his mother through rehabilitation, as well as attempting to ameliorate the isolation caused by her health crisis. He taught her how to drive a car again, and encouraged her to get out and resume socializing with friends. His strong sense of responsibility and care-giving efforts lasted about a year before feelings of resentment began to simmer, along with a strong sense of guilt due to the growing resentment. Patrick reflected:

I felt really uncomfortable knowing how much I resented them because . . . my mom is going through this really traumatic experience. My dad is just busting his ass with the store and a part of me feels like I have lost that year. I don't have a life of my own and I started to resent them and told very few people that because I felt so guilty for feeling that. . . . I was just so negative and I was so pessimistic and cynical. . . . I'd be thinking about my mom constantly. . . . I just thought, this is going to go on till she passes away. Yeah, it was just so big, you know? The pain is just all encompassing and overwhelming. Everywhere, you know?

After one year, Patrick applied to graduate programs. Although he ultimately decided to attend an out-of-state university based on the funding it offered and faculty who were willing to work with him, he admitted that his choice was motivated as much by desperation to escape his emotional turmoil as it was by the practical aspects. He reflected on the impact of his mother's illness on his family. Before her health scare, he was a college student who viewed his parents as "authority figures," but the health crisis and the care giving year had shifted the hierarchical relationship.

It made me kind of reassess my own values. My relationship with my parents. Seeing them as—realizing that my parents are people too, you know? They're not just these—beforehand, I just saw them as authority figures. They can tell me what to do and then finally my dad just opening up so much to me, and being there with my mom on a daily basis, and seeing her go through just his struggle to become like herself again. . . . It was a really humbling experience.

Respondents tried to balance their own needs and those of their parents, and also find meaning in their care-taking. This attempt to balance, though ongoing, becomes urgent as they come to terms with their parents' vulnerability and mortality. Moreover, if a parent was widowed, divorced, or separated, adult children often felt greater urgency to be there as they were thrust into a primary care-giving role, yet still sought to retain a sense of balance. Adult children care-giving for frail parent(s) coped in various ways. Earlier in the chapter, Carrie shared how she served as her divorced father's primary care-giver and advocate as he faced his dying days. Although she describes their relationship as "rocky" for much of her life, she worked to ease his fears at the end so that he did not feel alone in his terminal condition. As the oldest daughter and the one with the health care background, Carrie put her own life and relationships on the backburner to take care of her father and to provide financial and emotional support for her mother and younger sister. In the process, she feared that she was taking too much time off from work, especially when she needed the income to support the rest of the family, including her mother. She reached out and relied on close friends and other supportive networks, not her family, when things became unbearable. She found meaning in the responsibility and care work that she did, but also recounts the sacrifices she made:

> There wasn't anyone else to do it, me being the eldest and me knowing what his dire condition really meant. . . . The biggest thing that helped me was that I felt like I was doing everything I possibly could to let my dad know that he was not alone—as mean as he was—he still wasn't all alone, and that gave me peace. I feel that he knows that I gave it my all to make sure he was not alone and was taken care of at the end of his life.
>
> Next to giving birth, it was the hardest time in my life [laughs]. I took lots of time off from work, which made me feel horrible. I needed to make money and financially take care of my other parent so there was this huge stress over me. I sacrificed others around me to take care of my Dad, including not being able to see my husband, my fiancé at the time, being deployed . . . but the docs said my dad might pass soon so I stayed back.

Overall, the experience of taking care of her terminally ill father made Carrie more empathetic as a health care provider, especially toward those taking care of aging immigrant parents.

> I'm very sympathetic when adult children come in for their parents' medication. I had one grown adult, son of Chinese immigrants, whose mom just got discharged and her medications were not covered so I personally made sure they were taken care of. I sympathized with him and told him that, too. Inside, I thought—he was one of the lucky ones; his parents were getting out of the hospital alive.

Others may feel overwhelmed by their parents' and their own pain; one way to cope is to become distanced emotionally and physically from their parents. Michelle, whose father unexpectedly passed away from cancer, describes what it was like to support her widowed mother while the two of them tried to deal with his loss:

> Because you don't know how to process grief, and we didn't know how to do it well. And it was so sudden. And nobody told me about therapy— I didn't know. I would have gone to a therapist but I didn't know and clearly, my mom thinks therapists are for crazy people so she's not going to go. So it was two of us, home, not going anywhere.

One way for Michelle's mother to cope with her loss was to do everything with her daughter. Michelle explains she became her mother's "boyfriend" as a replacement for her father, which resulted in growing resentment and anger during this period:

> I felt very resentful and very angry. I felt like I was wasting my life. I felt like I should be going out. I should be dating. I was twenty-three, twenty-four. And I wasn't doing those things. So I had a lot of resentment and I blamed my mom for everything bad in my life.

After her sister returned and settled near their mother, Michelle went to a graduate school outside California, partly for the reputation of the program in her field and partly to reduce the built-up resentment. At the university, she was able to utilize the counseling and psychological student services where she began to address her own grief and anger over her father's passing away.

Respondents like Carrie, Michelle, and Patrick have experienced the short-term, intense health crisis of one parent and its overwhelming impact on other family members, including themselves. Other respondents like Andrew reflect on managing care for an aging parent after the efforts of "early heroic rush" must be adjusted to the "new normal" of chronic conditions and slow decline.[29] He has become a self-described "modified Confucianist" as he has realized that realistically and practically, he is unable to live out the expectations of the eldest son with its attendant filial duties. Despite the pressure he feels, he recognizes the gap between cultural expectations of sons and actual care-giving by daughters and daughter-in-laws. His sister, who lives closer to their mother, provides crucial day-to-day assistance, and his wife takes care of her mother-in-law's finances and calls several times a week to check in with her. He has to learn to accept his own limitations, thank his siblings and wife for the division of labor, and balance his life with the needs of his widowed mother, so that he can be financially, emotionally, and physically present for everyone, for the long-term. Andrew remembers:

> I've done this before. I dropped everything, canceled my appointments here at work and just flew out. Sometimes you need to do that, but I've also got to be realistic and reasonable as well. So one of the ways that I've come to accept is acceptance. Just accepting the fact that pain and suffering and death are part of life. . . . I think the other thing is just reminding myself that I cannot—physically and emotionally—I cannot always be there for my mom and [now I am] just accepting my limitation. That I can do the best I can but even my best will not be enough sometimes, and then just having to live with that. . . . I don't want to be callous, but at the same time, I don't want to exceed my capabilities . . . because that's not going to make me more effective either. I can lose my concentration at work; it could affect my productivity. It can take away some of the potential money that can go to my mom. Or the strength that I would need to drive out there in a month from now and be with here and help her—so it's self-preservation, so I can help other people.

Caring for parents is a balancing act, wherein the adult children's time, energy, and emotional reserves might be divided among several competing priorities. Adult children may also agonize over unheeded medical directives. Some discuss how they have criticized or fought with their parents when they become stubborn and refuse treatments or do not comply with medication, diet, and other care instructions. Respondents in return have been accused of belittling and patronizing their parents. These respondents discuss how frustrated and guilty they have become in the care-giving process, adding fuel to already manifest family conflicts and dynamics. For example, Andrew laments:

> Sometimes you go there with [the] best of intentions, and then something gets sabotaged and so you wind up arguing or you get frustrated

because she won't do this or she won't see the doctor. . . . Maybe we have so much *jeong*? So much love. We care so much, but then you leave feeling less satisfied. It's worse. You went back like two or three steps. And then, somehow, we have this amnesia about all that. We get delusional thinking our next trip, everything will get better. . . . Maybe it's genetically built in—this fantasy of this idea of home and family and we're always longing to repair whatever damages and we have these idealistic ideas that we project into our parents and into our family. [30]

Andrew and his family are fortunate in many ways. His mother, despite her chronic conditions, is still healthy enough to live independently and enjoy a full life in her church community, with help from her attentive children. But apart from cultural expectations regarding filial duties (whether these are deeply held or not) and the desire to give back to aging parents for lifelong sacrifices, caring is, in reality, difficult work. Idealism and good intentions clash with problems and crises that arise, and the ups and downs of taking care of aging—not to mention strong-willed and independent—parents become taxing. Those respondents who have experienced the illness or death of a parent have needed to make difficult decisions about medical treatments, finances, and care-work while managing emotions, relationships, logistics, and demands of their own lives, other family members, and jobs, from near and far. They discuss intertwined feelings and responses of satisfaction, love, duty, anger, resentment, and guilt as they have tried to make meaning of their care-giving experiences and create balance in their lives.

Conclusion

This chapter examines the experiences of respondents familiar with care work—those who have lost a parent to an unexpected acute illness, nursed a parent through a serious illness, or had a parent who needed long-term care. The often invisible work that sons and daughters of Korean immigrants have done has been crucial to the well-being of the parents and the family unit as a whole. The urgency and extent of this care work becomes more visible as aging parents become more fragile and more dependent on the advocacy and support of their English-speaking adult children. Although this work is crucial to the lives of older adults in general, it is especially critical for immigrants who rely on their children to access and translate information about managing their chronic illnesses, navigate through the health care system, locate the right specialists, understand their medications, and even communicate with their doctors.

Aging immigrants face numerous challenges that could be viewed as "double jeopardies."[31] These include the language barriers, economic vulnerabilities, and a whole range of issues associated with aging. Moreover, parents who are widowed, separated, or divorced have even greater need for the support of their adult children. Thus, a recurring central theme in this chapter is how the lives of adult children of immigrants are interconnected with those of their parents. Their relationships and care-work often grow more complex as adult children become the voices, brokers, and translators for their parents who face acute and chronic illnesses, while also managing their own lives, finances, work, and spouses or partners, and children. In most families, siblings were cooperatively and willingly sharing support and tasks rather than relying on the eldest son; the sibling most available tended to serve as the main coordinator of care.

As adult children try to step up to the plate to "be there" for their parents, the job often proves to be complicated because of the first-generation parents' limited English ability and understanding of the health care system. They try to navigate the health care system and provide or coordinate home care, as well as access the best professional care, information, and expertise that is available and affordable. They learn to be fierce advocates for their parents. They learn from their experiences and become more empathetic to other families facing decline and death. However, they also become overwhelmed. They become angry and resentful and may move temporarily in order to take a break or to permanently set limits and reclaim their own lives. They grieve over the losses affecting their parents, including chronic pain and other impairments, whether due to cancer, dementia, or simply old age. In middle adulthood, some adult children become "modified Confucianists" as they accept their own limitations. The accumulated combination of stresses creates enormous burdens, but many in this study nevertheless view caring for their parents as a form of reciprocity, involving duty, gratitude, and cultural expectations.

Adult children of aging Korean immigrants draw upon aspects of ethnic culture and immigrant experiences to explain their care-giving attitudes and practices. However, as we discuss in the beginning of the chapter, we are entering an unprecedented period in which elder care will be a pressing national and global agenda. Many more persons in the United States and other industrialized nation-states are living longer; families are decreasing in size and living farther away from each other; more women (traditionally the care-givers to the young, old, and the infirm) are participating full-time in the workforce, and government officials and policy makers are battling over health care and safety net programs. Meanwhile, adult children and their families are beginning a challenging journey through informational mazes, new responsibilities, role-reversals, and dedicating substantial time and resources to the family member's care— a physically, emotionally, and financially involved task. While this book illuminates the invisible and visible work accomplished by the children of Korean immigrants in their families, it also aims to highlight the need to view old age and elder care in the United States as a national and public responsibility and not simply as a cultural or private family matter.

6

Linked Lives

Where Do We Go from Here?

This book focuses on narratives of adult children of Korean immigrants and the roles they play in relationship to their aging parents, particularly in regards to the support they have provided in the face of structural constraints and both Korean and American cultural norms. The narratives of adult children of immigrants do not negate or minimize the lifelong work of their parents who came to a new country, raised their families, and navigated economic, political, and structural systems.[1] Many parents, if they were able, provided their children with emergency short-term or long-term support, such as financial assistance or childcare. And although adult children cared for parents when they became ill, they discussed how one parent (especially mothers) became the primary care-giver of the other parent, and worked hard not to burden their children. While parents navigated the health care system with assistance from spouses and adult children, they also found ways to accomplish self-care through their own networks.[2] In fact, a growing body of literature has demonstrated that older immigrants choose self-sufficiency for as long as they can manage.[3]

However, we have seen how respondents have empowered their parents through their fluency in English, access to higher education, and their entry into the mainstream work force. In a way, the children of immigrants construct their own notions of privilege in U.S. society. Given the prejudice and racism immigrants like their parents have suffered, they in turn speak up, to bridge divides and to advocate for their immigrant parents and others like them. Children of Korean immigrants navigate structural barriers for their parents and become brokers and advocates for their health as they age or develop illnesses and conditions. While this study has explored how respondents have modified cultural norms of respecting and honoring elders, we have suggested that the children of Korean immigrants have created their own responses to political, economic, and social constraints that immigrants parents face lifelong in the United States.[4]

Model Minority Children, Care Work, and Linked Lives

The responsibility to care for parents evokes significant social, cultural, political, and familial pressure to do it perfectly—to be the good daughter or son who embodies the model minority image. In both mainstream U.S. and ethnic media, Korean and other Asian immigrants and their children have been simultaneously praised for their educational achievement and socioeconomic upward mobility and excoriated for promoting strict parenting styles and community values that prioritize and reward academic achievement.[5] Asian Americans have long critiqued the model minority image as a rosy myth created by a dominant society that denies the existence of structural racism and the challenges and barriers that diverse Asian groups face.[6] Reading across fields in the area of Asian American literature, erin Khuê Ninh has argued that the critique of the model minority needs to be reassessed as it is "mythical no longer."[7] Rather than viewing the model minority as an externally imposed subjectivity, Ninh insightfully argues, with reference to literary texts, that the immigrant nuclear family, as a "special form of capitalist enterprise," seeks to produce children who fit the model minority model in the "hope of profiting in the Western capitalist economy."[8] Likewise, our subjects in this study affirm the pressure—imposed by self, parents, community, and the dominant society—to fulfill their parents' hopes and aspirations, "capitalist enterprise" and all.

Despite assumptions and stereotypes about Korean culture and care for elderly, the narratives of respondents were driven by the concept of linked lives and the need to care for the previous generation. Adult children interviewed varied in disposition while their parents differed in English fluency, occupations, and ability to prepare for retirement. Moreover, differences existed in the proximity of family members and in the health of parents. A common theme, though, is that a majority of female respondents recalled participating in emotion work from childhood to the present day. Often, it is the daughters of Korean immigrants who take on the role being in the middle for their parents from childhood to adulthood. Both sons and daughters are motivated by a need to "repay" their parents' sacrifices, yet daughters expressed greater concerns about their parents' advancing age, their limited English ability, their health, and/or their limited retirement savings. They more often participated in invisible emotion work in their parents' lives in order to help parents feel understood, stable, proud, happy, and well. Many grew up translating and interpreting for their parents, thereby acting as family representatives or helping support their parents' work. Others sought to alleviate the stress their immigrant parents faced by doing well in school. Although there are similarities and differences in the degree and level of care and emotion work respondents have provided, the key theme throughout these narratives is that children, and especially daughters, of immigrants participated in emotional work in immigrant families. This book illustrates the work of children over a lifetime and the need for adult children to care for themselves as well.

Remembering Parents' Histories and Sacrifices: Finding Meaning in Care Work

Korean immigrants and their adult children in this study represent a growing cohort of second- generation Korean Americans in the United States. The adult children are a unique cohort in that their experiences were forged in a particular place and time in Korean and Korean

American history. Compared to the more recent wave of immigrants (arriving after 1990) who were raised during a time of growing affluence and political stability in South Korea, our respondents' parents (and other kin) lived through the Korean War and came of age in a politically volatile and impoverished post-war period focused on nation-building and rapid modernization.[9]

Moreover, the costs of migration for the cohort of immigrants and their children we have studied here were also quite different from those experienced by the later waves of Korean immigrants who benefit from increasing globalization and technological developments. The Internet and forms of communication such as emails, texts, and social media have made staying connected to family and friends abroad easier, instantaneous, and affordable, in contrast to the 1970s, for example, when international phone call rates were exorbitant and letters took a couple of weeks to be delivered via air mail.[10] Today, families can maintain connections more easily across nations and time zones. Previous immigrants faced lost connections and also often settled in places where there were few Asian Americans. These places may have also been hostile to Asian Americans, in comparison to the greater number of ethnic enclaves available to contemporary immigrants. Given these vulnerabilities and others such as language barriers and downward mobility for the first generation, these immigrants' children became their vehicle for not only maneuvering through society, but also meeting unfulfilled dreams for both generations. Growing up in this context, many children have seen parents make sacrifices in terms of taking jobs for which they are overqualified and working excessively long hours, and, as they themselves have grown up, they may have found meaning in living out parents' dreams and missed opportunities.

The current myth of the "tiger parent" aside, many of our respondents discussed their parents having lofty dreams for them but not necessarily being involved in the details of their children's success.[11] Because of language barriers, lack of time, and unfamiliarity with the educational system, it was the children who were the ones to navigate their education. Cultural socialization also provides a backdrop for children of immigrants to find meaning in their experience of care work. Immigrant parents teach their children Korean cultural values of filial piety that emphasize obedience and obligations to parents. Filial piety also entails parents' nurturing their children when they are young and children respecting and caring for their parents in their old age.[12] Studies have indicated that while Korean culture and South Korean society traditionally have emphasized the eldest son's (or the eldest daughter-in-law's) duties to parents and care-giving responsibilities, urbanization and industrialization have changed these patriarchal and patrilocal customs.[13] Contemporary South Koreans, especially after the financial crisis of the late 1990s, and after the change in primogeniture laws, are more likely to draw on both sons *and* daughters, and both patrilineal *and* matrilineal ties and kin, for support and interaction.[14] In our study, whether or not their parents expressed their wishes (or demands) outright, many respondents placed expectations on themselves to care for their parents. And while many respondents' parents are financially secure, others see themselves as their parents' retirement plan. Many respondents are supplementing their parents' limited incomes and coordinating with their siblings to be present for their parents. Those whose parents face unexpected or life-threatening illnesses have found ways to be advocates. Often, adult children have fought against the structural and racial barriers that impacted their parents' access to and quality of health care.

Viewing these structural constraints through a cultural lens, respondents find a sense of personal identity as Korean Americans in their care of immigrant parents. Doing well is not an individual act but one that also involves helping families emotionally and tangibly. They also reassess past intergenerational conflicts as parent-children roles reverse in later years. Other studies have found that adult children—women in particular—across the board find meaning in their life-long care work for their parents.[15] Hyeong Kang and fellow researchers find that the exposure of children to the adversity experienced by Korean immigrant parents may deepen the meaning they attain from hard work and upward mobility especially as they support their family's mobility. Building on work by Jeanne A. Schaefer and Rudolf H. Moos, Kang and his colleagues suggest that meaning in life not only provides a way of coping but also contributes to the development of resilience and to personal growth.

In the outside world, children of immigrants have fought the prejudice, invisibility, marginalization, and vilification of their parents who speak with accents or who may not speak English at all. Respondents discuss how they involved themselves when a parent faced dehumanizing experiences with institutions that failed to listen to or serve their parent because of his or her limited English ability. Adult children can find meaning in their ability to speak up for their parents and for other immigrants like their parents. Other studies have shown how the challenges and difficulties experienced by their own parents and other immigrants around them can serve as catalysts for the development of meaning and purpose in their own lives, and in their careers, volunteer work, or activism in the community.[16]

Ambivalence and Working at Maximum Capacity

As aging immigrants face retirement and various losses in friendships, family, and health, many navigate these changes with their adult children. Although immigrants of diverse backgrounds possess an incredible will to make it in the United States, they also face a lifetime of "cumulative disadvantage" that puts them at risk for morbidity and mortality in later years.[17] Korean Americans continue to exhibit one of the highest uninsured rates among all racial and ethnic groups in the United States.[18] Inadequate health care coverage over the life course for the first generation impacts the second generation of Korean American adults, who may need to pay for health expenses or manage long-ignored chronic health conditions that aging parents now face.

Some respondents with parents who are under sixty-five are waiting for their parents to be eligible for Medicare. At the same time, many discuss their parents' lack of access to preventative health care screenings, which may result in abruptly entering into a medical nightmare, wherein they find out through a phone call or a meeting with a doctor that their parent had stage-four cancer, kidney failure, or another fatal condition. Because their parents did not have health care checkups, many adult children were unaware that parents had health issues until the situation became catastrophic. Moreover, when parents do obtain Medicare, many are already suffering from chronic health conditions. And then, regardless of insurance, many need their adult children's help to navigate health care, especially through bureaucratic HMOs and/or changes in informational technology (such as electronic health records). In short, adult children find themselves in the position of brokering the life, health, and even the death of aging immigrant parents.

Despite ideals of familial responsibility to "take care of one's own," many Korean immigrant families are ill equipped or not prepared for life in old age. Many families have not discussed practical matters such as wills, advance directives and other important legal and health particulars, so they are often unprepared when an aging family member starts to need care.[19] Moreover, care work is complicated by adult children's distance from parents, their own financial limitations, and the juggling of demanding jobs, young children, spouses or partners, and in-laws.

Life-course theorists often describe parent-child relations late in life as an arena ripe for feelings of ambivalence.[20] Ambivalence arises from the tensions associated with caring for family while trying to live one's own life; the sons and daughters of Korean immigrants are more likely to contend with structured ambivalence, compared with more privileged counterparts.[21] Some find themselves overwhelmed as they cope with ambivalence and psychological stresses within their own lives and especially in the care of their parents when cultural socialization and expectations collide with the difficulties and demands of care-giving.

Whether in the role of the "good" child or the one who "fell through the cracks," children of immigrants, in particular daughters, share how they have learned to care for themselves in their adulthood. Most respondents report that intergenerational relations improved and became smoother as they grew older and family lives stabilized. Many have adjusted through psychotherapy or just through aging and life experiences; they have come to realize that they cannot do it all for everyone. Most respondents grew up in households where parents were overworked and mothers in particular went above and beyond for their children. While these sacrificial models uphold the ideals of motherhood (Korean, Confucian, Christian, and/or other), children of immigrants also remembered that their parents (particularly mothers) did not or were not able to take care of themselves. Growing research supports the importance for those who are caring for others to also ensure they are caring for their own emotional and physical health needs.[22]

As parents age, there are multiple costs of time, money, emotion, and energy involved in meeting obligations to care for them. Past studies show that Asian Americans who are "sandwiched" between generations experience more guilt compared to other racial and ethnic groups about not doing enough for aging parents.[23] In fact, two out of five Asian

Americans caring for an aging parent have taken time off work for this purpose, and one in two regularly accompany their parents on doctor's visits.[24] Caring for the older generation comes at many costs including care-giver stress. One in three Asian Americans providing care to aging parents experiences exhaustion, loss of concentration, and feelings of being overwhelmed.[25] Yet our respondents illustrated how they adapted, and learned how to be flexible and balance caring for themselves and others as their parents grow more reliant on others in their old age.

Aging Immigrants and Policy Issues

Korean Americans have been impacted by and responded to different issues regarding racial representation, social mobility, and political power in recent decades. Debates around long-term care and health care reform have the potential to resonate with the children of immigrants especially when these and other aging and health care issues appear on the policy agendas of local, state, and national governments. Given their intimate connection to immigrant experiences and to the complicated and convoluted processes of survival and adaptation in the United States, their role as an intergenerational bridge could extend to supporting a social reform agenda because aging and health care are not just private family matters, but universal social issues.

Jill, a second generation Korean American in her late twenties, discussed how her parents who do not qualify for Medicare yet and are uninsured, make frequent trips to South Korea to utilize its advanced and affordable health care system:

> I would say my mom has probably been uninsured for most of my memory, and that's because the job my dad had would only provide insurance for him but not for family members, and then purchasing insurance is too expensive. So a lot of times, she will go to Korea to get stuff done or stuff taken care of. . . . I think that it's something that is not common but it's not unheard of. I think there are other Korean Americans who are uninsured that will go to Korea because it's more affordable.

Her entrepreneur parents have chosen to go without health care due to costs, and are baffled by the difficulties associated with passing health

care reform legislation in the United States, especially when compared to the affordable, universal health care system available in South
Korea—the nation they had long considered less wealthy and advanced
than the United States. Jill shares:

> I feel like my dad has expressed my outrage at how he doesn't understand
> why Republicans would try to block this kind of legislation. . . . And I
> think it's also more international in scope, not understanding how this
> country cannot provide this type of service to you. Even a country like
> Korea can, which they left in the 1980s—and so I think a lot of Ameri-
> cans don't have that perspective. It can seem possible or too costly, but I
> think that my parents know that it is an issue of political will.

With the establishment of the Patient Protection and Affordable Care
Act, U.S. citizens and legal residents are now required to have health
insurance or pay a fine.[26] Individuals who do not have access to job-
based insurance should be able to access coverage through an affordable state health insurance plan. Moreover, health insurers are required
to provide coverage regardless of any pre-existing condition. Under this
act, it will be interesting to see how the newer Americans—immigrants
and their adult children—will be affected in terms health care access
and utilization. New studies estimate that an additional two million
Asian Americans will gain or be eligible for health insurance coverage
by 2016 as a result of the new law.[27]

Despite the barriers that immigrants and their families face throughout their lives, the larger national political discourse is often anti-immi-
grant. National and various statewide legislation throughout the United
States has only fueled the notion that immigrants are not wanted, and
if in need, should not burden our safety nets. The 1994 passage of California's Proposition 187 conveyed to immigrants the message that they
were not welcomed in the state's publicly funded schools, clinics, and
hospitals.[28] Moreover, on August 22, 1996, President Clinton signed a
federal welfare reform law (the Personal Responsibility and Opportunity for Work Reform Act—PL 104-193) that ended legal immigrants'
eligibility for federal means-tested entitlements.[29] There have been
increasing political action and media portrayals to construct immigrants as undeserving of any government and sometimes institutional

support.[30] Subsequent legislation has conveyed to immigrant families that in order to move upward, they and their American-raised children must do so on their own. As the United States grapples with the current economic recession, safety nets for non-citizens (documented or undocumented immigrants) are the first to be eliminated.

Viewed through a cultural lens, the efforts that adult children make to help their families maintain financial stability and stay healthy are presumed to be their individual, familial responsibility. However, caregiving for the elderly is a social issue that most adult children of both immigrant and non-immigrant parents must wrestle with in the United States and other rapidly aging industrialized societies. In fact, although we have discussed the impact of baby boomers on aging, baby boomers are managing the financial, physical, and emotional efforts of caring for their *own* parents. The continued cutbacks to federal safety-net entitlements for the elderly including Social Security, Medicare, Medicaid, and other state and local aging and health resources have an impact on Asian immigrant elders and their children.[31] Their lack of access to traditional retirement savings, such as pension benefits, means that older Asian immigrants are more likely to rely on their adult children.[32] With such fiscal challenges looming ahead, the voices of elderly immigrants and their adult children must be included within discussions that address and seek to improve social, economic, and psychological conditions of the growing aging population.

In the United States, persons sixty-five years and older numbered 39.6 million in 2010.[33] By 2030, there will be about 72.1 million older persons— more than twice the number in 2000.[34] This growth means that those in the sandwich generation, who may be parenting their own children and thinking about their own retirement, will most likely have to juggle the responsibilities for ill and frail parents. Roughly, 5.7 million care-givers, primarily adult daughters, make up 29 percent of the U.S. adult population providing care to someone who is ill, disabled, or aged.[35]

It is also projected that in the next four decades the aging population will substantially increase in its racial and ethnic diversity. By 2050, 22 percent of the Asian American population is expected to be at least sixty-five years of age and older.[36] Between 2000 to 2010, the sixty-five and older population in the Korean American community grew the most compared to other age groups.[37] This growth highlights the need to work and collaborate with others in the immigrant and aging communities. Koreans Americans, as an ethnic group, may think about themselves as mostly family-oriented and caring but so do other groups; our study demonstrates that family cannot and should not do it alone. Immigrant elders face double jeopardy, a lifetime of cumulative disadvantages, which their sons and daughters must navigate. Adult children may draw from a combination of available and accessible unpaid and paid resources, including family, friends, neighbors, in-home care-givers, nurses, and others, combined with government social service agencies, community-based organizations, online communities, and other institutions to take care of elders. Those families with older immigrant parents like many Korean Americans may need to navigate a system rife with cultural and linguistic challenges. Although they may feel that their concerns are private matters, or that they would fall on deaf ears, adult children of immigrants can be forceful advocates and can inform researchers, service providers, gerontologists, and policymakers in creating social policies that will address the needs of the old and young, native-born and immigrant, in the context of historically unprecedented socioeconomic shifts and trends in the United States. Demographer Dowell Myers writes that a mutual self-interest binds immigrants and boomers together—the needs of an aging population that is mostly white and native-born (but becoming more racially and ethnically diverse) inextricably depends on a U.S. labor force that is increasingly racially and ethnically diverse and foreign-born.[38] Even in the face of statewide and federal budgetary cut-backs, it is important to protect and support safety nets across generations, including anti-poverty, unemployment, and other measures; childcare; and high-quality, affordable education.[39]

Looking to the Church and Beyond

For many first-generation Korean Americans, the church is a sanctuary from the everyday experience of racism and linguistic and cultural barriers, and a comfortable place to interact with other Koreans. Korean immigrant churches were established as early as 1903 and continue to be a community force and institution for more than two-thirds of the population. Studies continue to show that immigrant churches are the dominant form of social organization in Korean American communities; 74

percent of our respondents who attend church stated that they attended a Korean ethnic church.[40] A potential exists for Korean churches or Korean American organizations to foster dialogue and discussion about the issues considered in this book, to organize, and to provide a vehicle for a collective call for equity.

As one of the strongest and most accessible institutions in the Korean community, the church provides critical social networks and support and has the potential to help Korean American families sort out their expectations and plan consciously and realistically for the care of aging family members. Research shows that like other faith community leaders, Korean church leaders already provide a range of social and health services to their members and neighboring communities. Historically, the role of the clergy in Korean churches has not only been to be spiritual leaders but also to be in the forefront of support for immigrants adjusting to life in the United States. One study finds that pastors and other church leaders (e.g., pastor's wife, elders, and deacons) have devoted up to 50 percent of their time to meeting the health and social needs of many of their elderly immigrant members, and that their roles have included explaining health and legal issues and transporting and accompanying members to doctor's appointments, which often entail translating.[41]

Immigrant parents generally indicate they want to live independently and not burden their children, and for Korean parents, participating actively in a church or faith community is an important part of that independence. In addition to the programs, services, and interaction that faith and regular attendance provide, churches can play a valuable role in disseminating helpful information to aging immigrants and their adult children on issues such as Medicare, Medicaid, affordable housing, volunteer opportunities, and retirement planning—information that older adults (and their children) need and desire to know.[42]

The children of Korean immigrants continue to be involved in ethnic churches and congregations. Churches and parachurch ministries have provided both spiritual support for young Korean Americans (especially within a college campus setting) and opportunities to share similar struggles and experiences. They also provide ways to cope not only with marginalization but also with bicultural and intergenerational conflicts, much as language schools have done for Chinese American communities.[43] Second-generation Korean Americans have also engaged in social, political, and civic participation through their church communities, and many of our respondents—especially those who reside in the greater Los Angeles area—share that Christianity continues to be if not the most important, certainly an important aspect of their identity, and that they are actively involved in their churches. Korean American and other faith communities can partner with community-based organizations, government agencies, and ethnic media for effective outreach to older adults and their adult children.[44]

Korean American churches and Christians did receive criticisms from our respondents, even from those who identify as Christians. Many pointed out that churches are not advocating actively for the rights of disenfranchised Korean immigrants, and that imitating white, right-wing fundamentalist churches, many Korean American churches are vocal about "moral" issues but not social justice issues. For example, Korean American churches have taken an anti-gay rights stance as a major priority for political organizing. One respondent, Jacob critiques:

> My church does not really talk about politics, but my pastor sometimes does, and when he does he talks about anti-gay issues and says if you could vote, you should vote this way or that way. It's always against homosexuals. My wife and I just roll our eyes. I have never told him this—that's not the only issue there is in this world. If I could pinpoint the issues he could talk about affecting us Korean Americans, it could be health care.

Although a potential exists for Korean American churches to address disparities and inequities faced by members of Korean American communities, many churches have focused their attention on other issues.[45] Lydia would like to see Korean American churches address the needs of older adults and broader social justice issues.

> As such, the Korean American community has a responsibility to care for seniors in order to repay their debt for the things that they have done for us, either personally or collectively, when we were young. Also, I think that a community in general, regardless of ethnicity, has a moral responsibility to care for their elders because they are weaker. . . . Churches have not been active in advocating in the political realm—with the exception of advocating against gay marriage—what a terrible way to spread

the message of God's love. Until the Korean American churches embrace Jesus's social justice message, I don't think that they will play much of a role in general public policy issues. . . . Maybe when the second generation takes over church leadership, this will change. . . . They'll spend hundreds of dollars to go on a mission trip to bring the gospel to unchurched areas, but they won't spend much time or energy advocating on social justice issues. I can't believe the energy or time that was spent in Korean American churches against the gay marriage initiative when even a tenth of that could have been spent on immigration or health care issues.

Jacob agrees that the Korean American church, with its ability to unite Korean Americans across generational differences, could be a potential site for organizing:

It's a great place to organize around issues affecting our community. As Christians, there is something we could organize around, but all I get from my church are gay issues or abortion issues. It really turns me off.

In response to the marriage equality movement and in particular, California's legalization of same-sex marriages in 2008 (upheld by the U. S. Supreme Court in 2013), many Korean American churches joined other evangelical churches and organizations to oppose same-sex marriages in recent years, while issues of the aged or those who are uninsured have been considered to be private or non-religious. However, there is clearly a need for church leaders, both first-and second-generation, to understand care-giving and aging issues such as the lack of availability of affordable, and culturally and linguistically appropriate, long-term care, as these issues will affect the congregation and the community as a whole; in fact, many churches already provide such care work and support to their members.

One of the most difficult decisions for a family can be to place a frail loved one in a nursing home. Over the last four decades, Asian American communities in different parts of the United States have established nonprofit community-based long-term care facilities that are linguistically and culturally familiar. Given their role and the demographic trends in the ethnic community, Korean American churches and affiliates have the potential to serve as a powerful advocate for meeting the needs of older adults by partnering with public and private sectors to provide culturally and linguistically appropriate programs and/or living facilities for aging Korean immigrants. Most immigrant churches already provide informal services for older Korean immigrant adults, but more formalized attention and planning would better serve the existing needs and could ease the burdens of members and the greater community.

Parting Thoughts

This book documents how adult children of Korean immigrants care for and support their parents, but our narratives are not comprehensive. For example, although our respondents grew up and lived in different regions of the United States, all eventually settled in two metropolitan areas of California. And although many of our respondents grew up in blue-collar or working-class families, almost all did relatively well in school and were working professionals. However, many also mentioned siblings, cousins, or friends who have faced addiction to alcohol or drugs, dealt with a debilitating physical or mental illness, or had troubles with the law and thus have been unable not able to support their parents as they themselves have struggled along their own pathways to self-sufficiency. These friends and family members have not been able to take on the task of caring for parents. In fact, some of our respondents are in the middle between a sibling who is not well and parents struggling to accept their child's addiction or illness. Respondents also shared stories of friends and family members estranged from their parents and/or siblings. Illuminating these difficulties, recent studies challenge the model minority myths by focusing on those who have "fallen through the cracks."[46] Further studies need to be undertaken to examine how Korean immigrant families care for each other in the face of unmet dreams and expectations.

Beyond the model minority image and the glowingly high socioeconomic status of some Asian Americans, are the less documented stories of immigrants and their American dreams in the twilight years. As one of the main groups to have immigrated in the post–World War II period and especially after 1965, Korean Americans have pursued new lives in the United States, but these lives have largely been captured in snapshots of intergenerational conflicts between younger immigrant parents and their school-aged children. This book attempts to capture family structures, cultural transmissions, and universal joys and challenges of linked lives as children of immigrants come of age and parents grow older. It also contributes to the scholarship of the work, emotional and otherwise, that children of immigrants continue to provide in order to support their families and the larger society, and how they broker the dreams of their parents in different ways in their middle adulthood even as they negotiate what is meaningful and significant in their own lives, as well as for the third generation and the broader community.

The stories of these respondents attest to adult children's tireless work, active reciprocity, and sacrificial love for other generations as immigrant families experience changing relationships, expectations, and responsibilities in next life stages. However, finding solutions and allocating resources for an aging society in a racially, ethnically, economically, and linguistically diverse United States cannot only draw upon cultural orientations and the goodness, capabilities, and resources of individual children and kin. There is too much at stake, because caregiving and the challenges around illness and old age are public and institutional issues that encompass and stretch beyond a private, ethnic, or immigrant matter.

APPENDIX: DEMOGRAPHIC BACKGROUND

Table 1: Demographic Background of Participants (N=137)

	N=137 (%)
Age	Range: 22–50 (Mean=34)
Place of Birth	
Korea	81 (59.1%)
United States	52 (38.0%)
Other country	4 (2.9%)
Mean Age at Arrival in United States (Mean=7)	Range: 1 to 15 years of age
Gender	
Female	73 (53.3%)
Male	64 (46.7%)
Marital Status	
Single	61 (44.5%)
Married/Partnered	73 (53.3%)
Divorced	3 (2.2%)
Highest Educational Attainment	
Some High School	1 (.7%)
Some College	9 (6.6%)
College Graduate	43 (31.4%)
Graduate School	84 (61.3%)
Region of Residence	
Southern California	65 (47.4%)
Northern California	72 (52.6%)
Mean Age of Parents at Time of First Interview	
Fathers	Range: 55 to 84 years (Mean=66)
Mothers	Range: 50 to 83 years (Mean=63)

NOTES

NOTES TO THE INTRODUCTION

1. Elder, Johnson, and Crosnoe, "The Emergence and Development of Life Course Theory."
2. Settersten, "It Takes Two to Tango."
3. Elder, "The Life Course as Developmental Theory"; Elder, "Beyond Children of the Great Depression"; Elder, "Time, Human Agency, and Social Change."
4. Settersten, "It Takes Two to Tango"; King and Elder, "American Children View Their Grandparents"; Pyke and Bengtson, "Caring More or Less"; Bengtson, Elder, and Putney, "The Life Course Perspective on Ageing."
5. Hochschild, *The Managed Heart*.
6. Brody, *Women in the Middle*. See also Yoon, Eun, and Park, "Korea: Demographic Trends, Sociocultural Context, and Public Policy"; Savundranayagam, Montgomery, and Kosloski, "A Dimensional Analysis of Caregiver Burden among Spouses and Adult Children."
7. Hochschild, *The Managed Heart*; Hochschild, *The Second Shift*; Yoo et al., "Emotion Work: Disclosing Cancer."
8. Louie, *Compelled to Excel*; Park, *Consuming Citizenship*; Pyke, "'The Normal American Family.'"
9. Kim, "Korean-American Family Postcaregivers on Dementia Caregiving"; AARP, *In the Middle*.
10. Capps et al., *The New Demography of America's Schools*.
11. Yu and Singh, "High Parenting Aggravation among U.S. Immigrant Families"; Yu et al., "Parental Awareness of Health and Community Resources among Immigrant Families."
12. Huynh, Devos, and Smalarz, "Perpetual Foreigner in One's Own Land."
13. Tuan, *Forever Foreigners or Honorary Whites?*; Huynh, Devos, and Smalarz, "Perpetual Foreigner in One's Own Land."
14. Chao, "The Prevalence and Consequences of Adolescents' Language Brokering for Their Immigrant Parents"; Morales and Hanson, "Language Brokering"; Orellana, *Translating Childhoods*; McQuillan and Tse, "Child Language Brokering in Linguistic Minority Communities"; Song, *Helping Out*.
15. Ibid.

16. Ibid.

17. Chao, "The Prevalence and Consequences of Adolescents' Language Brokering for Their Immigrant Parents"; Morales and Hanson, "Language Brokering"; Orellana, *Translating Childhoods.*

18. Pyke and Bengtson, "Caring More or Less"; Sung, "An Asian Perspective on Aging East and West."

19. Wong, Yoo, and Stewart, "The Changing Meanings of Family Support among Older Chinese and Korean Immigrants"; Wong, Yoo, and Stewart, "Examining the Types of Social Support and the Actual Sources of Support in Older Chinese and Korean Immigrants"; Yoo and Kim, "Remembering Sacrifices"; Louie, *Compelled to Excel*; Park, *Consuming Citizenship*; Pyke, "'The Normal American Family.'"

20. U.S. Census Bureau, *Korean Age Groups.*

21. Danico, *The 1.5 Generation*; Rumbaut and Komaie, "Immigration and Adult Transitions."

22. Chin, "Korean Birthday Rituals."

23. Chavez, "Conceptualizing from the Inside."

24. Yoo was born in the United States while Kim emigrated at age six.

25. Park, *The Korean American Dream.*

26. Myers, *Immigrants and Boomers*; Schulz and Binstock, *Aging Nation;* Yoo and Kim, "Remembering Sacrifices."

NOTES TO CHAPTER 1

1. Rumbaut and Komaie, "Immigration and Adult Transitions," 44–45.

2. Myers, *Immigrants and Boomers*; Rumbaut and Komaie, "Immigration and Adult Transitions"; Settersten, Furstenberg, and Rumbaut, eds., *On the Frontier of Adulthood*; Waters and Alba, *The Next Generation.*

3. Park, *The Korean American Dream.*

4. Ibid.; Min, Adam, and Watkinson, *Caught in the Middle*; Yoon, *On My Own.*

5. Chung, "A Snapshot of the Korean American Community."

6. Min, *Changes and Conflicts*; Song and Moon, eds., *Korean American Women*; Park, *The Korean American Dream.*

7. Kibria, *Becoming Asian American;* Lew, "A Structural Analysis of Success and Failure of Asian Americans"; Dhingra, *Managing Multicultural Lives*; Chung, *Legacies of Struggle.*

8. Park, *Consuming Citizenship.*

9. Song, *Helping Out.*

10. Ibid., 58.

11. Yu and Singh, "High Parenting Aggravation among U.S. Immigrant Families"; Yu et al., "Parental Awareness of Health and Community Resources among Immigrant Families."

12. Hochschild, "Working on a Feeling," 94.

13. Wharton and Erickson, "The Consequences of Caring"; Devault, "Comfort and Struggle"; Illouz, *Cold Intimacies: The Making of Emotional Capitalism.*

14. Ibid.

15. Louie, *Compelled to Excel*; Pyke, "'The Normal American Family.'"

16. Ibid.

17. Louie, *Compelled to Excel*, 133.

18. Park, *The Korean American Dream*; Min, *Caught in the Middle*.

19. Jezewski, "Culture Brokering in Migrant Farm Worker Health Care."

20. McQuillan and Tse, "Child Language Brokering in Linguistic Minority Communities"; Orellana, *Translating Childhoods*; Vasquez, Pease-Alvarez, and Shannon, *Pushing Boundaries*.

21. Ibid.

22. Orellana, *Translating Childhoods*, 2–3.

23. Chao, "The Prevalence and Consequences of Adolescents' Language Brokering"; Orellana, *Translating Childhoods*.

24. Dorner, Orellana, and Jiménez, "'It's One of Those Things That You Do to Help the Family'"; McQuillen and Tse, "Child Language Brokering in Linguistic Minority Communities"; Tse, "Language Brokering in Linguistic Minority Communities: The Case of Chinese and Vietnamese American Students."

25. Dorner, Orellana, and Jiménez, "'It's One of Those Things That You Do to Help the Family'"; McQuillen and Tse, "Child Language Brokering."

26. Buriel et al., "The Relationship of Language Brokering to Academic Performance, Biculturalism, and Self-Efficacy among Latino Adolescents"; Orellana, "Responsibilities of Children in Latino Immigrant Homes."

27. Orellana, *Translating Childhoods*.

28. Straus and Gelles, *Physical Violence in American Families*; Farrington, "Stress and Family Violence"; Kim and Sung, "Conjugal Violence in Korean American Families."

29. Lee et al., "Improving Access to Mental Health Services."

30. Ibid.; Yick and Oomen-Early, "A 16-Year Examination of Domestic Violence among Asians and Asian Americans"; Kim and Sung, "Conjugal Violence in Korean American Families"; Yick, "Role of Culture and Context"; Lee and Hadeed, "Intimate Partner Violence among Asian Immigrant Communities."

31. Lee et al., "Improving Access to Mental Health Services"; Lee and Hadeed, "Intimate Partner Violence among Asian Immigrant Communities."

32. Chao, "The Prevalence and Consequences of Adolescents' Language Brokering"; Dorner, Orellana, and Jiménez, "'It's One of Those Things That You Do to Help the Family.'"

NOTES TO CHAPTER 2

1. Park, *The Korean American Dream*, 3.

2. Ibid., 2–3.

3. Ibid.

4. Smetana, "Culture, Autonomy, and Personal Jurisdiction in Adolescent-Parent Relationships."

5. Juang and Umana-Taylor, "Family Conflict among Chinese and Mexican-Origin Adolescents and Their Parents in the U.S."; Orellana, *Translating Childhoods*; Park, *The Korean American Dream*.

6. Grotevant and Cooper, "Patterns of Interaction in Family Relationships and the Development of Identity Exploration in Adolescence."

7. Juang and Umana-Taylor, "Family Conflict among Chinese and Mexican-Origin Adolescents and Their Parents in the U.S."

8. Ibid.

9. Tuason and Friedlander, "Do Parents' Differentiation Levels Predict Those of Their Adult Children?"; Piercy and Sprenkle, *Family Therapy Sourcebook*. In fact, in a study of adolescent children of Chinese immigrant parents, conflict peaks at the ages of seventeen to eighteen while for European American adolescents and their parents, conflict peaks at ages twelve to thirteen; see Fugilini, Tseng, and Lam, "Attitudes toward Family Obligations among American Adolescents with Asian, Latin American, and European Backgrounds."

10. Usita, "Interdependency in Immigrant Mother-Daughter Relationships."

11. Settersten, Furstenberg, and Rumbaut, eds., *On the Frontier of Adulthood*.

12. For research on childhoods, see Juang, Syed, and Takagi, "Intergenerational Discrepancies of Parental Control among Chinese American Families"; Kang et al., "Redeeming Immigrant Parents"; Ahn, Kim, and Park, "Asian Cultural Values Gap, Cognitive Flexibility, Coping Strategies, and Parent-Child Conflicts among Korean Americans." For research on the new second generation, see Kasinitz et al., *Inheriting the City*; Nancy Foner, ed., *Across Generations* ; Rumbaut and Komaie, "Immigration and Adult Transitions."

13. Park, *The Korean American Dream*, 7.

14. Cho, *Haunting the Korean Diaspora*; Liem, "History, Trauma, and Identity,"; Yoo, "A Not So Forgotten War."

15. Ibid.; Liem, "Still Present Pasts."

16. Ibid.; Kim and Yoo, *Stories Untold*; MU Films, "Memory of Forgotten War" [in production].

17. Liem, "History, Trauma, and Identity."

18. In May 1980, South Korean military leaders sent paratroopers to the city of Gwangju to quell pro-democracy demonstrators who were demanding a repeal of the martial law. Although the official government figures at the time put the death toll at one hundred people, it is estimated that about two thousand citizens, mainly college students, were brutally killed by the Korean army during the Gwangju Massacre (also known as May 18 Uprising or Massacre). See Cumings, *Korea's Place in the Sun*.

19. Chang, "Compressed Modernity and Its Discontents."

20. See Settersten, Furstenberg, and Rumbaut, eds., *On the Frontier of Adulthood*, for a discussion of how the age, sequence, and social expectations and significance of these conventional markers of adulthood have shifted dramatically in the last century.

21. Louie, *Compelled to Excel*.

22. Rhee and Yoo, "'It's For the Family.'"

23. See Rhee and Yoo for a discussion of queer Korean Americans, dating, and marriage, and normative ideologies of the Korean immigrant family.

24. Lee et al., "Improving Access to Mental Health Services."

25. Jo et al., "Conducting Health Research in Korean American Churches."

26. Park, *The Korean American Dream*.

NOTES TO CHAPTER 3

1. Kibria, *Becoming Asian American*; Thai, "'Splitting Things in Half Is So White!'"

2. Cornell and Hartmann, *Ethnicity and Race*; Yetman, ed., *Majority and Minority*.

3. Nagel, "Constructing Ethnicity," 152.

4. Min and Park, "Second Generation Asian Americans' Ethnic Identity," ix.

5. Kasinitz et. al, *Inheriting the City*, 66–67.

6. Alba and Nee, *Remaking the American Mainstream*; Kasinitz et al., *Inheriting the City*; Rumbaut and Komaie, "Immigration and Adult Transitions."

7. Davey et al., "Parenting Practices and the Transmission of Ethnic Identity."

8. Tuan, *Forever Foreigners or Honorary Whites?*

9. Park and Sarkar, "Parents' Attitudes toward Heritage Language Maintenance for Their Children."

10. Hovey, Kim, and Seligman, "The Influences of Cultural Values, Ethnic Identity, and Language Use on the Mental Health of Korean American College Students."

11. Kasinitz et al., *Inheriting the City*.

12. Ibid.; Park and Sarkar, "Parents' Attitudes toward Heritage Language Maintenance for Their Children."

13. Kasinitz et al., *Inheriting the City*; Zhou and Guoxuan, "Chinese Language Media in the United States."

14. Park and Sarkar, "Parents' Attitudes toward Heritage Language Maintenance for Their Children."

15. Kasinitz et al., *Inheriting the City*; Louie, *Compelled to Excel*.

16. Kibria, *Becoming Asian American*.

17. Ibid., 52.

18. Kasinitz et al., *Inheriting the City*.

19. Ibid.; Ong, *Flexible Citizenship*.

20. One recent study drawing from the Integrated Public Use Microdata (IPUMS) 2000 Decennial Census and 2008–2010 American Community Survey (ACS) data found that while Koreans made up 22 percent of Los Angeles Koreatown's residents, Latinos of Mexico, El Salvador, Guatemala, and other Latin American national origins composed 58 percent of the population. See Sanchez et al., in collaboration with Koreatown Immigrant Workers Alliance, "Koreatown: A Contested Community at a Crossroads," 3.

21. Kasinitz et al., *Inheriting the City*, 20–21.

22. Kim, "The Social Reality of Korean American Women," 23. Kim notes that Korean American women have been impacted by traditional Confucian views of

gender hierarchy, and that these have traditionally shaped the image and roles of the ideal Korean woman as a "submissive wife and sacrificial mother" (27). Similarly, respondents were much more vocal about challenging gendered hierarchy.

23. Hochschild, *The Second Shift*.

24. *Chuseok* or *Hangawi* ("the ides of August") is observed on the fifteenth day of the eighth month of the lunar calendar, like the Mid-Autumn or Moon Festival. Traditionally, it was a time to celebrate the year's harvest, give thanks to ancestors with gravesite visits and/or worship ceremonies, and gather with family. Very few respondents said that their immigrant families observed *jesa*, in which family elders perform a ceremony to honor those ancestors who have passed away. However, some, like Lauren, visited their grandparents' gravesites.

25. Korean Independence Day is observed annually on August 15 to commemorate the end of Japanese rule in 1945.

26. According to a February 2012 Korean Gallup poll of 1,511 South Korean adults, 92 percent said they observed only *Gujeong*, or Lunar New Year. Korea Gallup Report, "2013년 한국인의 설 풍경 [2013 New Year Landscape of Koreans]."

27. National Archives of Korea, "기록으로 보는 '설날 이야기' [The Story of New Year's Day' through Records]."

28. Ibid.

29. Yoo, "서울시 강남구 땅값, 부산시 전체와 비슷 [The Land Value of Gangnam District is Equivalent to the Entire City of Busan]." In 2011, the land value of Gangnam district (which occupies about 40 km², or 15 square miles) within the greater Seoul metropolitan area was equal to the land value of Busan, the second largest city in South Korea. As accumulation of capital, wealth, and privilege, and the number of two-parent families increase, children's birthday celebrations have become a lucrative industry, and restaurants and *dol* banquet facilities have become popular places to host *dol* parties, complete with professional photographers, event coordinators, decorators, and/or entertainers. In contemporary South Korea, especially among Seoulites residing in and around the wealthy Gangnam District, *doljanchi* can be an elaborate affair rivaling wedding banquets.

In the U.S., *dol* parties can range from small dinners at homes to larger parties at restaurants and banquet facilities. In one example, Andrew Ahn portrays *dol* as an intimate family celebration in his award-winning 2011 short film, "Dol," which explores a gay Korean American man's dilemma as he contemplates coming out to his immigrant Christian parents (http://www.andrewahnfilms.com/index/dol-first-birthday).

In another example, Lawry's the Prime Rib, with several locations in the United States has created a specific marketing flyer for Korean birthday celebrations, which reads, "Time-honored traditions like the dol deserve the timeless style and elegance of Lawry's, where animal-shaped food and balloon-lined archways are created with care, and every guest enjoys a legendary dining experience." (http://www.lawrysonline.com/Files/A_1stbday.pdf).

30. Chin, "Korean Birthday Rituals." Although traditional items on the *dol* table include thread (symbolizing long life), money (fortune), pencils or books (scholarship), and a bow and arrow (warrior), contemporary parents in both South Korea and Korean America have added different items to represent an updated list of successful occupations. Hence, Korean one-year-olds can now choose from items such as stethoscope and microphone to predict their future professions.

31. Ibid., 151.

32. Ibid. For example, Little Seouls Party (www.littleseoulsparty.com) is an online store that sells and rents supplies for dol parties and caters to English-speaking customers. DolUSA (www.dolUSA) is a Korean-language online community website, according to its tagline, for "mothers in the U.S."

33. Hochschild, *The Outsourced Self*, 12.

34. Waters, *Ethnic Options*.

35. Chin, "Korean Birthday Rituals."

36. Ibid., 145. For example, Chin notes that *hwangap* was once considered to be a form of ancestor worship for a living ancestor, but it has become secularized and familiarized in response to social changes, including living arrangements. For example, whereas *hwangap* was traditionally held in the (rural) home of the celebrant, it is more often held in restaurants and other outside venues in contemporary urban South Korea (a more convenient place for their children to host the event).

37. Ibid., 150.

38. Kibria, "Marry into a Good Family."

39. One type of trip that has been heavily advertised in the Korean immigrant community is a "medical" or "filial piety" trip to Korea that combines sightseeing and/or travel with an affordable and comprehensive health examination, screenings, and/or treatment at a state-of-the-art hospital or medical facility, all of which are part of a national effort to promote Korea's medical tourism. For an example, see Korea Tourism Organization's "About Korean Medical Tourism" (http://english.visitkorea.or.kr/enu/mt/guide/mt_infomation.jsp.

40. Tuan, *Forever Foreigners or Honorary Whites?*

NOTES TO CHAPTER 4

1. Brody, *Women in the Middle*.

2. Ibid.

3. Ibid.

4. Silverstein, Gans, and Yang, "Intergenerational Support to Aging Parents"; Dwyer and Coward, "A Longitudinal Study of Residential Differences in the Composition of the Helping Networks of Impaired Elders."

5. Stoller, Forster, and Duniho, "Systems of Parent Care within Sibling Networks."

6. Di Leonardo, "The Female World of Cards and Holidays."

7. Wong, Yoo, and Stewart, "Examining the Types of Social Support and the Actual Sources of Support in Older Chinese and Korean Immigrants."

8. Kim and Cook, "The Continuing Importance of Children Relieving Elder Poverty"; Sung, "An Asian Perspective on Aging East and West."

9. Abelmann, *The Melodrama of Mobility*; Chung and Das Gupta, "The Decline of Son Preference in South Korea"; Mui and Shibusawa, *Asian American Elders in the Twenty-First Century*.

10. Chee, "Elder Care in Korea."

11. Kim, "The Legacy of Institutionalized Gender Inequality in South Korea"; Nam, "The Women's Movement and the Reformation of the Family Law in South Korea."

12. Di Leonardo, "The Female World of Cards and Holidays." Di Leonardo defines kin work as "conception, maintenance, and ritual celebration of cross-household kin ties, including visits, letters, telephone calls, presents, and cards to kin; the organization of holiday gatherings; the creation and maintenance of quasi-kin relations; decisions to neglect or to intensify particular ties; the mental work of reflection about all these activities; and the creation and communication of altering images of family and kin vis-á-vis the images of others, both folk and mass media" (442–43).

13. Brody, *Women in the Middle*; Rosenthal, "Kinkeeping in the Familial Division of Labor."

14. Di Leonardo, "The Female World of Cards and Holidays."

15. Ibid.

16. Brody, *Women in the Middle*; Chee, "Elder Care in Korea"; Lee, Yoon, and Kropf, "Factors Affecting Burden of South Koreans."

17. Seery and Crowley, "Women's Emotion Work in the Family"; See also: Yoo et al., "Emotion Work"; Gray et al., "To Tell or Not to Tell"; Reay et al., "'He Just had a Different Way of Showing It.'"

18. Seery and Crowley, "Women's Emotion Work in the Family."

19. Brody, *Women in the Middle*; Chee, "Elder Care in Korea"; Di Leonardo, "The Female World of Cards and Holidays"; Seery and Crowley, "Women's Emotion Work in the Family."

20. Chee, "Elder Care in Korea"; Lee, Yoon, and Kropf, "Factors Affecting Burden of South Koreans."

21. Lee and Bauer, "Motivations for Providing and Utilizing Child Care by Grandmothers in South Korea."

22. Ferguson, "Challenging Traditional Marriage."

NOTES TO CHAPTER 5

1. Werner, "The Older Population: 2010."

2. Ibid.

3. Jayson, "Caregivers Cope with Stress, Mixed Emotions about Aging Parents."

4. Doty, Jackson, and Crown, "The Impact of Female Caregivers' Employment Status on Patterns of Formal and Informal Eldercare"; Kramer and Kipnis, "Eldercare and Work-Role Conflict"; Levande, Herrick, and Sung, "Eldercare

in the United States and South Korea"; Spitze and Logan, "Sons, Daughters, and Intergenerational Social Support."

5. Levande, Herrick and Sung, "Eldercare in the United States and South Korea."

6. Han et al., "Experiences and Challenges of Informal Caregiving for Korean Immigrants"; Kim, "Korean-American Family Postcaregivers on Dementia Caregiving"; Kwak and Salmon, "Attitudes and Preferences of Korean-American Older Adults and Caregivers on End-of-Life Care."

7. National Alliance for Caregiving, *Caregiving in the U.S.*

8. Ibid.

9. AARP, *In the Middle.*

10. Ibid., 86.

11. AARP, *In the Middle*; Kamo and Zhou, "Living Arrangements of Elderly Chinese and Japanese in the United States."

12. Kalmijn and de Graaf, "Life Course Changes of Children and Well-Being of Parents." In their longitudinal study of a nationally representative sample of parents with grown children in the Netherlands, Kalmijn and de Graaf found that children's life course transitions affected their parents. For example, children's divorces were linked to decline in mothers' well-being, while children's marriage and parenthood were linked to increased well-being of both mother and father.

13. Kaiser Family Foundation and Asian and Pacific Islander Health Forum, "Health Coverage and Access to Health Care among Asian Americans, Native Hawaiians, and Pacific Islanders."

14. Lynch, "Race, Socioeconomic Status, and Health in Life-Course Perspective."

15. Ibid.

16. Institute of Medicine, *Living Well with Chronic Illness.*

17. Ferraro and Farmer, "Double Jeopardy, Aging as Leveler, or Persistent Health Inequality?"

18. Moy, Greenberg, and Borsky, "Community Variation."

19. Ponce, Hayes, and Cunningham, "Linguistic Disparities in Health Care Access and Health Status among Older Adults."

20. Kim and Yoo, "Korean Immigrant Entrepreneurs."

21. KAC-CIC, "Korean Employment, Poverty, and Naturalization in the United States."

22. Kim and Yoo, "Korean Immigrant Entrepreneurs"; Brown et al., *The State of Health Insurance in California.*

23. Charmaz, *Good Days, Bad Days.*

24. Ngo-Metzger, Legedza, and Phillips, "Asian Americans' Reports of Their Health-care Experiences."

25. Ibid.

26. Moy, Greenberg, and Borsky, "Community Variation."

27. Pyke, "The 'Normal American Family'"; Park, *Consuming Citizenship*; Chung, *Legacies of Struggle.*

28. Schulz, Visintainer, and Williamson, "Psychiatric and Physical Morbidity Effects of Caregiving"; Ziemba and Lynch-Sauer, "Preparedness for Taking Care of Elderly Parents: 'First You Get Ready to Cry.'"

29. Gross, *A Bittersweet Season*.

30. The concept of *jeong* has no direct translation in English. The Chinese character and its concept can be used to mean "feeling, empathy, affinity, attachment, bonding, affection, and love" as well as loyalty. It is an "emotional bond and an inter-personal glue that connects people together" in Korea. See Kim, "The Mental Health of Korean American Women."

31. Ferraro and Farmer, "Double Jeopardy, Aging as Leveler, or Persistent Health Inequality?"; Norman, *Triple Jeopardy*.

NOTES TO CHAPTER 6

1. See Light and Bonacich, *Immigrant Entrepreneurs*; Min, *Caught in the Middle*; Park, *The Korean American Dream*; Yoon, *On My Own*.

2. Pang, "Self-Care Strategy of Elderly Korean Immigrants in the Washington, D.C., Metropolitan Area."

3. Ibid.

4. Kim and Yoo, "Korean Immigrant Entrepreneurs"; Moy, Greenberg, and Borsky, "Community Variation." See the 1993, 1994, and 1995 editions of National Asian Pacific American Legal Consortium, *Audit of Violence against Asian Pacific Americans*; Ngo-Metzger, Legedza, and Phillips. "Asian Americans' Reports of Their Healthcare Experiences"; Yoo, "The Fight to Save Welfare for Low-Income Older Asian Immigrants"; Yoo and Kim, "Korean Immigrants."

5. Suzuki, "Asian Americans as the 'Model Minority'"; Chua, *Battle Hymn of the Tiger Mother*.

6. Ngo and Lee, "Complicating the Image of Model Minority Success"; Suzuki, "Education and the Socialization of Asian-Americans"; Tuan, *Forever Foreigner or Honorary Whites?*

7. Ninh, *Ingratitude*, 9. The economic and political gains by women and people of color in the post–civil rights era, the continuous immigration of Asian professionals since 1965, and the transnational movement and settlement of Asian elites have resulted in a contemporary Asian America composed dominantly of first and second generation who identify with the characteristics of the model minority. See also Koshy, "Morphing Race into Ethnicity"; Su, "Jade Snow Wong's Badge of Distinction in the 1990's"; Ong, *Flexible Citizenship*.

8. Ninh, *Ingratitude*, 2.

9. Chang, "Compressed Modernity."

10. Bacigalupe, Gonzalo, and Lambe, "Virtualizing Intimacy"; Peng, Yinni, and Wong, "Diversified Transnational Mothering via Telecommunication"; Uy-Tioco, "Overseas Filipino Workers and Text Messaging."

11. Chua, *Battle Hymn of the Tiger Mother*.

12. Sung, "An Asian Perspective on Aging East and West."

13. Kim and Cook, "The Continuing Importance of Children Relieving Elder Poverty"; Lee and Bauer, "Motivations for Providing and Utilizing Child Care by Grandmothers in South Korea."

14. Ibid.; Nam, "The Women's Movement and the Reformation of the Family Law in South Korea."

15. McLennon, Habermann, and Rice, "Finding Meaning as a Mediator of Burden on the Health of Caregivers of Spouses with Dementia"; Romero-Moreno et al., "Motives for Caring."

16. Kang et al., "Redeeming Immigrant Parents"; Lam, "The Power of Privilege and the Privilege of Power."

17. Dannefer, "Aging as Intracohort Differentiation"; Ferraro, "Health and Aging"; Ferraro and Kelley-Moore, "Cumulative Disadvantage and Health"; O'Rand, "The Precious and the Precocious."

18. Chu et al., "ASPE Research Brief: The Affordable Care Act and Asian Americans and Pacific Islanders"; Kim and Yoo, "Korean Immigrant Entrepreneurs."

19. Yoo and Kim, "Remembering Sacrifices"; Kim and Yoo, "Korean Immigrant Entrepreneurs."

20. Pillemer and Suitor, "Collective Ambivalence"; Willson, Shuey, and Elder, "Ambivalence in the Relationship of Adult Children to Aging Parents and In-Laws."

21. Ibid.

22. AARP, *In the Middle*.

23. Ibid.

24. Ibid.

25. Ibid.

26. Chu et al., "ASPE Research Brief."

27. Ibid.

28. Ibid.

29. Yoo, "Immigrants and Welfare"; Yoo, "Constructing Deservingness"; Yoo, "Shaping Public Perceptions of Elderly Immigrants on Welfare."

30. Ibid.

31. Ibid.; Vincent and Velkoff, *The Next Four Decades*.

32. Vincent and Velkoff, *The Next Four Decades*.

33. Ibid.

34. Ibid.

35. Family Caregiver Alliance, "Women and Caregiving— Facts and Figures."

36. Mui and Shibusawa, *Asian American Elders in the Twenty-First Century*.

37. Ibid.; U.S. Census Bureau, *Korean Age Groups*.

38. Myers, *Immigrants and Boomers*.

39. Ibid.

40. Kim, Warner, and Kwon, "Korean American Religion in International Perspective."

41. Jo et al., "Conducting Health Research in Korean American Churches."

42. Ibid; Kim, "Korean American Churches," 43.
43. Ibid.
44. Jo et al., "Conducting Health Research in Korean American Churches."
45. Lee, "Whither Immigrant Churches/Hello Next Generation"; Rhee, "Towards Community."
46. Hovey, Kim, and Seligman, "The Influences of Cultural Values, Ethnic Identity, and Language Use on the Mental Health of Korean American College Students"; Korean Churches for Community Development, *Pushed to the Edge*; Otsuki, "Substance Use, Self-Esteem, and Depression among Asian American Adolescents"; Suh, Suhyun, and Satcher, "Understanding At-Risk Korean American Youth."

REFERENCES

AARP. *In the Middle: A Report on Multicultural Boomers Coping with Family and Aging Issues*. Washington, D.C.: AARP, 2001. http://assets.aarp.org/rgcenter/il/in_the_middle.pdf.

Abelmann, Nancy. *The Melodrama of Mobility: Women, Talk, and Class in Contemporary South Korea*. Hawaii: University of Hawaii Press, 2003.

Ahn, Annie J., Bryan S. K. Kim, and Yong S. Park. "Asian Cultural Values Gap, Cognitive Flexibility, Coping Strategies, and Parent-Child Conflicts among Korean Americans." *Asian American Journal of Psychology* S, no. 1 (2009): 29–44.

Alba, Richard, and Victor Nee. *Remaking the American Mainstream: Assimilation and Contemporary Immigration*. Cambridge, MA: Harvard University Press, 2003.

Allen, Katherine, Rosemary Blieszner, and Karen A. Roberto. "Families in the Middle and Later Years: A Review and Critique of Research in the 1990s." *Journal of Marriage and Family* 62, no. 4 (2000): 911–26.

Bacigalupe, Gonzalo, and Susan Lambe. "Virtualizing Intimacy: Information Communication Technologies and Transnational Families in Therapy." *Family Process* 50, no. 1 (2011): 12–26.

Banerjee, Sudipto. "Effects of Nursing Home Stays on Household Portfolios," EBRI Issue Brief, no. 372 (June 2012).

Bengtson, Vern L., Kyong-Dong Kim, George Myers, and Ki-Soo Eun, eds. *Aging in East and West: Families, States, and the Elderly*. New York: Springer Publishing Company, 2000.

Bonacich, Edna. "A Theory of Middlemen Minorities." *American Sociological Review* 38, no. 5 (1973): 583–94.

Brody, Elaine. *Women in the Middle: Their Parent Care Years*. New York: Springer Publishing, 2006.

Bromley, Mark C., and Rosemary Blieszner. "Planning for Long-Term Care: Filial Behavior and Relationship Quality of Adult Children with Independent Parents." *Family Relations* 46, no. 2 (1997): 155–62.

Brown, E. Richard, Shana Alex Lavarreda, Thomas Rice, Jennifer R. Kincheloe, and Melissa S. Gatchell. *The State of Health Insurance in California: Findings from the 2003 California Health Interview Survey*. UC Los Angeles: UCLA Center for Health Policy Research, 2005. http://escholarship.org/uc/item/5kr7g285.

Buriel, Raymond, William Perez, Terri L. de Ment, David V. Chavez, and Virginia R. Moran. "The Relationship of Language Brokering to Academic Performance, Biculturalism, and Self-Efficacy among Latino Adolescents." *Hispanic Journal of Behavioral Sciences* 20, no. 3 (1998): 283–97.

Capps, Randy, Michael Fix, Julie Murray, Jason Ost, Jefferey S. Passel, and Shinta Herwontoro. *The New Demography of America's Schools: Immigration and the No Child Left Behind Act.* Washington, DC: Urban Institute, 2005. http://www.urban.org/publications/311230.html.

Chang, Kyung-Sup. "Compressed Modernity and Its Discontents: South Korean Society in Transition." *Economy and Society* 28, no. 1 (1999): 30–55.

Chao, Ruth K. "The Prevalence and Consequences of Adolescents' Language Brokering for Their Immigrant Parents." In *Acculturation and Parent-Child Relationships: Measurement and Development,* eds. Marc H. Bornstein and Linda R. Cote, 271–96. Mahwah, NJ: Lawrence Erlbaum, 2006.

Charmaz, Kathy. *Good Days, Bad Days: The Self in Chronic Illness and Time.* New Brunswick, NJ: Rutgers University Press, 1991.

Chavez, Christina. "Conceptualizing from the Inside: Advantages, Complications, and Demands on Insider Positionality." *The Qualitative Report* 13, no. 3 (2008): 474–94.

Chee, Yeon Kyung. "Elder Care in Korea: The Future is Now." *Ageing International* 26, nos. 1–2 (2000): 25–37.

Chin, Soo Y. "Korean Birthday Rituals." *Journal of Cross-Cultural Gerontology* 6, no. 2 (1991): 145–52.

Cho, Grace M. *Haunting the Korean Diaspora: Shame, Secrecy, and the Forgotten War.* Minneapolis, MN: University of Minnesota Press, 2008.

Chu, Rose, Daniel Wong, Wilma Robinson, and Kenneth Finegold. "The Affordable Care Act and Asian Americans and Pacific Islanders," ASPE Research Brief, April 2012 (July 8, 2013), http://aspe.hhs.gov/health/reports/2012/ACA&AsianAmericans&PacificIslanders/rb.shtml.

Chua, Amy. *Battle Hymn of the Tiger Mother.* New York, NY: The Penguin Press, 2011.

Chung, Angie Y. *Legacies of Struggle: Conflict and Cooperation in Korean American Politics.* Palo Alto, CA: Stanford University Press, 2007.

Chung, Woojin, and Monica Das Gupta. "The Decline of Son Preference in South Korea: The Roles of Development and Public Policy." *Population and Development Review* 33, no. 4 (2007): 757–83.

Cornell, Stephen, and Douglas Hartmann. *Ethnicity and Race: Making Identities in a Changing World.* Thousand Oaks, CA: Pine Forge Press, 1998.

Cumings, Bruce J. *Korea's Place in the Sun: A Modern History.* New York: W. W. Norton, 2005.

Davey, Maureen, Linda Stone Fish, Julie Askew, and Mihaela Robila. "Parenting Practices and the Transmission of Ethnic Identity." *Journal of Marital and Family Therapy* 20, no. 2 (2003): 195–208.

Dannefer, Dale. "Aging as Intracohort Differentiation: Accentuation, the Matthew Effect, and the Life Course." *Sociological Forum* 2 (1987): 211–36.

Devault, Marjorie L. "Comfort and Struggle: Emotion Work in Family Life." *American Academy of Political and Social Science* 561, no.1 (1999): 52–63.

Dhingra, Pawan. *Managing Multicultural Lives: Asian American Professionals and the Challenge of Multiple Identities*. Palo Alto, CA: Stanford University Press, 2007.

Di Leonardo, Micaela. "The Female World of Cards and Holidays: Women, Families, and the Work of Kinship." *Signs* 12, no. 3 (1987): 440–53.

Dorner, Lisa M., Marjorie Faulstich Orellana, and Rosa Jiménez. "'It's One of Those Things That You Do to Help the Family': Language Brokering and the Development of Immigrant Adolescents." *Journal of Adolescent Research* 23, no. 5 (2008): 515–43.

Doty, Pamela, Mary Jackson, and William Crown. "The Impact of Female Caregivers' Employment Status on Patterns of Formal and Informal Eldercare. *The Gerontologist*, 38, no. 3 (1998): 331–41.

Dwyer, Jeffrey W., and Raymond T. Coward. "A Longitudinal Study of Residential Differences in the Composition of the Helping Networks of Impaired Elders." *Journal of Aging Studies* 5, no. 4 (1991): 391–407.

Eisman, Gerry, Anoshua Chaudhuri, and Grace Yoo. *Impact of Budget Cuts on the Lives of In-Home Support Services Consumers in San Francisco*. Prepared for the San Francisco In-Home Supportive Services Public Authority, 2009.

Elder, Glen H., Jr. "Beyond Children of the Great Depression." In *Children of the Great Depression: Social Change in Life Experience, 25th Anniversary Edition*, ed. Glen H. Elder, Jr., 301–43. Boulder, CO: Westview Press, 1999.

———. "Time, Human Agency, and Social Change: Perspectives on the Life Course." *Social Psychology Quarterly* 57, no.1 (1994): 4—15.

———, Monica Kirkpatrick Johnson, and Robert Crosnoe. "The Emergence and Development of Life Course Theory." In *Handbook of the Life Course*, eds. Jeylan T. Mortimer and Michael J. Shanahan, 3–19. New York: Kluwer Academic/Plenum Publishers, 2003.

Family Caregiver Alliance. "Women and CaregivingFacts and Figures: Who are the Caregivers?" http://www.caregiver.org/caregiver/jsp/content_node.jsp?nodeid=892.

Farrington, Keith. "Stress and Family Violence." In *The Social Causes of Husband-Wife Violence*, eds. Murray A. Straus and Gerald T. Hotaling, 94–114. Minneapolis, MN: University of Minnesota Press, 1980.

Fass, Paula. *Children of a New World: Society, Culture, and Globalization*. New York: New York University Press, 2007.

———, and Mary Ann Mason. *Childhood in America*. New York: New York University Press, 2000.

Ferguson, Susan. "Challenging Traditional Marriage: Never Married Chinese American and Japanese American Women. *Gender & Society* 14, no. 1(2000): 136–59.

Ferraro, Kenneth F. "Health and Aging." In *Handbook of Aging and the Social Sciences*, 6th ed., eds. R. H. Binstock, and L. K. George, 238–56. Amsterdam, Netherlands: Elsevier, 2006.

———, and Jessica Kelley-Moore. "Cumulative Disadvantage and Health: Long-Term Consequences of Obesity?" *American Sociological Review* 68 (2003): 707–29.

———, and Melissa M. Farmer. "Double Jeopardy, Aging as Leveler, or Persistent Health Inequality? A Longitudinal Analysis of White and Black Americans." *The Journals of Gerontology, Series B: Social Sciences* 51, no. 6 (1996): S319–S328.

Fingerman, Karen L., Karl A. Pillemer, Merril Silverstein, and J. Jill Suitor. "The Baby Boomers' Intergenerational Relationships." *The Gerontologist* 52, no. 2 (2012): 199–209.

Fuligni, Andrew J., Vivian Tseng, and May Lam. "Attitudes towards Family Obligations among American Adolescents with Asian, Latin American, and European Backgrounds." *Child Development* 70, no. 4 (1999): 1030–44.

Gray, Ross E., Margaret Fitch, Catherine Phillips, Manon Labrecque, and Karen Fergus. "To Tell or Not to Tell: Patterns of Disclosure among Men with Prostate Cancer." *Psycho-Oncology* 9, no. 4 (2000): 273–82.

Gross, Jane. *A Bittersweet Season: Caring for Our Aging Parents—and Ourselves.* New York: Vintage Press, 2011.

Grotevant, Harold D., and Catherine R. Cooper. "Patterns of Interaction in Family Relationships and the Development of Identity Exploration in Adolescence." *Child Development* 56, no.2 (1985): 415–28.

Hall, Nigel, and Sylvia Sham. "Language Brokering as Young People's Work: Evidence from Chinese Adolescents in England." *Language and Education* 21 (2007): 16–30.

Hallberg, Lillemor R. "The 'Core Category' of Grounded Theory: Making Constant Comparisons." *International Journal of Qualitative Studies on Health and Well-Being* 1, no. 3 (2006): 141–48.

Han, Hae-Ra, Yun Jung Choi, Miyong T. Kim, Jong Eun Lee, and Kim B. Kim. "Experiences and Challenges of Informal Caregiving for Korean Immigrants." *Journal of Advanced Nursing* 63, no. 5 (2008): 517–26.

Hochschild, Arlie Russell. *The Managed Heart: Commercializing of Human Feeling.* Berkeley, CA: University of California Press, 1983.

———. *The Outsourced Self: What Happens When We Pay Others to Live Our Lives for Us.* New York: Picador, 2013.

———. *The Second Shift: Working Parents and the Revolution at Home.* New York: Viking, 1989.

———. *The Commercialization of Intimate Life: Notes from Home and Work.* Berkeley, CA: University of California Press, 2003.

Hoffman, Eva. *Lost in Translation: A Life in a New Language.* New York: Penguin, 1989.

Hovey, Joseph D., Sheena E. Kim, and Laura D. Seligman. "The Influences of Cultural Values, Ethnic Identity, and Language Use on the Mental Health of Korean American College Students." *The Journal of Psychology* 140, no. 5 (2006): 499–511.

Illouz, Eva. *Cold Intimacies: The Making of Emotional Capitalism.* Boston, MA: Polity, 2007.

Institute of Medicine. *2010 IOM Annual Meeting.* Renaissance Washington Hotel: Washington, DC, October 11, 2010.

———. *Living Well with Chronic Illness: A Call for Public Health Action.* Washington, DC: The National Academies Press, 2012.

Jang, Yuri, Giyeon Kim, David A. Chiriboga, and Soyeon Cho. "Willingness to Use a Nursing Home: A Study of Korean American Elders." *Journal of Applied Gerontology* 27, no. 1 (2008): 110–17.

Jayson, Sharon. "Caregivers Cope with Stress, Mixed Emotions about Aging Parents." *USA Today,* 2008. http://www.usatoday.com/money/perfi/eldercare/2007-06-25-elder-care-emotional-support_N.htm.

Jezewski, Mary Ann. "Culture Brokering in Migrant Farm Worker Health Care." *Western Journal of Nursing Research* 12, no. 4 (1990): 497–513.

———, and Paula Sotnik. *Culture Brokering: Providing Culturally Competent Rehabilitation Services to Foreign-Born Persons.* Buffalo, NY: Center for International Rehabilitation Research Information and Exchange, 2001. http://cirrie.buffalo.edu/monographs/cb.pdf

Jo, Angela M., Annette E. Maxwell, Brian Yang, and Roshan Bastani. "Conducting Health Research in Korean American Churches: Perspectives from Church Leaders." *Journal of Community Health* 35, no. 2 (2010): 156–64.

Juang, Linda P., and Jeffrey T. Cookston. "Acculturation, Discrimination, and Depressive Symptoms among Chinese American Adolescents: A Longitudinal Study." *The Journal of Primary Prevention* 30, no. 3–4 (2009): 475–96.

———, and Adriana J. Umana-Taylor, "Family Conflict among Chinese and Mexican-Origin Adolescents and Their Parents in the U.S." In *New Directions for Child and Adolescent Development,* eds. Lene Arnett Jensen and Reed W. Larson, 1–12. San Francisco, CA: Wiley Subscription Services, 2012.

———, Moin Syed, and Miyuki Takagi. "Intergenerational Discrepancies of Parental Control among Chinese American Families: Links to Family Conflict and Adolescent Depressive Symptoms." *Journal of Adolescence* 30, no. 6 (2007): 965–75.

KAC-CIC. "Korean Employment, Poverty, and Naturalization in the United States: Tables and Highlights." *Korean American Coalition—Census Information Center and Center for Korean American and Korean Studies News Release.* Los Angeles: California State University, Los Angeles, 2008. http://www.calstatela.edu/centers/ckaks/census/PR_112202.pdf.

Kaiser Family Foundation and Asian and Pacific Islander Health Forum, "Health Coverage and Access to Health Care among Asian Americans, Native Hawaiians, and Pacific Islanders." *Race, Ethnicity, and Health Care Fact Sheet, Publication #7745.* Menlo Park, CA: Kaiser Family Foundation, 2008. http://www.kff.org/minority-health/upload/7745.pdf.

Kalmijn, Matthijs, and Paul M. de Graaf. "Life Course Changes of Children and Well-Being of Parents." *Journal of Marriage and Family* 74, no. 2 (2012): 269–80.

Kamo, Yoshinori, and Min Zhou. "Living Arrangements of Elderly Chinese and Japanese in the United States." *Journal of Marriage and the Family* 56, no. 3 (1994): 544–58.

Kang, Hyeyoung, Sumie Okazaki, Nancy Abelmann, Chu Kim-Prieto, and Shanshan Lan. "Redeeming Immigrant Parents: How Korean American Emerging Adults Reinterpret Their Childhood." *Journal of Adolescent Research* 25, no. 3 (2010): 441–64.

Kang, K. Connie, and Azia Kim. "Rethinking an Emphasis on Achievement." *Los Angeles Times*, October 23, 2007. http://articles.latimes.com/2007/oct/23/local/me-korean23.

Kasinitz, Philip, John H. Mollenkopf, Mary C. Waters, and Jennifer Holdaway. *Inheriting the City: The Children of Immigrants Come of Age*. Cambridge, MA: Harvard University Press, 2008.

Kauh, Tae-Ock. "Changing Status and Roles of Older Korean Immigrants in the United States." *International Journal of Aging and Human Development* 49, no. 3 (1999): 213–29.

———. "Intergenerational Relations: Older Korean Americans' Experience." *Journal of Cross-Cultural Gerontology* 12, no. 3 (1997): 245–71.

Kibria, Nazli. *Becoming Asian American: Second-Generation Chinese and Korean American Identities*. Baltimore, MD: The Johns Hopkins University Press, 2002.

———. *The Family Tightrope: The Changing Lives of Vietnamese Americans*. Princeton, NJ: Princeton University Press, 1993.

———. "Marry into a Good Family: Transnational Reproduction and Intergenerational Relations in Bangladeshi American Families." In *Across Generations: Immigrant Families in America*, ed. Nancy Foner, 98–113. New York: New York University Press, 2009.

Kim, Barbara W., and Grace J. Yoo. "Korean Immigrant Entrepreneurs: Saving for the Health and the Future." In *Korean American Economy and Community in the 21st Century*, eds. Eui-Young Yu, Hyojoung Kim, Kyeyoung Park, and Moonsong David Oh, 545–570. Los Angeles: Korean American Economic Development Center, 2009.

Kim, El-Hannah. "The Social Reality of Korean American Women: Toward Crashing with the Confucian Ideology." In *Korean American Women: From Tradition to Modern Feminism*, eds. Young I. Song, and Ailee Moon, 23–34. Westport, CT: Praeger, 1998.

Kim, Erin Hye-Won, and Philip J. Cook. "The Continuing Importance of Children Relieving Elder Poverty: Evidence from Korea." *Ageing & Society* 31, no. 6 (2011): 953–76.

Kim, Hyungsoo, and Won-Young Choi. "Willingness to Use Formal Long-Term Care Services by Korean Elders and Their Primary Caregivers." *Journal of Aging & Social Policy* 20, no. 4 (2008): 474–92.

Kim, Jae Yop, and Kyu-taik Sung. "Conjugal Violence in Korean American Families: A Residue of the Cultural Tradition." *Journal of Family Violence* 15, no. 4 (2000): 331–345.

Kim, Kwang Chung, R. Stephen Warner, and Ho-Youn Kwon. "Korean American Religion in International Perspective." In *Korean Americans and their Religions: Pilgrims and Missionaries from a Different Shore*, eds. Ho-Youn Kwon, Kwang Chung Kim, and R. Stephen Warner, 3–24. University Park, PA: The Pennsylvania State University Press, 2001.

———, Shin Kim, and Won Moo Hurh. "Filial Piety and Intergenerational Relationships in Korean Immigrant Families." *International Journal of Aging and Human Development* 33, no. 3 (1991): 233–45.

———, Won Moo Hurh, and Shin Kim. "Generational Differences in Korean Immigrants' Life Conditions in the United States." *Sociological Perspectives* 36, no. 3 (1993): 257–70.

Kim, Luke I. "The Mental Health of Korean American Women." In *Korean American Women: From Tradition to Modern Feminism*, eds. Young I. Song and Ailee Moon, 209–24. Westport, CT: Praeger, 1998.

Kim, Rosa. "The Legacy of Institutionalized Gender Inequality in South Korea: The Family Law." *Boston College Third World Law Journal* 14, no. 1 (1994): 145–62.

Kim, Sharon. "Korean American Churches." In *Koreans in America*, ed. Grace Yoo, 259–66. San Diego, CA: Cognella, 2012.

Kim, Shin, and Kwang Chung Kim. "Intimacy at a Distance, Korean American Style: Invited Korean Elderly and Their Married Children." In *Age through Ethnic Lenses: Caring for the Elderly in a Multicultural Society*, ed. Laura Katz Olson, 45–58. Lanham, MD: Rowman and Littlefield, 2001.

Kim, Sulgi, and Grace Yoo. *Stories Untold: Memories of Korean War Survivors*. San Francisco State University: Asian American Studies, 2002. DVD.

Kim, Yujin. "Korean-American Family Postcaregivers on Dementia Caregiving: A Phenomenological Inquiry." *Journal of Gerontological Social Work* 52, no. 6 (2009): 600–17.

King, Valerie, and Glen H. Elder, "American Children View Their Grandparents, Linked Lives across Three Rural Generations," *Journal of Marriage and the Family* 57, no.1 (1995): 165–78.

Korea Gallup Report, "2013년 한국인의 설 풍경 [2013 New Year Landscape of Koreans]." February 7, 2013. http://www.gallup.co.kr/gallupdb/reportDownload. asp?seqNo=388.

Korean Churches for Community Development. *Pushed to the Edge: Asian American Youth at Risk*. June 2008. http://www.kccd.org/sites/default/files/pushed_to_the_ edge_asian_youth_profile_updated_version_0.pdf.

Korean Ministry of Health and Welfare. *Research on the Development of the Long-Term Care System for Older People. Policy Report 2004-19-1*, 2004.

Koshy, Susan. "Morphing Race into Ethnicity: Asian Americans and Critical Transformations of Whiteness." *boundary* 28, no. 1 (2001): 153–94.

Kramer, Betty J., and Stuart Kipnis, "Eldercare and Work-role Conflict: Toward Understanding of Gender Differences in Caregiver Burden." *The Gerontologist* 35, no. 3 (1995): 340–48.

Kwak, Jung, and Jennifer R. Salmon. "Attitudes and Preferences of Korean-American Older Adults and Caregivers on End-of-Life Care." *Journal of the American Geriatrics Society* 55. no. 11 (2007): 1867–72.

Lam, Amy Grace. "The Power of Privilege and the Privilege of Power," January 28, 2013. http://www.asianweek.com/2013/01/28/the-power-of-privilege-and-the-privilege-of -power/—.

LeBlanc, Allen J., and Richard G. Wight. "Reciprocity and Depression in AIDS Caregiving Relationships." *Sociological Perspectives* Winter 43, no. 4 (2000): 631–49.

Lee, Hochang B., Jennifer A. Hanner, Seong-Jin Cho, Hae-Ra Han, and Miyong T. Kim. "Improving Access to Mental Health Services for Korean American Immigrants: Moving Toward a Community Partnership between Religious and Mental Health Services." *Psychiatry Investigation* 5 (2008):14–20.

Lee, Jaerim, and Jean W. Bauer, "Motivations for Providing and Utilizing Child Care by Grandmothers in South Korea," *Journal of Marriage and Family* 75, no. 2 (2013): 381–402.

Lee, K. W. "Whither Immigrant Churches/Hello Next Generation." In *Koreans in America,* ed. Grace Yoo, 268–70. San Diego, CA: Cognella, 2012.

Lee, Minhong, Eunkyung Yoon, and Nancy P. Kropf. "Factors Affecting Burden of South Koreans Providing Care to Disabled Older Family Members." *The International Journal of Aging and Human Development* 64, no. 3 (2007): 245–62.

Lee, Yeon-Shim, and Linda Hadeed. "Intimate Partner Violence among Asian Immigrant Communities: Health/Mental Health Consequences, Help-Seeking Behaviors, and Service Utilization." *Trauma, Violence and Abuse* 10, no. 2 (2009): 143–70.

Levande, Diane I., John M. Herrick, and Kyu-taik Sung, "Eldercare in the United States and South Korea: Balancing Family and Community Support," *Journal of Family Issues* 21, no. 5 (2000): 632–51.

Lew, Jamie. "A Structural Analysis of Success and Failure of Asian Americans: A Case of Korean Americans in Urban Schools." *Teachers College Record* 109, no. 2 (2007): 369–90.

Liem, Ramsay. "History, Trauma, and Identity: The Legacy of the Korean War for Korean Americans." *Amerasia Journal* 29, no. 3 (2003): 111–30.

———. "Still Present Pasts." In *Koreans in America,* ed. Grace Yoo, 291. San Diego, CA: Cognella, 2012.

Light, Ivan, and Edna Bonacich. *Immigrant Entrepreneurs: Koreans in Los Angeles, 1965–1982.* Berkeley: University of California Press, 1991.

Louie, Vivian. *Compelled to Excel: Immigration, Education and Opportunity among Chinese Americans.* Palo Alto, CA: Stanford University Press, 2004.

Luborsky, Mark, and Robert L. Rubinstein. "The Dynamics of Ethnic Identity and Bereavement among Older Widowers." In *The Cultural Context of Aging: Worldwide Perspectives,* ed. Jay Sokolovsky, 304–15. Westport, CT: Bergin and Garvey, 1997.

Luescher, Kurt, and Karl Pillemer. "Intergenerational Ambivalence: A New Approach to the Study of Parent-Child Relations in Later Life." *Journal of Marriage and Family* 60, no. 2 (1998): 413–25.

Lynch, Scott M. "Race, Socioeconomic Status, and Health in Life-Course Perspective." *Research on Aging* 30, no. 2 (2008): 127–36.

Mancini, Jay, and Rosemary Blieszner. "Aging Parents and Adult Children: Research Themes in Intergenerational Relations." *Journal of Marriage and Family* 51 (1989): 275–90.

McElroy, Ann, and Mary Ann Jezewski. "Cultural Variation in the Experience of Health and Illness." In *Handbook of Social Studies in Health and Medicine,* eds. Gary Albrecht, Ray Fitzpatrick, and Susan C. Scrimshaw, 191–209. London: Sage Publications, 2000.

McLennon, Susan M., Barbara Habermann, and Marti Rice. "Finding Meaning as a Mediator of Burden on the Health of Caregivers of Spouses with Dementia." *Aging and Mental Health* 15, no. 4 (2011): 522–30.

McQuillan, Jeff, and Lucy Tse. "Child Language Brokering in Linguistic Minority Communities: Effects on Cultural Interaction, Cognition, and Literacy." *Language and Education* 9, no. 3 (1995): 195–215.

Min, Pyong Gap. *Caught in the Middle: Korean Merchants in America's Multiethnic Cities.* Berkeley: University of California Press, 1996.

———. *Changes and Conflicts: Korean Immigrant Families in New York.* New York: Prentice Hall, 1998.

———, and Chigon Kim. "Patterns of Intermarriages and Cross-Generational In-marriages among Native-Born Asian Americans." *International Migration Review* 43 (2009): 447–70.

———, and Kyeyoung Park. "Second Generation Asian Americans' Ethnic Identity." *Amerasia Journal* 23, no.1 (1999): ix–xiii.

Morales, Alejandro, and William Hanson. "Language Brokering: An Integrative Review of the Literature." *Hispanic Journal of Behavioral Sciences* 27, no. 4 (2005): 471–503.

Moy, Ernest, Linda Greenberg, and Amanda E. Borsky. "Community Variation: Disparities in Health Care Quality between Asian And White Medicare Beneficiaries." *Health Affairs* 27, no. 2 (2008): 538–49.

MU Films. "Memory of Forgotten War" (in production). http://www.mufilms.org/films/memory-of-forgotten-war/.

Mui, Ada C. and Tazuko Shibusawa. *Asian American Elders in the Twenty-First Century: Key Indicators of Well-Being.* New York: Columbia University Press, 2008.

Myers, Dowell. *Immigrants and Boomers: Forging a New Social Contract for the Future of America.* New York: Russell Sage Foundation, 2007.

Nagel, Joane. "Constructing Ethnicity: Creating and Recreating Ethnic Identity and Culture." *Social Problems* 41, no. 1 (1994): 152–76.

Nam, Sanghui. "The Women's Movement and the Reformation of the Family Law in South Korea: Interactions between Local, National, and Global Structures." *European Journal of East Asian Studies* 9, no. 1 (2010): 67–86.

National Alliance for Caregiving. *Caregiving in the U.S.: A Focused Look at the Ethnicity of Those Caring for Someone Age 50 or Older.* Executive Summary, November 2009.

———, in collaboration with AARP. *Caregiving in the U.S.* Bethesda, MD, and Washington, DC), November 2009. http://www.caregiving.org/pdf/research/CaregivingUSAllAgesExecSum.pdf.

National Archives of Korea, "기록으로 보는 '설날 이야기 [The Story of New Year's Day through Records]." January 2012. http://m.archives.go.kr/next/m/monthly/detail.do?page=2&designateYear=2012&designateMonth=01.

National Asian Pacific American Legal Consortium. *Audit of Violence against Asian Pacific Americans: The Consequences of Intolerance in America.* Washington, DC, 1995.

———. *Audit of Violence against Asian Pacific Americans: The Consequences of Intolerance in America.* Washington, DC, 1994.

——. *Audit of Violence against Asian Pacific Americans: The Consequences of Intolerance in America*. Washington, DC, 1993.

Ngo-Metzger, Quyen, Anna Legedza, and Russell Phillips. "Asian Americans' Reports of Their Healthcare Experiences: Results of a National Survey." *Journal of General Internal Medicine* 19, no. 2 (2004): 111–19.

Ngo, Bic, and Stacey J. Lee, "Complicating the Image of Model Minority Success: A Review of Southeast Asian American Education." *Review of Educational Research* 77, no. 4 (2007): 415–53.

Ninh, erin Khuê. *Ingratitude: The Debt-Bound Daughter in Asian American Literature*. New York: New York University Press, 2011.

Norman, Alison. *Triple Jeopardy: Growing Old in a Second Home Land*. London: Centre for Policy on Ageing, 1985.

Northouse, Laurel, Anna-leila Williams, Barbara Given, and Ruth McCorkle. "Psychosocial Care for Family Caregivers of Patients with Cancer." *Journal of Clinical Oncology* 30, no. 11 (2012): 1227–34.

Oh, Eun-Hui, Moon-Doo Kim, and Seong-Chul Hong. "The Effect of the Traditional Living Arrangement, Anpakkori, on Depressive Symptoms in Elderly People Residing on Jeju Island." *Psychiatry Investigation* 6, no. 3 (2009): 131–40.

Omi, Michael, and Howard Winant. *Racial Formation in the United States: From the 1960s to the 1990s*. New York, NY: Routledge, 1994.

Ong, Aihwa. *Flexible Citizenship: The Cultural Logics of Transnationality*. Durham, NC: Duke University Press, 1999.

O'Rand, Angela M. "The Precious and the Precocious: Understanding Cumulative Disadvantage and Cumulative Advantage over the Life Course." *The Gerontologist* 36, no.2 (1996): 230–38.

Orellana, Majorie Faulstich. "Responsibilities of Children in Latino Immigrant Homes." *New Directions for Youth Development* 100 (2003): 25–39.

——. *Translating Childhoods: Immigrant Youth, Language, and Culture*. Rutgers, NJ: Rutgers University Press, 2009.

Otsuki, Teresa A. "Substance Use, Self-Esteem, and Depression among Asian American Adolescents." *Journal of Drug Education* 33, no. 4 (2003): 369–90.

Pang, Keum Young Chung. "Self-Care Strategy of Elderly Korean Immigrants in the Washington, D.C., Metropolitan Area." *Journal of Cross-Cultural Gerontology* 11, no. 3 (1996): 229–54.

Parham, Thomas A. "Cycles of Psychological Nigrescense." *The Counseling Psychologist* 17, no.2 (1989): 187–226.

Park, Edward J. W., and John S. W. Park. *Probationary Americans: Contemporary Immigration Policies and the Shaping of Asian American Communities*. New York, NY: Routledge, 2005.

Park, Kyeyoung. *The Korean American Dream: Immigrants and Small Businesses in New York City*. Ithaca, NY: Cornell University Press, 1997.

Park, Lisa Sun-hee. *Consuming Citizenship: Children of Asian Immigrant Entrepreneurs*. Palo Alto, CA: Stanford University Press, 2005.

Park, Seong Man, and Mela Sarkar. "Parents' Attitudes toward Heritage Language Maintenance for Their Children and Their Efforts to Help Their Children Maintain the Heritage Language: A Case Study of Korean-Canadian Immigrants." *Language, Culture and Curriculum* 20, no. 3 (2007): 223–35.

Peng, Yinni, and Odalia M.H. Wong. "Diversified Transnational Mothering via Telecommunication: Intensive, Collaborative, and Passive." *Gender & Society* 27, no. 4 (2013): 491–513.

Phinney, Jean. "Ethnic Identity in Adolescents and Adults: Review of Research." *Psychological Bulletin* 108, no. 3 (1990): 499–514.

Piercy, Fred P., and Douglas H. Sprenkle. *Family Therapy Sourcebook.* New York: Guitford Press, 1986.

Pillemer, Karl, and J. Jill Suitor. "Collective Ambivalence: Considering New Approaches to the Complexity of Intergenerational Relations." *Journal of Gerontology: Social Sciences* 63 (2008): S94–96.

Ponce, Ninez, Ron D. Hayes, and William E. Cunningham, "Linguistic Disparities in Health Care Access and Health Status among Older Adults." *Journal of General Internal Medicine* 21, no. 7 (2006): 786–91.

Pyke, Karen. "'The Normal American Family' as an Interpretive Structure of Family Life among Grown Children of Korean and Vietnamese Immigrants." *Journal of Marriage and Family* 62, no. 1 (2000): 240–55.

———, and Vern. L. Bengtson. "Caring More or Less: Individualistic and Collectivist Systems of Family Eldercare." *Journal of Marriage and the Family* 58, no. 2 (1996): 379–92.

Radina, M. Elise, Hailee Gibbons, and Ji-Young Lim. "Explicit Versus Implicit Family Decision-Making Strategies Among Mexican American Caregiving Adult Children." *Marriage & Family Review* 45 (2009): 392–411.

Raj, Anita, and Jay Silverman. "Violence Against Immigrant Women: The Roles of Culture, Context, and Legal Immigrant Status on Intimate Partner Violence." *Violence against Women* 8, no. 3 (2002): 367–98.

Reay, Deay, Sarah Bignold, Stephen J. Ball, and Alan Cribb. "'He Just Had a Different Way of Showing It': Gender Dynamics in Families Coping with Childhood Cancer." *Journal of Gender Studies* 7 (1998): 39–52.

Reay, Diane. "Gendering Bourdieu's Concepts of Capitals? Emotional Capital, Women and Social Class." *The Sociological Review* 52 (2004): 57–74.

Rhee, Margaret. "Towards Community: *KoreAm Journal* and Korean American Cultural Attitudes on Same-Sex Marriage." *Amerasia Journal—Special Issue: Asian Americans and the Marriage Equality Debate* 32, no. 1 (2006): 75–88.

———, and Grace Yoo. "'It's For the Family': Negotiating Love and Marriage within Korean American Families." In *Koreans in America,* ed. Grace Yoo, 149–55. San Diego, CA: Cognella, 2012.

Robiso, Julie, Richard Fortinsky, Alison Kleppinger, Noreen Shugrue, and Martha Porter. "A Broader View of Family Caregiving: Effects of Caregiving and Caregiver Conditions on Depressive Symptoms, Health, Work, and Social Isolation." *Journal of Gerontology: Social Sciences* 64, no. 6 (2009): 788–98.

Romero-Moreno, R., M. Márquez-González, A. Losada, and J. López. "Motives for Caring: Relationship to Stress and Coping Dimensions." *International Psychogeriatrics* 23, no. 4 (2011): 573–82.

Rook, Karen S. "Reciprocity of Social Exchange and Social Satisfaction among Older Women." *Journal of Personality and Social Psychology* 52, no. 1 (1987): 145–54.

Rosenthal, Carolyn J. "Kinkeeping in the Familial Division of Labor." *Journal of Marriage and the Family* 47, no. 4 (1985): 965–74.

Rumbaut, Ruben G., and Kenji Ima. *The Adaptation of Southeast Asian Refugee Youth: A Comparative Study.* Final Report to the U.S. Department of Health and Human Services, Office of Refugee Resettlement. Washington, DC: U.S. Department of Health and Human Services, 1988.

———, and Golnaz Komaie. "Immigration and Adult Transitions." *The Future of Children* 20, no.1 (2010): 43–66.

Sanchez, Jared, Mirabai Auer, Veronica Terriquez, and Mi Young Kim. "Koreatown: A Contested Community at a Crossroads." Koreatown Immigrant Workers Alliance and Program for Environmental and Regional Equity, University of California, April 2012. http://dornsife.usc.edu/pere/documents/Koreatown_Contested_ Community_Crossroads_web.pdf

Schulz, James H., and Robert H. Binstock. *Aging Nation: The Economics and Politics of Growing Older in America.* Baltimore, MD: The Johns Hopkins University Press, 2006.

Schulz, Richard, Paula R. Visintainer, and Gail Williamson. "Psychiatric and Physical Morbidity Effects of Caregiving." *Journals of Gerontology* 45, no. 5 (1990):P181–P191.

Seery, Brenda L., and M. Sue Crowley. "Women's Emotion Work in the Family: Relationships Management and the Process of Building Father-Child Relationships." *Journal of Family Issues* 21, no.1 (2000): 100–27.

Settersten, Richard A., Jr. "It Takes Two to Tango: The (Un)easy Dance between Life-Course Sociology and Life-Span Psychology." *Advances in Life Course Research* 14, no. 1–2 (2009): 74–81.

———, Frank F. Furstenberg, and Ruben G. Rumbaut, eds. *On the Frontier of Adulthood: Theory, Research, and Public Policy.* Chicago: University of Chicago Press, 2005.

Silverstein, Merril, Daphna Gans, and Frances M. Yang. "Intergenerational Support to Aging Parents: The Role of Norms and Needs." *Journal of Family Issues* 27, no. 8 (2006): 1068–84.

Smetana, Judith G. "Culture, Autonomy, and Personal Jurisdiction in Adolescent-Parent Relationships." *Advances in Child Development and Behavior* 29 (2002): 51–87.

Sohn, Linda. "The Health and Health Status of Older Korean Americans at the 100-Year Anniversary of Korean Immigration." *Journal of Cross-Cultural Gerontology* 19, no. 3 (2004): 203–09.

Song, Miri. *Helping Out: Children's Labor in Ethnic Business.* Philadelphia, PA: Temple University Press, 1999.

Song, Young I., and Ailee Moon, eds. *Korean American Women: From Tradition to Modern Feminism.* Westport, CT: Praeger Publishers, 1998.

Spitze, Glenna, and John J. Logan. "Sons, Daughters, and Intergenerational Social Support." *Journal of Marriage and the Family*, 52, no. 2 (1990): 420–30.

Still Present Pasts: Korean Americans and the "Forgotten War." "About Still Present Pasts." http://stillpresentpasts.org/about-english.

Stoller, Palo Eleanor, Lorna Earl Forster, and Tamara Sutin Duniho. "Systems of Parent Care within Sibling Networks." *Research on Aging* 14, no. 1 (1992): 28–49.

Straus, Murray A., and Richard J. Gelles. *Physical Violence in American Families: Risk Factors and Adaptations to Violence in 8,145 Families.* New Brunswick, NJ: Transaction, 1990.

Strauss, Anselm, and Julie Corbin. *Basics of Qualitative Research: Grounded Theory Procedures and Techniques.* Newbury Park, CA: Sage Publications, 1990.

Su, Karen. "Jade Snow Wong's Badge of Distinction in the 1990's." *Critical Mass: A Journal of Asian American Cultural Criticism* 2, no. 1 (1994): 3–42.

Suh, Suhyun, and Jamie Satcher. "Understanding At-Risk Korean American Youth." *Professional School Counseling* 8, no. 5 (2005): 428–36.

Suitor, Jill, and Myra Sabir. "Race and Ethnic Differences in Intergenerational Relations." *The Gerontologist* 48 (2008): 137.

Sung, Kyu-Taik. "An Asian Perspective on Aging East and West: Filial Piety and Changing Families." In *Aging in East and West: Families, States, and the Elderly*, eds. V. L. Bengston, K. Kim, G. C. Myers, and K. Eun, 41–56. New York: Springer Publishing Company, 2000.

Suzuki, Bob H. "Asian Americans as the 'Model Minority': Outdoing Whites? Or Media Hype?" *Change: The Magazine of Higher Learning* 21, no. 6 (1989): 13–19.

———. "Education and the Socialization of Asian-Americans: A Revisionist Analysis of the Model Minority Thesis." *Amerasia Journal* 4 (1977): 23–51.

Takaki, Ronald. *A Different Mirror: A History of Multicultural America.* Boston, MA: Little, Brown and Company, 1993.

Thai, Hung C. "'Splitting Things in Half Is So White!': Conception of Family Life and Friendship and the Formation of Ethnic Identity among Second Generation Vietnamese Americans." *Amerasia Journal* 25, no.1 (1999): 53–88.

Treas, Judith, and Shampa Mazumdar. "Older People in America's Immigrant Families: Dilemmas of Dependence, Integration and Isolation." *Journal of Aging Studies* 16, no. 3 (2002): 243–58.

Trickett, Edison J., and Curtis J. Jones. "Adolescent Culture Brokering and Family Functioning: A Study of Families from Vietnam." *Cultural Diversity and Ethnic Minority Psychology* 13, no. 2 (2007): 143–50.

Tse, Lucy. "Language Brokering among Latino Adolescents: Prevalence, Attitudes, and School Performance." *Hispanic Journal of Behavioral Sciences* 17, no.2 (1995): 180–93.

———. "Language Brokering in Linguistic Minority Communities: The Case of Chinese- and Vietnamese-American Students." *The Bilingual Research Journal* 20, nos.3–4 (1996): 485–98.

Tuan, Mia. *Forever Foreigners or Honorary Whites? The Asian Ethnic Experience Today.* New Brunswick, NJ: Rutgers University Press, 1998.

Tuason, Maria Teresa, and Myrna L. Friedlander. "Do Parents' Differentiation Levels Predict Those of Their Adult Children? and Other Tests of Bowen Theory in a Philippine Sample." *Journal of Counseling Psychology* 47, no. 1 (2000): 27–35.

U.S. Census Bureau. *Census 2000 Summary File 2 (SF 2) 100-Percent Data.* Washington, DC: U.S. Department of Commerce, 2001. http://www.census.gov/.

———. *Korean Age Groups, Percentages of Foreign Born among Korean Americans.* Washington, DC: American Community Survey, 2010. http://factfinder2.census.gov/faces/tableservices/jsf/pages/productview.xhtml?pid=ACS_10_1YR_S 201&prodType=table.

U.S. Department of Labor. *A Chartbook of International Labor Comparisons: The Americas, Asia, Europe— June 2006.* Washington, DC: U.S. Department of Labor, 2006.

———. *Korean Age Groups, Percentages of Foreign Born among Korean Americans.* Washington, DC: American Community Survey, 2010. http://factfinder2.census.gov/faces/tableservices/jsf/pages/productview.xhtml?pi=ACS10_1YR_S 201&prodType=table.

Usita, Paula M. "Interdependency in Immigrant Mother-Daughter Relationships." *Journal of Aging Studies* 15, no. 2 (2001): 183–99.

Uy-Tioco, Cecilia. "Overseas Filipino Workers and Text Messaging: Reinventing Transnational Mothering." *Continuum: Journal of Media & Cultural Studies* 21, no. 2 (2007): 253–65.

Valenzuela, Angela. *Subtractive Schooling: U.S.-Mexican Youth and the Politics of Caring.* Albany, NY: States University of New York Press, 1999.

Vasquez, Olga, Lucinda Pease-Alvarez, and Sheila Shannon. *Pushing Boundaries: Language and Culture in a Mexicano Community.* Cambridge: Cambridge University Press, 1994.

Vincent, Grayson K., and Victoria A. Velkoff. *The Next Four Decades: The Older Population in the United States, 2010 to 2050.* Washington, DC: U.S Census Bureau, 2010. http://www.census.gov/prod/2010pubs/p25-1138.pdf.

Waters, Mary. *Ethnic Options: Choosing Identities in America.* Berkeley, CA: University of California Press, 1990.

———, and Richard Alba, eds. *The Next Generation: The Children of Immigrants in Europe and North America.* New York: New York University Press, 2010.

Werner Carrie A, "The Older Population: 2010." *2010 Census Briefs.* Washington, DC: U.S. Census Bureau, 2011. http://www.census.gov/prod/cen2010/briefs/c2010br-09.pdf.

Wharton, Amy S., and Rebecca J. Erickson. "The Consequences of Caring: Exploring the Links between Women's Jobs and Family Emotion Work." *Sociological Quarterly* 36, no.2 (1995): 273–96.

Williams, Natalia. "Watsonville High's Valedictorian Choi Called One in a Million." *Santa Cruz Sentinel,* 2011. http://www.santacruzsentinel.com/rss/ci_18169805.

Willson, Andrea E., Kim M. Shuey, and Glen H. Elder. "Ambivalence in the Relationship of Adult Children to Aging Parents and In-Laws." *Journal of Marriage and Family* 65, no. 4 (2003): 1055–72

Wong, Sabrina, Grace Yoo, and Anita Stewart. "The Changing Meanings of Family Support among Older Chinese and Korean Immigrants." *Journal of Gerontology: Social Sciences* 61, no.1 (2006): S4–S9.

———. "An Empirical Evaluation of Social Support and Psychological Well-Being in Older Chinese and Korean Immigrants." *Ethnicity and Health* 12, no. 1 (2007): 43–67.

———. "Examining the Types of Social Support and the Actual Sources of Support in Older Chinese and Korean Immigrants." *International Journal of Aging and Human Development* 61, no.2 (2005): 105–12.

Yetman, Norman, ed.. *Majority and Minority: The Dynamics of Race and Ethnicity in American Life*, 5th ed. Boston: Allyn and Bacon 1991.

Yick, Alice G. "Role of Culture and Context: Ethical Issues in Research with Asian Americans and Immigrants in Intimate Violence." *Journal of Family Violence* 22, no. 5 (2007): 277–85.

———, and Jody Oomen-Early. "A 16-Year Examination of Domestic Violence among Asians and Asian Americans in the Empirical Knowledge Base: A Content Analysis." *Journal of Interpersonal Violence* 23, no.8 (2008): 1075–94.

Yoo, Grace J. "A Not So Forgotten War." *Peace Review* 16, no.: (2004):169-179.

———. "The Fight to Save Welfare for Low-Income Older Asian Immigrants: The Role of National Asian American Organizations." *AAPI Nexus* 1, no.1 (2003): 85–103.

———. "Constructing Deservingness: Federal Welfare Reform, Supplemental Security Income, and Elderly Immigrants." *Journal of Aging and Social Policy*, 13 no. 4, (2002) 17–34.

———. "Shaping Public Perceptions of Elderly Immigrants on Welfare: The Role of Editorial Pages of Major U.S. Newspapers." *International Journal of Sociology and Social Policy*, 21 no. 7(2001): 47–62.

———. "Immigrants and Welfare: Policy Constructions of Deservingness." *Journal of Refugee and Immigration Studies* 6, no. 4 (2008): 490–507.

———, Caryn Aviv, Ellen Levine, Cheryl Ewing, and Alfred Au. "Emotion Work: Disclosing Cancer." *Supportive Care in Cancer* 18, no. 2 (2010): 205–13.

———, and Barbara W. Kim. "Korean Immigrants: Implications for the Uninsured and the Underinsured." *Research in the Sociology of Health Care* 25 (2008): 77–98.

———, and Barbara W. Kim. "Remembering Sacrifices: Attitudes and Beliefs among Second Generation Korean Americans Regarding Family Support." *Journal of Cross-Cultural Gerontology* 25, no.2 (2010): 165–81.

Yoo, Ha-ryong. "서울시 강남구 땅값, 부산시 전체와 비슷, [The Land Value of Gangnam District is Equivalent to the Entire City of Busan]." *ChosunBiz*, September 19, 2011. http://biz.chosun.com/site/data/html_dir/2011/09/18/2011091801100.html.

Yoon, Gene, Ki-Soo Eun, and Keong Suk Park. "Korea: Demographic Trends, Sociocultural Context, and Public Policy." In *Aging in East and West: Families, States, and the Elderly*, eds. V. L. Bengston, K. Kim, G. C. Myers, and K. Eun, 121–38. New York: Springer Publishing Company, 2000.

Yoon, In-Jin. *On My Own: Korean Businesses and Race Relations in America*. Chicago: University of Chicago Press, 1997.

Yu, Eui-Young, and Peter Choe. "Korean Population in the United States as Reflected in the Year 2000 U.S. Census." *Amerasia Journal* 29, no. 3 (2003): 2–21.

Yu, Stella M., and Gopal K. Singh. "High Parenting Aggravation among U.S. Immigrant Families." *American Journal of Public Health* (2012): 1–7.

———, Zhihuan J. Huang, Renee H. Schwalberg, and Michael D. Kogan. "Parental Awareness of Health and Community Resources among Immigrant Families." *Maternal and Child Health Journal* 9, no. 1 (2005): 27–34.

Zhou, Min. "Conflict, Coping, and Reconciliation: Intergenerational Relations in Chinese Immigrant Families." In *Immigrant Families*, ed. Nancy Foner, 21–46. New York: New York University Press, 2009.

———, and Cai Guoxuan. "Chinese Language Media in the United States: Immigration and Assimilation in American Life." *Qualitative Sociology* 25, no. 3 (2002): 419–41.

Ziemba, Rosemary A., and Judith M. Lynch-Sauer. "Preparedness for Taking Care of Elderly Parents: 'First You Get Ready to Cry.'" *Journal of Women and Aging* 17, no.1–2 (2005): 99–113.

INDEX

Ambivalence, 12, 107-108, 123, 171
Anjong, 40-41

Birthday observations, 89-99, 189n39;
   baek-il (hundred day), 89, 92, 97-98; *chil-soon* (seventieth), 86, 96-99; *dol* (first),
   88-93, 97-98, 188n29, 189n30, 189n32;
   hwangap (sixtieth), 86-99, 189n36;
   planned by female kin, 94-98, 100. *See
   also* Korean culture; Korean holiday
   observations
Borsky, Amanda E., 141
Boundaries, 42, 64-66; marriage and children, 57-68; work and career choices,
   53-56
Brody, Elaine, 4
Brokering, 4, 6-7; cultural 2, 5, 29; language,
   5, 29-34; between parents and the health
   care system, 141-146

Care-giving, 4-5; 102; to aging Asian American parents, 137, 171; from distance, 145-
   155; as duty, 122-123; emotional, 103-105,
   116, 129; financial, 103, 116, 124; gendered,
   105-108; and in-laws, 107-108; schoolwork
   as form of, 18-19, 21-22, 53; tangible, 22,
   103; women as main caregivers, 4, 102, 112,
   133-134, 136, 161, 174
Care-giving and negotiations: as balancing
   act, 121-130; 160-162; as only child, 128-129;
   between parents and children, 131-132;
   145 -149; among siblings, 106-107, 112-115,
   122-123, 125-127, 133, 146, 150-155; between
   spouses, 118-121
Chin, Soo-young, 89, 93-94, 189n30, 189n36
Church, 177; criticisms of, 177; and institutional support in the Korean American \

community, 175-176; leaders providing
   support, 176; and social justice, 177-178
Confucianism, 83-85, 97, 103, 152, 160; and
   gender hierarchy, 84-85; 113, 187n22; and
   Korean women, 187n21. *See also* Filial piety
Crowley, M. Sue, 108
Cumulative disadvantage, 138, 170

Daughters: as caregivers, 4-5, 16-17, 132-134,
   167, 169; and daughters-in-law, 97, 100-102;
   and emotion work, 104-118; as organizers
   of kin work, 94-97, 100-102. *See also* Care-
   giving; Intergenerational relations; Sons
Death of parent, 2-3, 135, 145-147, 158-160;
   grieving, 160
di Leonardo, Micaela, 104, 190n12
Domestic violence, 34-37
Double jeopardy, 138, 163

Elder, Glen H., 4
Emotion work, 4-5; and adult daughters,
   102-109, 129; of children, 12, 16-22;
   around the Korean War, 43-49. *See also*
   Care-giving
Ethnic entrepreneurship, 14-15; children's
   labor in, 15-16, 22-32; and lack of health
   insurance, 139
Ethnic groups, 72
Ethnic identity, 72-85; and authenticity, 71,
   74-75; and college, 71, 80, 82; and food,
   86; and Korean culture and history, 78-85;
   and language, 73-78, 82-83; and neighborhoods, 75-78, 80-81

Filial piety, 6-7, 82-84, 94-97, 103, 119, 168;
   and redefining gendered expectations,
   120. *See also* Confucianism

Grace J. Yoo is Professor of Asian American Studies at San Francisco State University. She is the editor/co-editor of *Koreans in America: History, Identity, and Community,* the *Handbook of Asian American Health,* and the *Encyclopedia of Asian American Issues Today.*

Barbara W. Kim is Professor of Asian and Asian American Studies at California State University, Long Beach.